I0729550

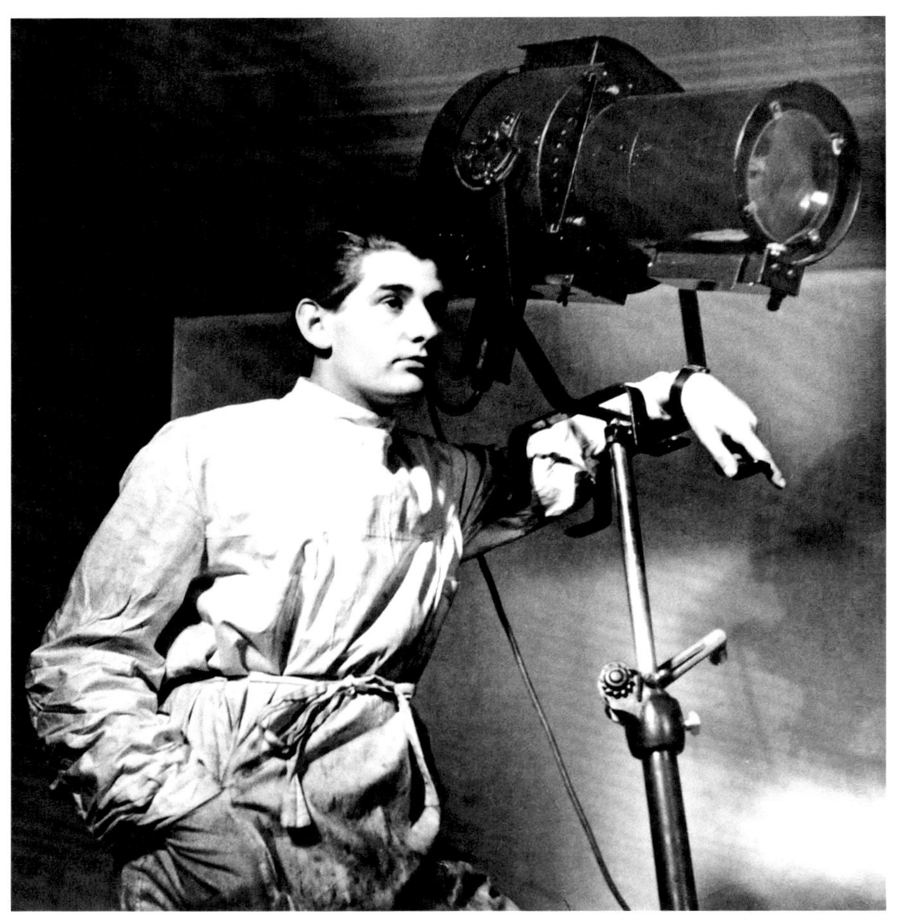

HELMUT NEWTON

TASCHEN

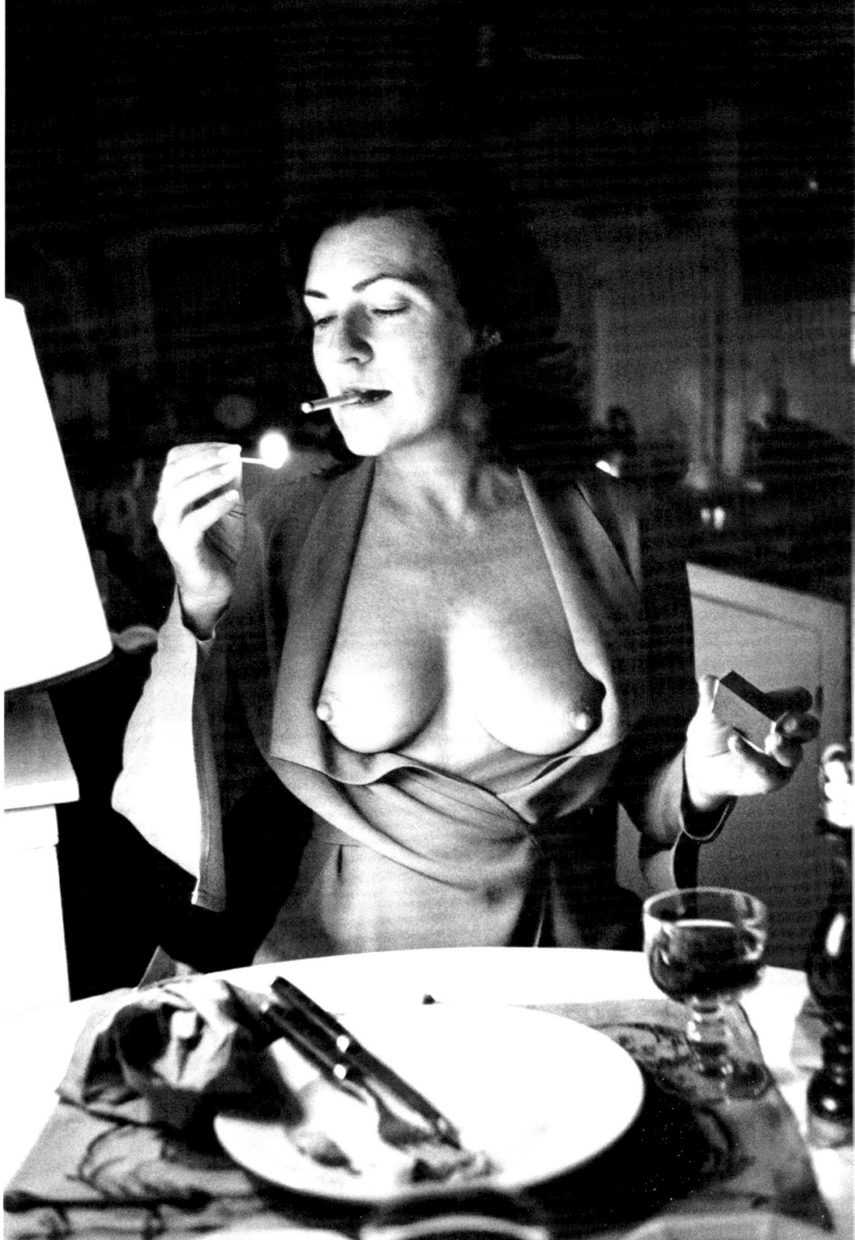

Contents

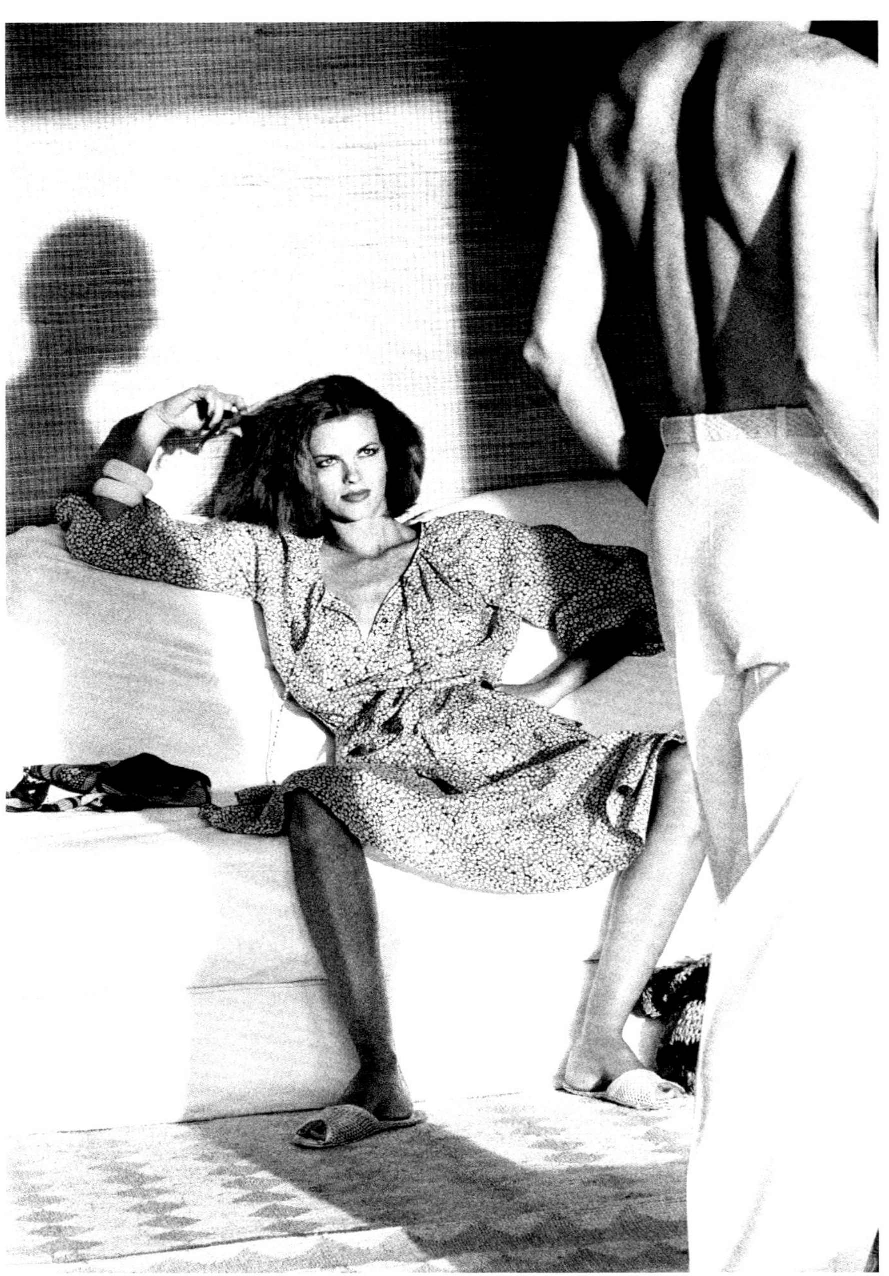

A fine line between
the illicit and the chic

By Sarah Mower

**"When American *Vogue* hit the news stands in the summer of 1975 with
The Story of Ohhh..., all hell broke out...This was the beginning of my notoriety,
and I never looked back."**

The gleeful satisfaction that Helmut Newton enjoyed at the uproar caused by his
twelve-page American *Vogue* shoot in May 1975 is a good place to start to discuss who
he was and where he stands in the histories of photography and fashion. In what has
long been regarded as an epoch-making Helmut Newton picture, the model Lisa Taylor
sits, legs apart, on a poolhouse banquette, wearing a Calvin Klein blouse and skirt
as she rests her gaze on a passing man. Newton frames the man's naked torso in
three-quarter profile, head cut off. It's clearly readable as a depiction of a woman's
desire. It is taken from an angle and deploys a model's pose which had never been
seen in a women's magazine.

Newton talked about his criteria for bending the conventions of fashion depiction
in *Helmut by June*, a documentary his wife June Newton made about him in 1995.
"The perfect fashion photo should look like something out of a movie, a souvenir shot,
a paparazzi shot," he said. "Anything but a fashion photograph." In the Lisa Taylor
image, it was more as if Newton had taken a shot at the forefront of a social revolution.
Arranged with the complicity of *Vogue*'s progressive fashion editor Polly Allen Mellen,
the photograph is cited frequently as glamorising the new potency of American
female-centred sexual liberation, taken as it was in the wake of legalised contraception
and the very recent Roe v. Wade decision of two years earlier. What shocked conserva-
tive viewers of *The Story of Ohhh...*, however, was something else they construed
as they inspected the entirety of Newton's three-way summer scenario. "I was accused
in the press of showing bestiality and advocating sex between two women and one
man," he happily exclaimed in his autobiography.[1]

Here were two women in bikinis and evening dresses, with one man and a dog –
the recurrent iconography of pools, sybaritic wealth, sexual tension and the occasional
canine which students of Newton will trace throughout his work. The editor Grace
Mirabella was left dealing with irate letters and *Vogue* being taken off newsstands in

Florida, while Newton claimed it did nothing but wonders for his career. "This was the beginning of my notoriety, and I never looked back."

Throughout his vast body of work, both editorial commissions and privately made Newton took pride and delight in balancing his work on knife-edges of ambiguity, allusion and social satire. In large part, his work is a dramatisation, documentation and skewering of the story of the second half of the twentieth century's attitudes about women and fashion, a coda to Western culture's sliding scale of its adjacencies to debates about female agency, pornography, and who gets to show or see what, in which contexts. When Newton was working, an old moral, political and gender order was supposedly being overthrown by the post-war "permissive society", and he took part in that. Yet his work constantly raised the question: What, then, is permitted in this society, and what is not? Nothing would have pleased him more than to know that contentious question still gets under the skin of viewers confronting it from different perspectives, in a different century.

For in many ways, too, his work should also be read as the coded autobiography of a German-Jewish Berliner who had endured the rise of Nazism; a sly, sophisticated series of acts of subversive, liberty-taking revenge, laced through with what he knowingly called "my rather nasty Berlin sense of humour." Celebrated, wealthy and courted by the city in his eighties, he decided that the perfect place for his archive, the Helmut Newton Foundation, to be housed was in a building opposite the Bahnhof Zoo station from which he escaped the city in 1938.

Page 4
June in Our Kitchen, Paris, 1976
Newton's portrait of his wife has the poise, intimacy and knowingly playful respect and love that came from an artistic relationship and marriage that lasted over five decades. She remembered: "He just said, 'Junie, open your dress.'"

June Newton adopted the pseudonym Alice Springs when she started taking photographs in 1970. The extent of their symbiotic but independent careers (they often photographed the same people), as well as the mutual importance to them of recording their domestic life, is recorded in the book *Us and Them*. June Browne had been an actress. The couple met in Australia, shortly after Newton set up his first studio, and married in Melbourne in 1948.

Page 6
Woman Regarding Man, American *Vogue*, Calvin Klein, Saint-Tropez, 1975
In the photograph of Lisa Taylor candidly gazing at a passing, bare-chested man at a pool house, every detail – pose, shadow, cropping – is considered, making it seem as if it's a spontaneously caught moment of sexual invitation. Part of Newton's lifelong strategy was to take fashion photographs as if they were reportage. He liked to work on location with as small a team as necessary, although he made meticulous preparatory plans in his notebooks.

The Story of Ohhh…, published by American *Vogue* in May 1975, caused a furore and cancelled subscriptions.

Opposite
***Queen*, Venice, 1966**

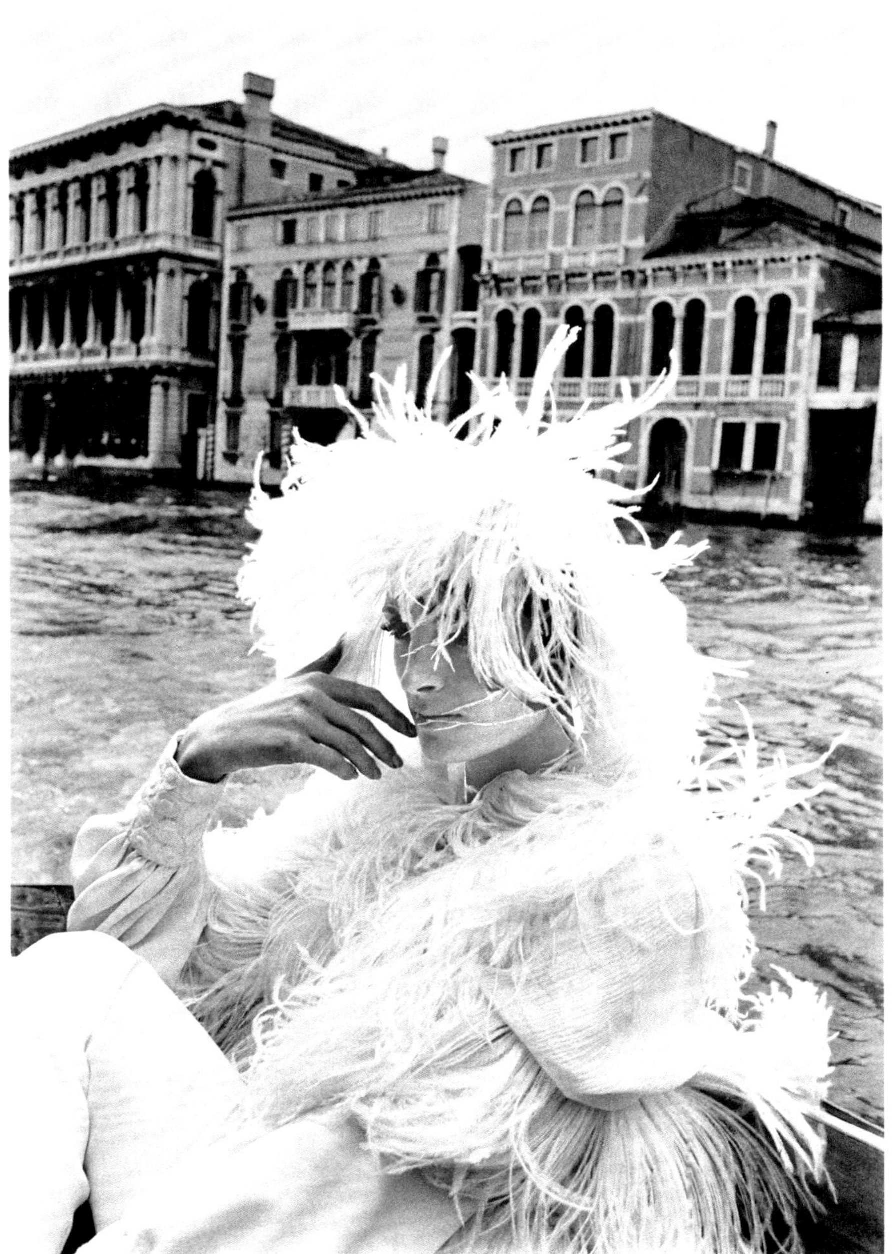

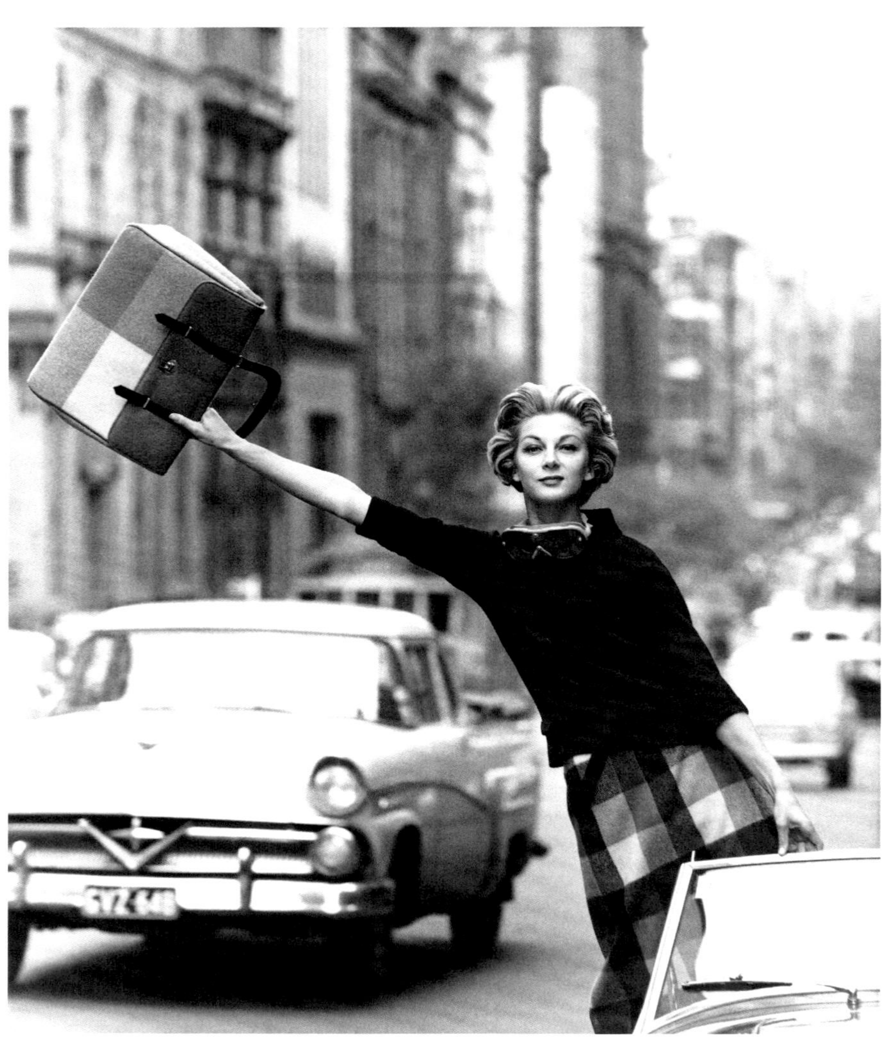

Queen Street,
Melbourne, 1959
Model: Janice Wakely

"Many of my fashion photographs have been taken in places that remind me of my childhood"

Helmut Neustädter was born in Berlin in 1920, his sensibility forged in the louche, ominous contemporary culture of the city's stylised high art and low-life prostitution in the last days of the German Weimar Republic. As a privileged Jewish boy, he enjoyed a happy, sex-and-photography-obsessed youth, until it was shattered by the rise of the Nazis. He escaped, alone, on a boat to Singapore in 1938, on a ticket his mother had risked everything to obtain. The last time he saw his family was when he set off, aged eighteen, on a train from Bahnhof Zoo station, carrying with him the two cameras with which he was destined to make a living. After two years, he was displaced to Australia and interned as a German "enemy alien." Eventually he joined the Australian army, finally setting up as a photographer upon being discharged, and changed his name to Helmut Newton in 1946. He met the actress June Browne when she applied to him for part-time modelling work. They married in Melbourne in 1948.

His autobiography mapped out the psychogeography imprinted on him by his Berlin upbringing – until then, he had confided the full extent of the story only to his wife June. "My parents gave me a great youth," he wrote. His father Max was a buckle and button manufacturer; his family lived in old-world comfort with domestic staff in attendance; his mother Claire read *Vogue*. On the first page, Newton claimed his first memory of erotic excitement was seeing his half-naked nanny "at the age of three or four," setting him off on a lifetime pursuit of sexual fantasies. He tied his fascination with prostitution back to a glimpse of a street-corner dominatrix known as Red Erna, whom his elder brother Hans made him ogle as a seven-year-old. Berlin, its economy in a state of hyperinflation, was full of women selling specialist services.

The settings of bourgeois life mingled with his imaginings of sexual behaviours conducted behind closed doors recur everywhere in Newton's work: he saw it in every society. "I've always been fascinated by hotels and hotel rooms. I used to travel with my parents through many of the big hotels of Europe. They still hold a special mystery for me," he remembered. "I've taken a great number of my fashion photographs in these places, as well as in smaller hotels, sometimes of dubious repute."[2]

Self-confessedly spoiled and uninterested in academic study, the young Helmut became an amateur teen swimming champ, spending summers chasing girls at open-air pools and Berlin lakes; swept up in the heady German health-and-fitness culture of the time. His only ambition was to become a photographer. "When I was twelve years old, I went into a kind of five- and ten-cent store and bought myself a camera with my pocket money." He credited his inspiration to poring over the groundbreaking photography of Martin Munkácsi, László Moholy-Nagy and Erich Salomon, which was published in mass-market weekly magazines such as *Berliner Illustrirte Zeitung*. For a time, he harboured a boyhood fantasy of "yellow press" crime reporting. Subjects which put the profession of press photography itself into the frame – the work of the paparazzi, his reenactments of lurid crime-scene reporting, his witty examinations of himself as a photographer – peppered his obsessions. Often, he returned to the theme of sex murders (*Murder Scene, Cannes 1975*, shot in broad, harsh daylight, twilight and in a hotel bathroom, is an example), pushing his need to shock ever further to the edge, right to the end of his life.

A dream came true when his mother organised a studio apprenticeship with Yva, the successful modernist photographer Else Neuländer-Simon. Perhaps it's significant that he first learned about cameras, lighting, darkroom processes and models from one of the powerful women who decisively influenced the course of his life. "Yva did fashion photography, portraits of ballet dancers, actors and actresses. We did a lot of underwear catalogues, which I loved," he remembered. "These were the happiest days of my life in Berlin…I worshipped the ground she walked on." His heroes Munkácsi Moholy-Nagy, Salomon and Yva all belonged to the progressive European wave of artistic talent of the twenties and thirties; they were also all Jewish. After he left Berlin Newton was devastated to learn that Yva had been murdered in a concentration camp. "I have always done my utmost to keep her memory alive," he wrote.

By the mid-seventies he was renowned in Europe as a fashion photographer for *Vogue Paris*, *Nova*, *Queen* and British *Vogue*. The sheer size of the 524-page book *Pages from the Glossies: Facsimiles 1956–1998*[3] is testament to the epic volume of his fashion magazine work alone. In this, a select few magazine art directors and fashion editors (Willy Landels at *Queen*; Caroline Baker at *Nova*; Francine Crescent and Jacques Faure at *Vogue Paris* and later Anna Wintour at American *Vogue*) enabled his meticulously dangerous visions. "Who else would have published these nudes, who else the crazy and sexually charged fashion photographs which I would submit?" he exclaimed of Crescent.[4] Even when photographing women fully clothed in high fashion, his talent for double commentary applied. In *Chez Yves Saint Laurent* (American *Vogue*, 1977), a scene populated by gorgeously dressed models in Yves Saint Laurent's gilded haute couture salon, it's impossible to evade the feeling that Newton has also made it look like a grand Parisian bordello.

> **"In Yves Saint Laurent's gilded haute couture salon, it's impossible to evade the feeling that Newton has also made it look like a grand Parisian bordello."**

Woman and Kangaroo,
American *Vogue*, 1964

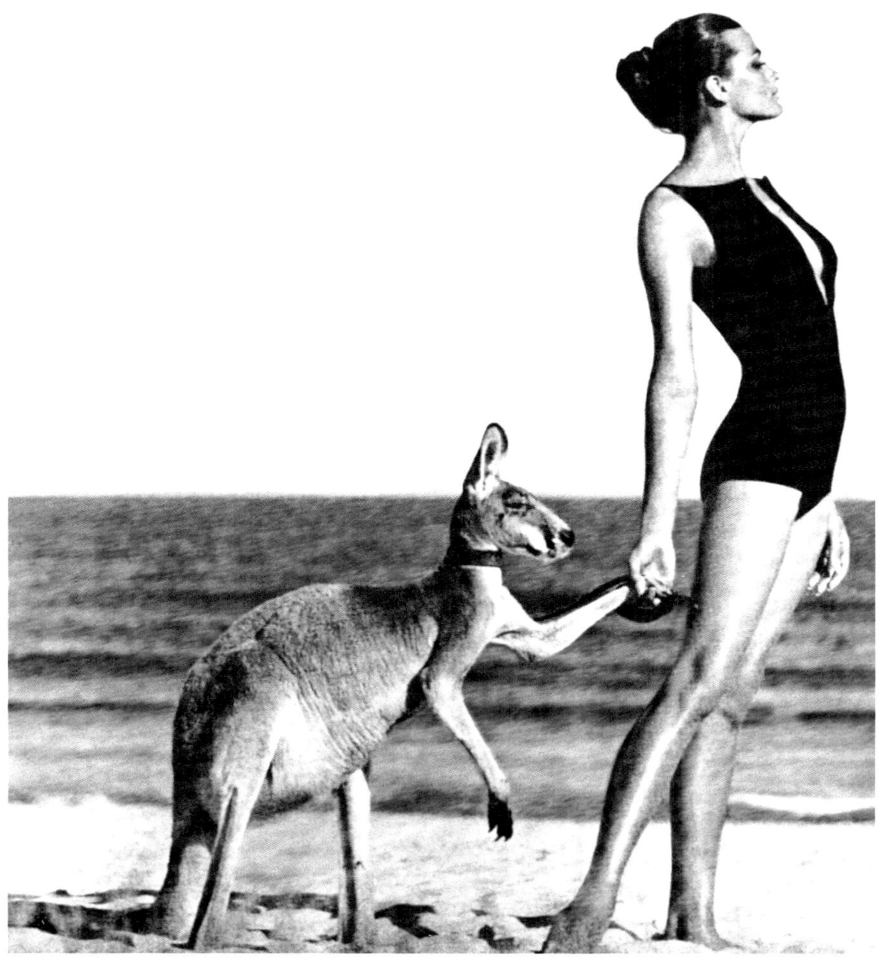

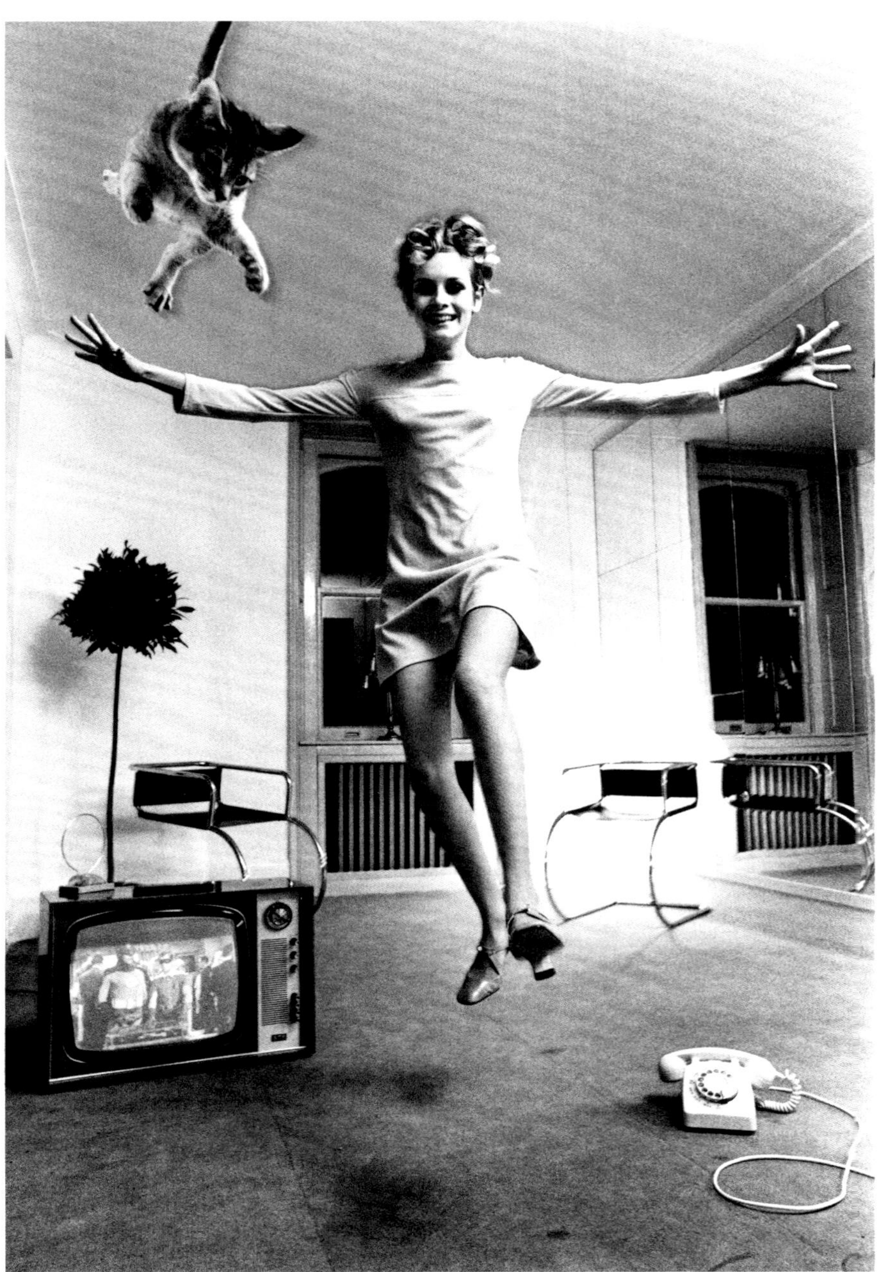

Provoking both desire and ire in a photograph was one of the benchmarks of success he set himself early on. "You've got to be able to live up to something, even a bad reputation," he once joked to his compatriot and friend Karl Lagerfeld.[5] In parallel with ring-fencing his independence as "a gun for hire" (as he liked to call himself) while also ensuring that he earned the best possible living for himself and June (who began her own career in photography under the pseudonym Alice Springs in 1970), Newton's constant concern was to keep the shock value of his work current. Thriving in the post-war decades of the consumer boom and the concomitant climate around the rise of liberated "power women", he achieved great financial success, made friends in high society, bought luxury cars – but most importantly, he achieved the freedom to live and work exactly as he desired. Whether living in Paris or near Ramatuelle in the south of France in the sixties and seventies, or in the eighties in Monte Carlo and at Chateau Marmont in Los Angeles in winter, Newton used all these exclusive locations – sometimes exposing their brutal underbellies. Even within the confines of the glossy enclave of Monaco, he found favourite rough corners – concrete walls, construction sites, the cliff edge of the Corniche and his own underground car park – all locations where he delighted in walking a very fine line between the illicit and what was considered chic. And very often, he deliberately stepped over it.

"A gun for hire"

To prepare his ideas and references, Newton would write detailed notes and then insist on the freedom to work quickly and directly with his subjects. "I have always been a lone wolf, and worked with one assistant." One model, sometimes two, the fashion editor or stylist and the hair and makeup artists were the only others allowed on a Helmut Newton shoot – the rule he applied as rigorously to advertising as to editorial clients. He prided himself on turning up with equipment which could mostly fit into one camera bag, with possibly a couple of small lights. So armed, he shot quickly, using just a few rolls of film over a day's work. His quick-fire professionalism tracked right back, he said, to his apprenticeship with Yva at age sixteen. "Nothing much has changed in my picture-taking technique since I was a boy in the 1930s," he declared in his autobiography. "I don't own a strobe light, rarely work in the studio."

It was this fascination for location photography that drove the development of the instantly recognisable Helmut Newton look. "My imagination needed the reality of the outdoors. I also realised that only as a fashion photographer could I create my kind of universe and make my models play the part of a certain kind of woman."[6]

British *Vogue*,
Foale & Tuffin, London, 1967
Model: Twiggy

Many of his most celebrated photographs were taken on the street at night, using only available light and occasionally a torch, deployed to pick up detail (he credited Brassaï's *Paris de Nuit* as an influence). Working in colour, his signature high-contrast technique, timed to be shot in the harsh overhead light of midday sun, looked like nobody else's. This was confident and fearless technical risk-taking. There were no guarantees of perfect results in the days of analogue photography. Yet Newton carried out all of this in the context of a huge volume of work, in the days of the low production budgets set by magazines which demanded speedy turnarounds.

He was in his element working quickly. (His self-confessed short attention span was the reason, as he told his film- and documentary-making friend Gero von Boehm, that he lacked the patience to transpose his distinctly narrative ideas into movies.) His attraction to the idea and appearance of spontaneity – although always captured within his precisely manufactured set-ups – made Newton often wonder whether his Polaroid first-takes (which preceded a shoot as a medium for checking composition) transmitted more visual electricity than the eventual image. Two exhibitions and a book[7] have been dedicated to this aspect of his work.

> **"He could go as far as he liked – at one point, chaining a favourite voluptuous 'model' naked to railings in one of the exclusive residential arrondissements of Paris."**

Newton never needed, nor ever wanted, to travel to exotic locations. His resourcefulness lay in the meticulous planning of scenarios in places familiar to him, sometimes just a short walk from where he lived. At one juncture, he problem-solved the difficulty of photographing the Paris collections for *Vogue Paris* through the night (when couture houses traditionally released clothes for magazine reports) by posing shop dummies in place of women. Convenient, funny, maybe – but it also controversially surfaced the male idea of seeing women as objects, dummies. That opened a whole new avenue of possibilities: many more shoots where he posed dummies, both male and female, to act out sexual scenarios in luxury apartments. He could go as far as he liked – at one point, chaining a favourite voluptuous "model" naked to railings in one of the exclusive residential arrondissements of Paris.

Arranging economical but outstandingly glamorous results worked for Helmut Newton's editorial clients for decades, but he also made certain it worked for him. He maintained an ambivalent, calculated attitude to what he wanted to achieve in earning a living from the press. No matter how clever he was at it, the job of shooting fashion was no more to Newton than a gateway to populating his own world with the subjects that interested him – chiefly women, naked or dressed.

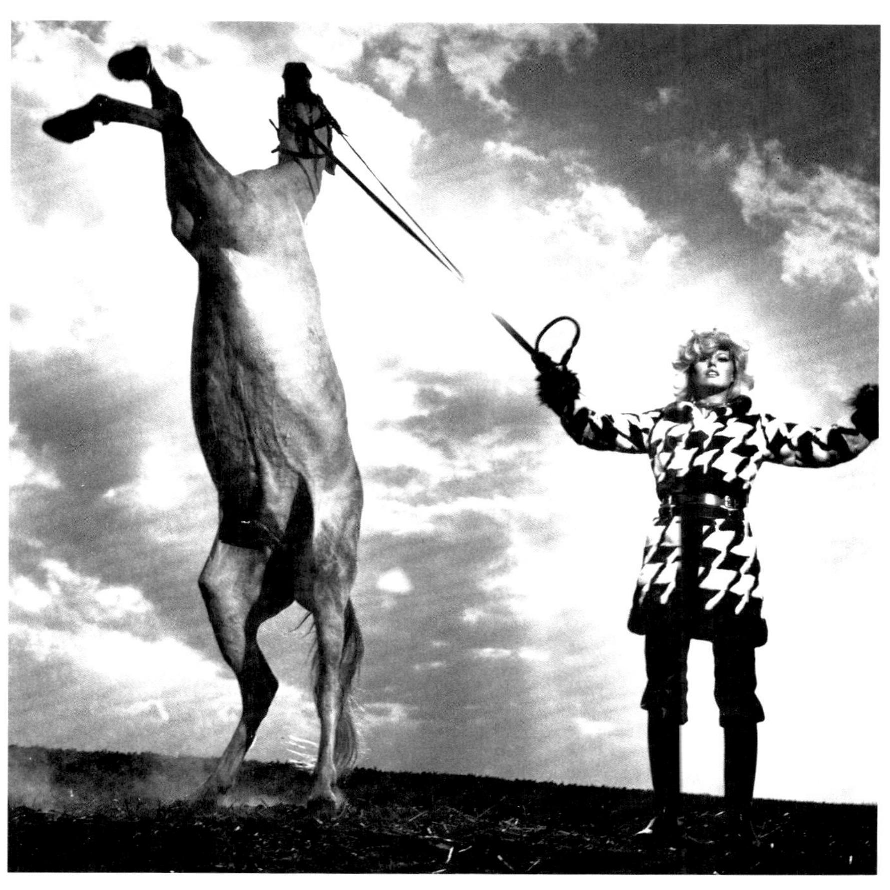

Vogue Paris,
Yves Saint Laurent,
near Paris, 1969
Model: Ulla Danielson

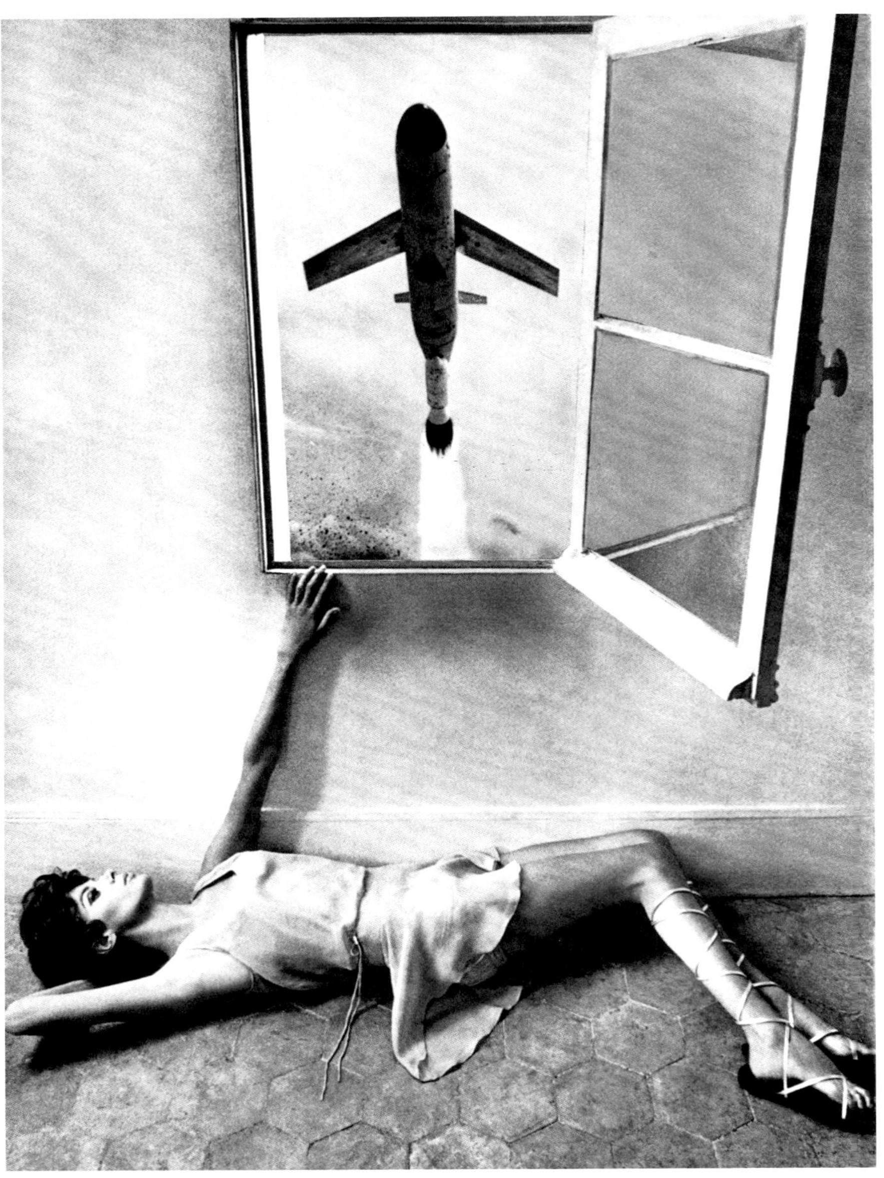

"I called it 'beating the system'"

Behind the margin of privacy that Newton stipulated as his modus operandi on commissions lay a strategy for creating his own, extra work. "I've always known how to use the resources of my clients – either advertising or editorial. I called it 'beating the system.' What I did was set aside one or two hours of the sitting for my own uses. Naturally I let them see the photographs, but these were generally of such a nature that they preferred to publish the straight versions rather than the private ones. In this way, over many years, I built up my personal archives."[8]

He revealed two of his after-hours plots in *White Women*,[9] the first book of his work, which earned him the soubriquet "The King of Kink". The "official" photograph of Saint Laurent's masculine "Smoking" trouser suit, taken in 1975 at night for *Vogue Paris* in the cobbled rue Aubriot in the Marais district (where the Newtons lived at the time) showed the clothed model alone. In the second, she's joined by a model who is naked, save for a veiled hat by Paulette. In another fashion double take, he photographed the blonde model Roselyne from behind, walking up a grand staircase of a chateau in a black Chloé evening dress by Karl Lagerfeld, described or the 1975 *Vogue Paris* page as "split from the waist down." In the twin shot, her naked backside is exposed.

The consent of the models to be photographed naked, sometimes in underwear – and always in high heels – presumably came into this. By the seventies, being chosen as a "Helmut Newton woman" had come to be considered an honour.

Long after Newton's death, Gero von Boehm went back to investigate that question in the 2020 documentary *The Bad and the Beautiful* when he interviewed Charlotte Rampling, Isabella Rossellini, Grace Jones, Hanna Schygulla and several other models who posed for him. Rampling testified that Newton's 1974 naked

Queen, Paris, 1967
Model: Jill Kennington

An interest in the symbolism of modern technology is a thread in Newton's work. This one exploded in the head office of the proprietor of *Queen* magazine in 1966, when he saw the combination of fashion photographs and photomontage that Newton and the art director Willy Landels had come up with. While the scenario ingeniously devised a way to depict the ever-rising miniskirt fashion of the time – showing this dress "with matching panties by Jean Muir" – it was the rockets, planes and warheads going off in the background which caused the enraged owner to demand to know why "phallic symbols are exploding outside their windows?" Growing up in Berlin, Newton was a young fan of the elegantly suggestive literature of Arthur Schnitzler and Stefan Zweig, whose novels and plays he surreptitiously took from his father's bookshelves. "Nothing was ever spelled out, but they were explicit enough for me to understand what they were all about," he wrote, a formative influence on his way of leaving the interpretation of his visual stories to the imagination of the viewer. Stepping back from whatever sexual content can be read nto this series, however, Newton's inclusion of rockets and warplanes referred to the sixties Space Race and the Cold War between the USA and USSR which was happening at the time – all readers would have seen that.

photograph of her "gave me an immense inner strength…if he had not taken these photographs of me, my whole career would have been different." Rossellini took the view that Newton was knowingly depicting the way that men see women in Western society and that she was knowingly complicit in acting that out in front of his camera. Jones joked that he was "a little bit perverted, but so am I." Newton made his perspective clear when he said he "loved women"; a comment which drew the acid and entirely subjective reply from Susan Sontag on a French TV arts show: "Well, that's what a lot of misogynists say."

Newton always credited June Newton, who had her own career as a photographer as his chief co-conspirator. "June and I worked on ideas that would astound the readers of the magazines."[10] It irritated him that "Journalists always ask, did I sleep with my models and was June jealous?"[11] His *Self Portrait with Wife and Models, Paris 1981*, showing June watching him photographing naked women, was presumably a retort, and a further provocation, on that subject. The closeness and collaboration in the Newtons' marriage, their professional respect for one another – as well as how they may have seen themselves as one unit against the world – might easily be read into the title of their joint book *Us and Them*.[12] Their frank, funny and sometimes poignant photographs of each other at home and at work are set alongside their portraits of *les autres*: Princess Caroline of Monaco, Catherine Deneuve, Karl Lagerfeld, Gianni Versace, Charlotte Rampling and Brassaï amongst them.

> "Newton's love of Berlin and the world he grew up in never left him. He often returned, to take photographs ambivalently loaded with both nostalgia and implied accusation."

June, as he was to make clear when he published his autobiography, was the only one who completely understood the landscapes and the ideas about women which were embedded in his mind; she knew exactly where his propensity for powerful and wickedly playful narratives were coming from. Whether – or whomever – he was photographing in Paris, Berlin, New York, Los Angeles or Monte Carlo, the truth was that the decades of Newton's oeuvre had all revolved around one location.

Newton's love of Berlin and the world he grew up in never left him. He often returned, to take photographs ambivalently loaded with both nostalgia and implied accusation. Invited to shoot for the relaunch of German *Vogue* in 1979, he retraced scenes from his youth – June had suggested he go back to his "old haunts". In 1963, he had stirred a Cold War political incident with his *Mata Hari* spy story shot at the Berlin Wall for *Vogue Paris*. Amongst the famous, inflaming series depicting women in surgical braces, published in *Sleepless Nights*,[13] he photographed the German fashion

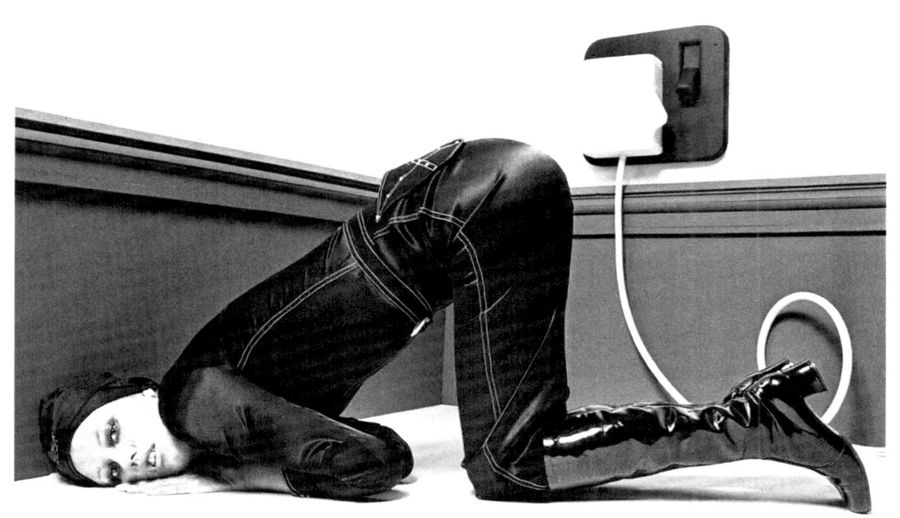

British *Vogue*, Mary Quant,
London, 1969

editor Jenny Capitain, naked except for a leg cast and neck brace, in the Pension Florian, a Berlin brothel.

He was at pains to restate his nuanced relationship with the specifics of the German culture that formed his sphere of reference: the reason that the type of women he photographed, his stylised lighting techniques and extreme-angled framing made so many uneasy. "At that time I was surrounded by Nazi imagery, like everybody in Germany, and for a boy obsessed with photography it left an indelible impression on me."[14] He had a hard-wired worship of the film-makers of the twenties and thirties – he said the influence of Erich von Stroheim's movies stood behind his series of women wearing medical corsets and neck braces. "The photography was very, very good in that period. Russian photography was interesting, too," he said in a *New York Times* interview in 2003. Between the end of World War I and the rise of National Socialism, the German film industry was flourishing, including a trade in "sex education", pornography and dark thrillers; he remembered sneaking into cinemas as a child. This was the Berlin of Brecht, the Bauhaus, cafés and cabaret, a liberal, avant-garde magnet for free-thinking creative people and visitors from all over Europe and America. As the actress Anita Loos once remarked: "Any Berlin lady of the evening might turn out to be a man," and vice versa. Decades later, he explained that it was seeing life-size identification photographs of the Baader-Meinhof terrorist gang in a German police office that inspired him to make his monumental series *Big Nudes*. "What certain persons in Germany have accused me of is making fascist images, referring to my *Big Nudes*. My answer was, I recognise that. It was a throwback to my youth."[15]

"To the question: 'What people do you like to photograph?' my answer is: 'Those I love, those I admire, and those I hate.'"

Whether he detected it coming from the Right or the Left, Newton harboured a lifelong, visceral distrust of anything he regarded as smacking of authoritarian control. "The term 'political correctness' has always appalled me, reminding me of Orwell's Thought Police and fascist regimes," he commented in his introduction to *SUMO*. His portrait photography for *Vanity Fair* and *The New Yorker* unleashed a fresh field of creative freedom in the nineties, years during which he increasingly baulked at what he saw as the narrowing constraints of fashion magazines and at the demands of Hollywood celebrity handlers. Society women, film stars and princesses of all ages – many of whom he had long friendships with – had been happy to pose for him from the seventies onward. But in later years, he turned his camera extensively on men – on a gallery of politicians, playboys, the rich and the powerful. The law came under his scrutiny again: a judge, a detective, the attorney Rudy Giuliani, then mayor of New York.

And for the first time, Helmut Newton savoured the rewarding opportunity to nail the infamous with all the forensic wit he applied to the famous. To his immerse satisfaction, he infuriated the far-right French politician Jean-Marie Le Pen by persuading him to pose, on the spur of the moment, with two pet Doberman dogs Newton spotted in the man's garden; thus causing an immediate furore when the press compared it to a notorious photograph of Hitler. He flattered the aged Leni Riefenstahl, the propaganda film-maker of the 1934 Nuremburg rallies and Hitler's 1936 Berlin Olympics, into sitting for him. They had struck up a weird friendship, which he described in his autobiography: "I got a lot of flak from people, June included, who can't understand how a Jew could have that kind of relationship with a person with such a dubious political past." But to look at one of his Riefenstah portraits, smiling winningly as she holds a film reel with both hands outstretched on her lap, is to see that Newton has caught her with a piece of film looped across both wrists, and to see, lastingly, exactly what he meant.

All the sexual foibles and fetishes Newton explored in his work, the bodies of the tall, statuesque women he cast, the pools and the interiors he set them in and the characters he liked to shoot were in one way or another his career-long way of processing, overcoming and sublimating the attraction and repulsion he felt about the factors that shaped him. It made the contrarian, cynical, laconic man whose visions produced some of the most important, contentious subject matter through which the latter half of the twentieth century's fashion can be viewed. In the final account, that is what will continue to astonish, thrill and appal in his vast body of work long into the future.

Pages 24/25
Linea Italiana, De Barentzen, Rome, 1970

Themes inspired by films and action photography pepper Newton's work. Commissioned by *Linea Italiana* to shoot a fashion story and inspired by the paparazzi scenes in Federico Fellini's *La Dolce Vita*, he went to Rome, where this "new breed of press photographers are". Working for several days with models and a pack of real paparazzi, he instructed models to behave like celebrities, shooting quickly to achieve the images he'd planned. The story ran into trouble, however, when the paparazzi discovered that Newton's day rate was considerably more than theirs and threatened to sell their own film to a tabloid. After much negotiation, only one photograph from those three days was printed.

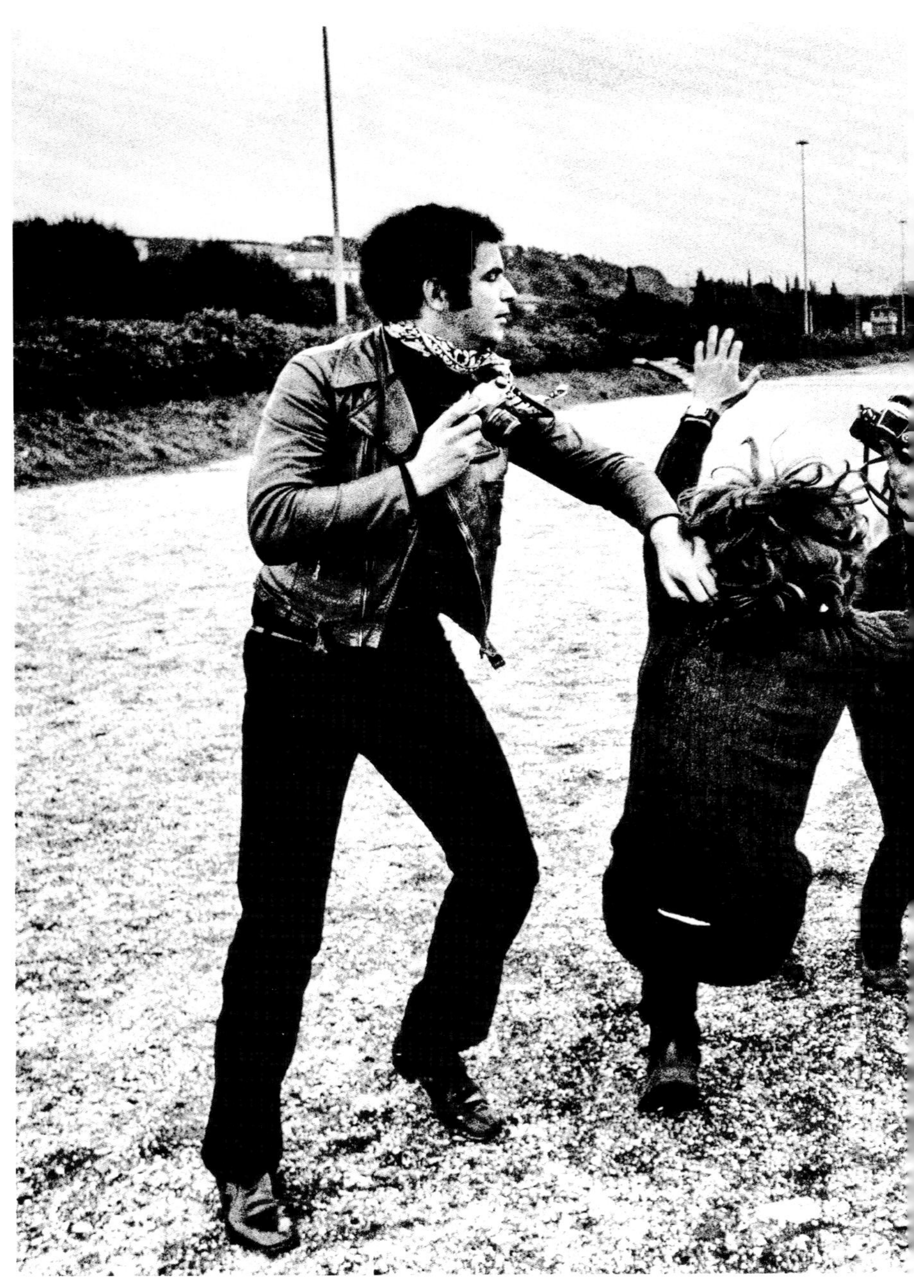

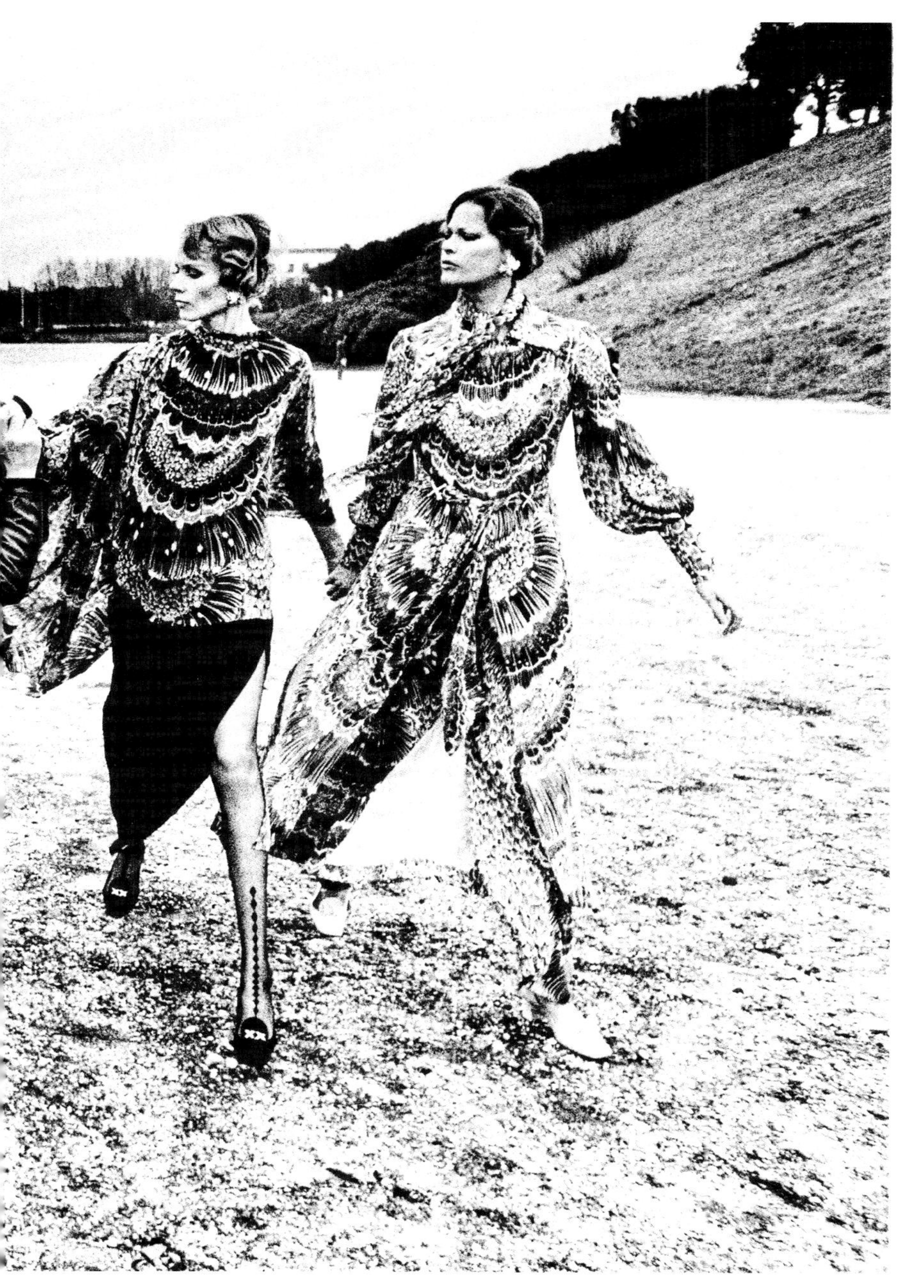

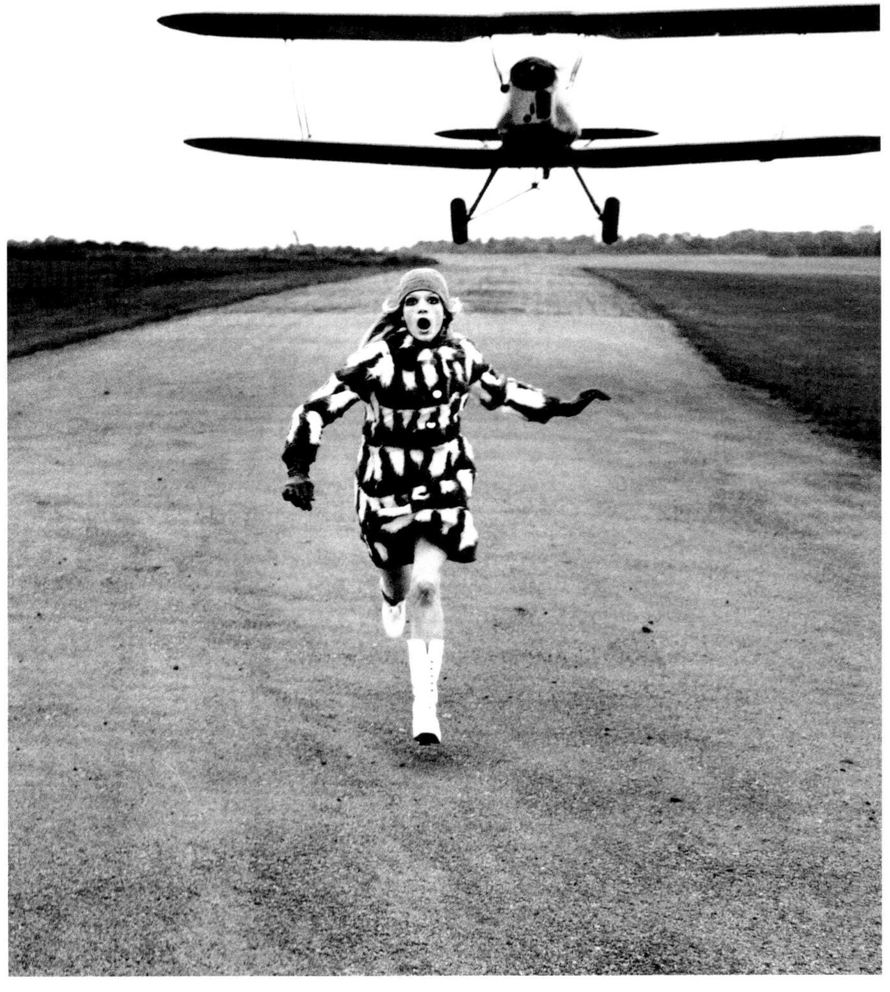

Der schmale Grat zwischen
dem Verbotenen und dem Stilvollen

Von Sarah Mower

„Als im Sommer 1975 die amerikanische *Vogue* mit *The Story of Ohhh…* in die Kioske kam, brach die Hölle los… Damit hatte ich meinen skandalösen Ruf weg, und ich habe es nie bereut."

Die fröhlich-schadenfrohe Genugtuung, die Helmut Newton angesichts des Aufruhrs empfand, den seine zwölfseitige Fotostrecke in der amerikanischen *Vogue* im Mai 1975 auslöste, ist ein guter Ausgangspunkt, um darüber nachzudenken, wer Newton war und wo er in der Fotografie- und Modegeschichte steht. Auf einem Foto, das schon lange als epochales Helmut-Newton-Bild gilt, sitzt das Model Lisa Taylor breitbeinig auf einer Bank vor einem Poolhaus. Taylor trägt Bluse und Rock von Calvin Klein und blickt einen vorbeigehenden Mann freimütig an. Den nackten Oberkörper des Mannes zeigt Newton im Dreiviertelprofil, sein Kopf ist nicht mehr im Bild. Das Foto ist eindeutig als Bild weiblichen Begehrens zu lesen. Es hat eine sehr spezielle Perspektive und zeigt das Model in einer Pose, die in einer Frauenzeitschrift bis zu diesem Zeitpunkt noch nicht zu sehen gewesen war.

In *Helmut by June*, einem Dokumentarfilm, den June Newton 1995 über ihren Mann machte, erzählt er, nach welchen Kriterien er sich über die Konventionen der Modefotografie hinwegsetzte: „Für mich soll das perfekte Modefoto aussehen, als komme es aus einem Film, wie ein Erinnerungsfoto oder ein Paparazzi-Bild, nur nicht wie ein Modefoto." Das Lisa-Taylor-Bild wirkt, als hätte Newton an der Frontlinie einer gesellschaftlichen Revolution fotografiert. Inszeniert mit dem stillen Einverständnis der fortschrittlichen *Vogue*-Redakteurin Polly Allen Mellen, wird es oft als Feier der von Frauen ausgehenden sexuellen Befreiung gedeutet in einer Zeit, in der erst zwei Jahre zuvor das Abtreibungsrecht in den USA liberalisiert und die Empfängnisverhütung legalisiert wurde. Konservative Betrachter und Betrachterinnen schockierte jedoch etwas anderes an der *Story of Ohhh…* und in Newtons sommerlichem Dreierszenario: „Die Presse beschuldigte mich, Sex mit Tieren und zwischen zwei Frauen und einem Mann zu propagieren."[1]

Zu sehen waren zwei Frauen, eine im Bikini, eine im Abendkleid, dazu ein Mann und ein Hund – also die immer wieder auftauchende Ikonografie aus Swimmingpools, genusssüchtigem Reichtum, erotischer Spannung und dem hier und da auftretenden Hund, die sich in Newtons gesamtem Werk wiederfinden lassen. *Vogue*-Kreativchefin Grace Mirabella bekam viele wütende Briefe, in Florida wurde das Heft sogar aus dem Verkauf genommen. Für seine Karriere hat es laut Newton Wunder gewirkt: „Damit hatte ich meinen skandalösen Ruf weg, und ich habe es nie bereut."

In seinem gesamten, umfangreichen Werk – egal, ob als Auftragsarbeiten für Zeitschriften oder privat entstanden – balanciert Newton mit Stolz und Freude auf dem schmalen Grat zwischen Doppeldeutigkeit, Anspielung und Gesellschaftssatire. Über weite Strecken dramatisieren, dokumentieren und kritisieren seine Fotos die sich in der zweiten Hälfte des 20. Jahrhunderts wandelnde Einstellung zu Frauen und Mode; sie sind wie ein Schlusspunkt der Abstufungen, mit denen die westliche Kultur das Nebeneinander von weiblicher Handlungsmacht, Pornografie und der Frage, wer was in welchem Kontext zeigen oder sehen darf, diskutiert. Zu Newtons aktiver Zeit trat an die Stelle der alten Ordnungen für Moral, Politik und die Geschlechter die „permissive Gesellschaft" der Nachkriegszeit. Und er nahm daran teil. Trotzdem warfen seine Arbeiten immer wieder diese Frage auf: Was ist erlaubt in unserer Gesellschaft – und was nicht? Nichts hätte ihn mehr gefreut, als zu wissen, dass diese strittige Frage die Betrachter seiner Bilder bis heute umtreibt, auch wenn sie sich ihnen nun mit gewandelter Perspektive, ja aus einem anderen Jahrhundert nähern.

In vielerlei Hinsicht sollte sein Werk als verschlüsselte Autobiografie eines jüdischen Berliners gelesen werden, der den Aufstieg des Nationalsozialismus miterleben musste, als eine freche und raffinierte Reihe subversiver Racheakte, für die er sich alle Freiheiten nahm und die von dem, was er „meinen ziemlich boshaften Berliner Humor" nannte, durchzogen sind. Als gefeierter, reicher und von der Stadt hofierter 80-Jähriger entschied er, sein Archiv, die Helmut Newton Foundation, in einem Gebäude direkt gegenüber vom Bahnhof Zoo unterzubringen, von wo aus er 1938 aus der Stadt floh.

„Viele meiner Modefotografien sind an Orten entstanden, die mich an meine Kindheit erinnern"

Helmut Neustädter wurde 1920 in Berlin geboren. Die späte Weimarer Republik prägte seine Wahrnehmung: das dekadente, ominöse Berliner Kulturleben jener Zeit mit seiner einerseits hochgradig stilisierten Kunst und andererseits mit Prostitution und zwielichtigen Milieus. Er war ein Junge aus einem wohlhabenden jüdischen Elternhaus und hatte eine glückliche, von Sex und Fotografie besessene Jugend, die durch den Aufstieg der Nazis ein jähes Ende fand. 1938 entkam er allein nach Singapur. Um das Ticket für seine Schiffspassage zu ergattern, hatte seine Mutter alles aufs Spiel gesetzt. Als 18-Jähriger stieg er am Bahnhof Zoo in den Zug, im Gepäck die beiden Kameras, mit denen er bald seinen Lebensunterhalt bestreiten sollte. Seine Familie sah er nie wieder. Zwei Jahre später wurde er als „feindlicher Ausländer" nach Australien gebracht und dort interniert. Dann trat er in die australische Armee ein und ließ sich nach seiner Entlassung schließlich als Fotograf nieder. 1946 änderte er seinen Namen in Helmut Newton. Die Schauspielerin June Browne lernte er kennen, als sie sich bei ihm um einen Modeljob bewarb. Die beiden heirateten 1948 in Melbourne.

In seiner Autobiografie zeichnet Newton die Psychogeografie seines Berliner Elternhauses nach – eine Geschichte, die er zuvor nur seiner Frau June anvertraut hatte. „Meine Eltern haben mir eine großartige Jugend beschert", sagte er in einem Interview mit der *New York Times*. Sein Vater Max war Schnallen- und Knopffabrikant, die Familie hatte Hauspersonal und lebte in gutbürgerlicher Annehmlichkeit, seine Mutter Claire las die *Vogue*. Schon auf der ersten Seite seiner Autobiografie schildert Newton seine früheste Erinnerung an eine erotische Erregung, als er sein Kindermädchen halb nackt sah: „Ich glaube, ich war drei oder vier Jahre alt." Von da an ließ er sich sein Leben lang von seinen sexuellen Fantasien leiten. Als er sieben war, nahm ihn sein älterer Bruder Hans mit, um die Rote Erna zu beobachten, eine Straßenstrich-Domina, auf die er seine Faszination für Prostituierte zurückführte. Im Berlin der Hyperinflation boten viele Frauen spezielle Dienstleistungen an.

Bürgerliche Kulissen, in die sich seine Fantasien von sexuellen Vorgängen hinter verschlossenen Türen mischen, gibt es in Newtons Arbeiten überall. Diese Verquickungen entdeckte er in jeder Gesellschaft. „Hotels und Hotelzimmer haben mich schon als Kind fasziniert. Ich bin mit meinen Eltern in vielen großen europäischen Hotels abgestiegen. Sie üben noch heute eine besondere Anziehungskraft auf mich aus", erinnerte er sich. „Jahrelang habe ich meine Modeaufnahmen in dieser Palästen gemacht – aber auch in kleineren Etablissements mit manchmal etwas zweifelhaftem Ruf."[2]

Der, wie er selbst von sich sagte, verzogene und nicht an einem Studium interessierte junge Helmut wurde als Teenager zu einem sehr guten Schwimmer der den Sommer im Freibad und an den Berliner Seen verbrachte, wo er, mitgerissen von der aufregenden deutschen Körper- und Fitnesskultur jener Zeit, den Mädchen nachstellte.

Page 26
How to Make Fur Fly,
British *Vogue*, Mansfield, London, 1967
Model: Willy van Rooy
During this period, Newton and his wife June would regularly brainstorm ideas until the early hours. Given a story on furs for British *Vogue*, June came up with the idea of taking a scene from Hitchcock's *North by Northwest*. It was not an easy shoot to pull off. For this shot, Newton stood on his camera case in the middle of the runway shooting slightly above the model running towards him. The pilot had to fly very low in order to keep the plane in the shot. Several times she had to hit the ground as the light aircraft got closer and closer. Newton knew he had the shot, but in his excitement misdirected the pilot in his approach, who almost crash-landed. Newton wrote in his autobiography that this was a time when fashion photographers were outdoing each other with fantastic ideas that were beyond just showing "the dress".

Sein einziger Ehrgeiz war es, Fotograf zu werden. Als Zwölfjähriger kaufte er sich in einem Berliner Billigladen von seinem Taschengeld die erste eigene Kamera. Dazu angeregt hatte ihn laut eigenem Bekunden die wiederholte Betrachtung der bahnbrechenden Fotos von Martin Munkácsi, László Moholy-Nagy und Erich Salomon, die in Massenblättern wie der Wochenzeitschrift *Berliner Illustrirte Zeitung* veröffentlicht wurden. Eine Zeit lang hegte er als Junge den Wunsch, Kriminalreporter bei einer Boulevardzeitung zu werden. Sujets, bei denen er den Beruf des Pressefotografen in Szene setzen konnte, gehörten auch später noch zu seinen Obsessionen: der Job der Paparazzi, die Nachstellung reißerisch aufgemachter Tatortreportagen, die witzige Reflexion der eigenen Rolle als Fotograf. Mehrfach widmete er sich auch dem Thema Sexualmorde (*Murder Scene, Cannes 1975*, aufgenommen in grellem Tageslicht, in der Dämmerung und in einem Hotelbadezimmer, ist ein Beispiel dafür). Das Bedürfnis, immer stärker zu schockieren, hielt bis an sein Lebensende an.

Als seine Mutter ihm eine Lehrstelle im Atelier der erfolgreichen modernistischen Fotografin Else Neuländer-Simon alias Yva organisierte, ging für ihn ein Traum in Erfüllung. Dass er die Handhabung von Kamera, Beleuchtung, Dunkelkammer und Modellen bei einer jener starken Frauen erlernte, die seinen Lebensweg entscheidend beeinflussten, ist sicher nicht unwichtig. „Yva machte Modefotos und Porträts von Balletttänzerinnen, Schauspielern und Schauspielerinnen. Wir illustrierten auch viele Unterwäschekataloge, eine Arbeit, die mir sehr zusagte", erinnert er sich. „Es war wahrscheinlich die glücklichste Zeit meiner Jugend in Berlin … Ich verehrte den Boden, auf dem sie ging." Seine Helden Munkácsi, Moholy-Nagy, Salomon und Yva gehörten alle zur progressiven Welle in der europäischen Kunst der 1920er- und 1930er-Jahre, und sie waren Juden. Nachdem er Berlin verlassen hatte, erfuhr Newton, dass Yva in einem Konzentrationslager ermordet worden war, und war am Boden zerstört. „Ich habe mir immer die größte Mühe gegeben, ihr Andenken hochzuhalten", schrieb er.

Mitte der 1970er-Jahre hatte sich Helmut Newton in Europa als Modefotograf für *Vogue Paris*, *Nova*, *Queen* und die britische *Vogue* einen Namen gemacht. Das 524-seitige Buch *Pages from the Glossies: Facsimiles 1956–1998*[3] zeugt vom gewaltigen Umfang seiner Arbeit für Modemagazine. Eine Handvoll Artdirectors und Moderedakteure machten ihm die Umsetzung seiner minutiös inszenierten, gefährlichen Visionen möglich (Willy Landels bei *Queen*, Caroline Baker bei *Nova*, Francine Crescent und Jacques Faure bei der *Vogue Paris* und später Anna Wintour bei der amerikanischen *Vogue*). Über Crescent sagte Newton: „Wer sonst hätte diese Akte, wer sonst hätte diese verrückten und sexuell aufgeladenen Modefotografien veröffentlicht, die ich einreichte?"[4] Denn sein Talent für Zweideutigkeit zeigte sich auch, wenn er

American *Vogue*, Maui, Hawaii, 1974
Models: Patti Hansen and Rene Russo

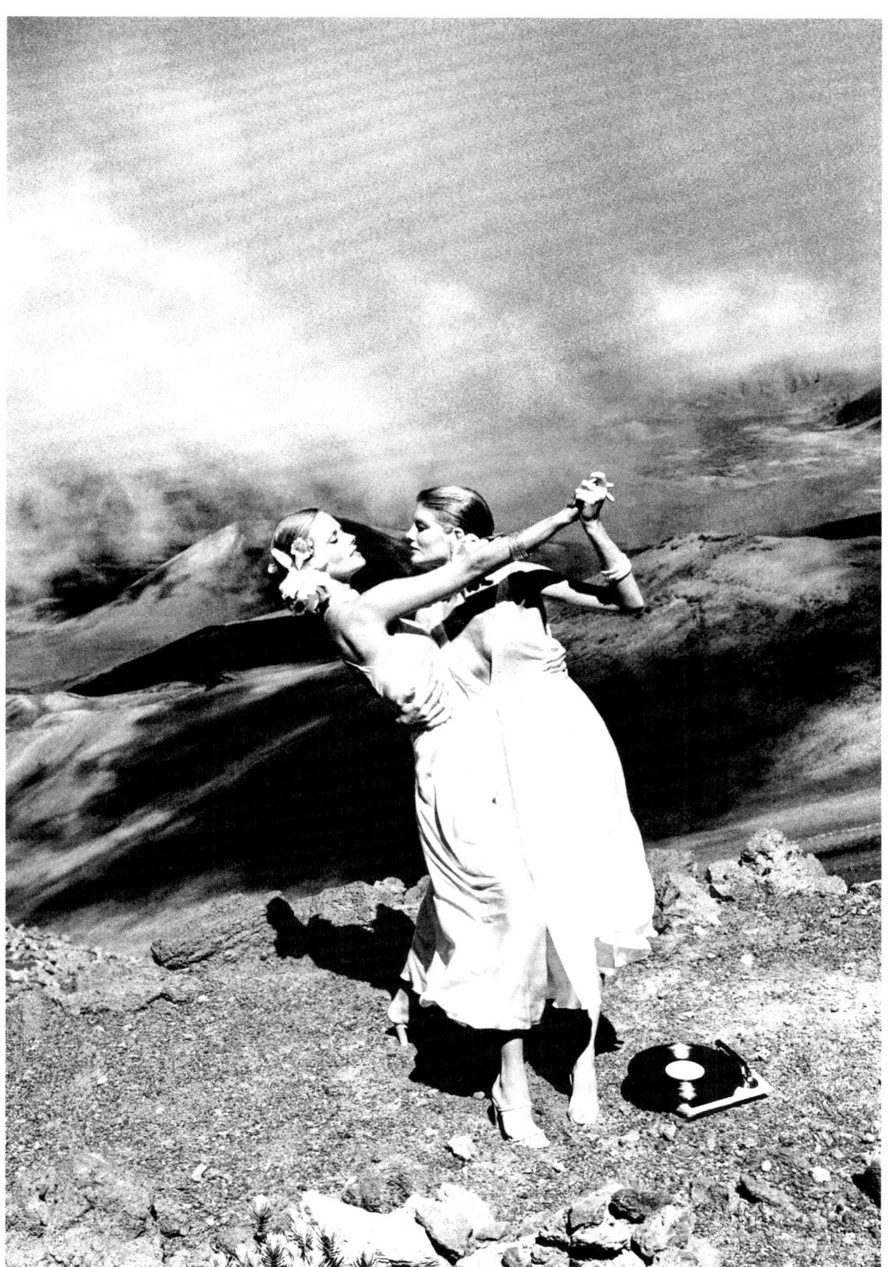

vollständig in Haute Couture gekleidete Frauen fotografierte. Auf dem Bild *Chez Yves Saint Laurent,* das 1977 in der amerikanischen *Vogue* erschien, bevölkern hinreißend gekleidete Models Yves Saint Laurents üppigen Haute-Couture-Salon – und trotzdem kann man sich des Eindrucks nicht erwehren, dass Newton ihn aussehen ließ wie eines der berühmten Pariser Bordelle.

Mit einem Foto sowohl Begehren als auch Empörung auszulösen, war eines seiner schon früh selbst gesetzten Kriterien für Erfolg. Sein Landsmann und Freund Karl Lagerfeld schrieb einmal im Vorwort eines Newton-Fotobands, man müsse seinem Ruf gerecht werden, auch einem schlechten.[5] Während Newton planvoll an seiner Unabhängigkeit als „Auftragskiller" (wie er sich gern bezeichnete) arbeitete und für sich und June (die 1970 unter ihrem Künstlernamen Alice Springs selbst eine Karriere als Fotografin begann) den bestmöglichen Lebensstil sicherte, war er gleichzeitig ständig damit beschäftigt, die Schockwirkung seiner Fotos aufrechtzuerhalten. Newton profitierte erfolgreich von den Nachkriegsjahrzehnten des Konsumbooms und den Vorstellungen, die im Zusammenhang mit dem Aufstieg der emanzipierter „Powerfrau" aufkamen, und er war finanziell sehr erfolgreich. Er hatte viele Freunde in der High Society, besaß Luxusautos und vor allem die Freiheit, so zu leben und zu arbeiten, wie er wollte. Ob er in Paris und im südfranzösischen Ramatuelle wohnte (in den 1960er- und 1970er-Jahren) oder im Sommer in Monte Carlo und im Winter im Hotel Chateau Marmont in Los Angeles (wie in den 1980er-Jahren): Newton nutzte all diese exklusiven Locations für seine Arbeit – und zeigte manchmal auch deren brutale Schattenseiten. Selbst in den engen Grenzen einer Hochglanz-Enklave wie Monaco entdeckte er noch die rauen Ecken, die er mochte: Betonmauern, Baustellen, die Felskante der Corniche und seine Tiefgarage. Überall bewegte er sich auf dem schmalen Grat zwischen dem Verbotenen und dem, was als stilvoll galt. Und oft überschritt er diese Grenze ganz bewusst.

„Auftragskiller"

Newton machte sich stets ausführliche vorbereitende Notizen zu seinen Ideen und Bezügen und bestand dann auf der Freiheit, schnell und unmittelbar zu arbeiten. „Ich war immer ein Einzelkämpfer und habe nur mit einem Assistenten gearbeitet." Ansonsten waren bei einem Helmut-Newton-Shooting nur ein, manchmal zwei Models, die Moderedakteurin oder Stilistin, die Friseurin und Maskenbildnerin zugelassen – eine Vorgabe, die Newton bei einem Werbekunden genauso rigoros durchsetzte wie bei einem Zeitschriftenauftrag. Er war stolz darauf, am Set immer nur mit einer Ausrüstung aufzutauchen, die in eine Kameratasche passte; vielleicht kamen noch ein paar kleine Lampen dazu. Derart ausgestattet, fotografierte er schnell und verbrauchte an einem Arbeitstag nur wenige Rollen Film. Seine Schnellschussprofessionalität führte er auf seine Ausbildung als 16-Jähriger bei Yva zurück. „An meiner Aufnahmetechnik hat sich nicht viel verändert, seit ich ein Kind war. Ich besitze kein Studioblitzgerät und arbeite nur ungern im Studio", schreibt er in seiner Autobiografie.

Diese Faszination für die Fotografie an Originalschauplätzen war es, die den typischen Helmut-Newton-Look mit seinem hohen Wiedererkennungswert hervorbrachte. „Meine Fantasie brauchte die Realität draußen unter freiem Himmel. Ich hatte außerdem begriffen, dass ich nur als Modefotograf mein persönliches Universum erschaffen konnte, in dem meine Models einen bestimmten Frauentyp verkörpern."[6] Viele seiner bekanntesten Fotos sind nachts auf der Straße bei natürlichem Licht entstanden. Nur gelegentlich kam eine Taschenlampe zum Einsatz (Newton nannte Brassaïs *Paris bei Nacht* als Einfluss). Beim Arbeiten in Farbe fotografierte er kalkuliert im grellen, senkrecht einfallenden Licht der Mittagssonne, was für die unverwechselbaren extremen Kontraste sorgte. Das damit einhergehende technische Risiko nahm er selbstbewusst und angstfrei in Kauf. In Zeiten der analogen Fotografie gab es keine Garantie für perfekte Ergebnisse. Doch Newton hielt an seiner Arbeitsweise fest, trotz des großen Auftragsvolumens und der kleinen Budgets, die von den Zeitschriften schnelle Gewinne verlangten.

Beim zügigen Arbeiten war er in seinem Element. (Dass er seine ausgesprochen narrativen Ideen nicht filmisch umsetzte, lag, wie er dem Regisseur und Freund Gero von Boehm anvertraute, an seiner kurzen Aufmerksamkeitsspanne und fehlender Geduld.) Begeistert von der Idee der Spontaneität – die aber immer in seinen präzise vorbereiteten Sets eingefangen wurde –, sah Newton oft in seinen Polaroid-Probeaufnahmen (die vor dem eigentlichen Foto zur Überprüfung des Bildaufbaus gemacht wurden) eine größere visuelle Spannung als in dem später entwickelten Film. Zwei Ausstellungen und ein Buch[7] wurden diesem Aspekt bereits gewidmet.

An exotische Orte wollte und musste Newton nie reisen. Sein Ideenreichtum zeigte sich, wenn er Szenarien für vertraute Orte austüftelte, die manchmal nur einen kurzen Fußmarsch von seiner Wohnung entfernt lagen. Einmal löste er das Problem, die Pariser Kollektionen für die *Vogue Paris* nachts fotografieren zu müssen (die Couture-Häuser gaben die Kleider für die Magazinstrecken immer nachts frei), indem er statt realer Frauen Schaufensterpuppen einsetzte. Was einerseits pragmatisch und vielleicht auch lustig war, verwies andererseits einigermaßen provokant auf den männlichen Blick, der Frauen als Objekte, als Puppen betrachtet. Dieser Kunstgriff eröffnete Newton neue Möglichkeiten: In vielen weiteren Shootings drapierte er sowohl männliche als auch weibliche Schaufensterpuppen in Luxuswohnungen in sexuellen Szenarien. Mit den Puppen konnte er so weit gehen, wie er wolte. Einmal kettete er eines seiner bevorzugten üppigen „Models" mitten in einem exklusiven Pariser Wohnviertel nackt an ein Geländer.

Dass Helmut Newton kostengünstig arbeitete und trotzdem ausnehmend glamouröse Ergebnisse brachte, funktionierte für seine redaktionellen Auftraggeber

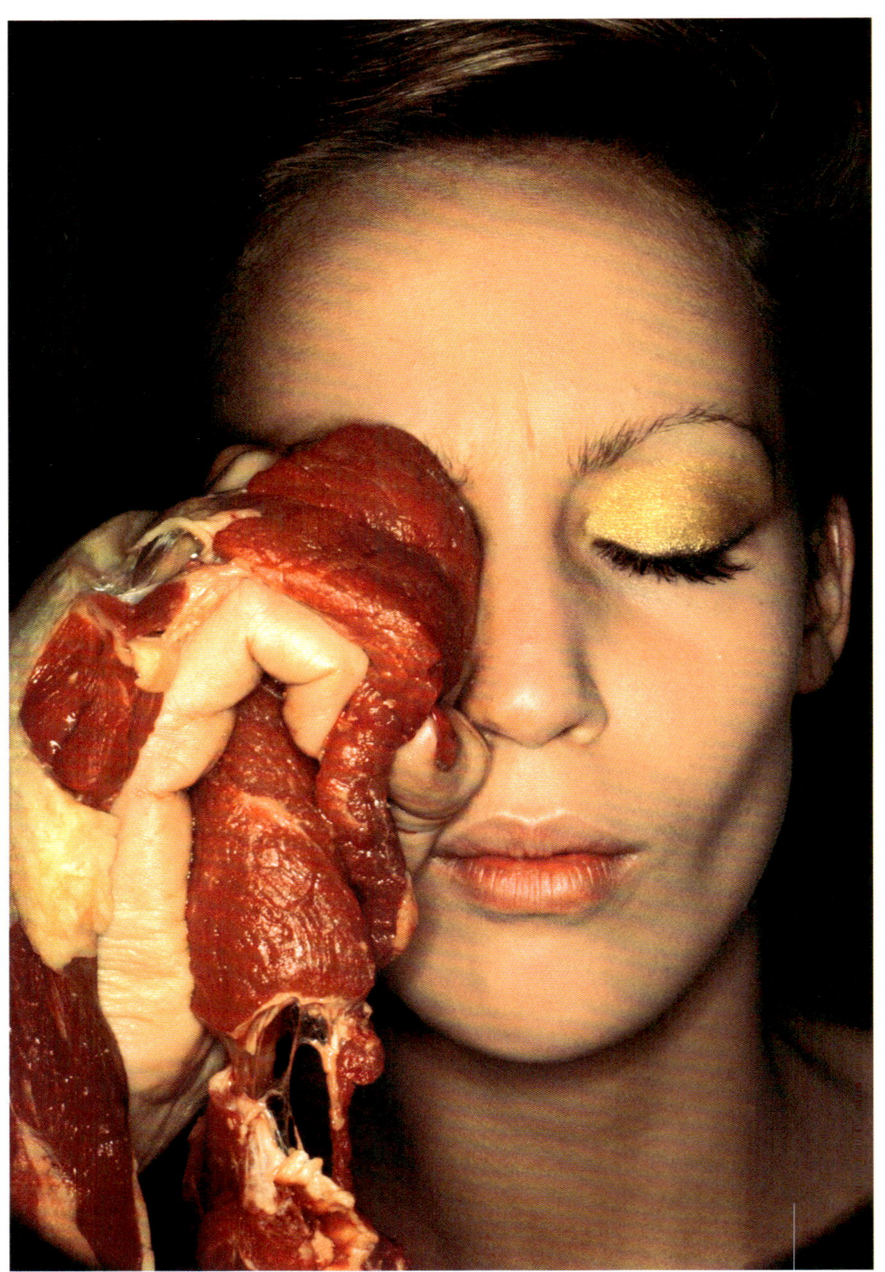

jahrzehntelang sehr gut. Für ihn selbst tat es das auch, dafür sorgte er. Für die Presse
zu arbeiten, war für ihn aber eine ebenso ambivalente wie kalkulierte Angelegenheit:
Obwohl er wirklich gut war, war die Modefotografie für ihn doch n e mehr als ein Tor,
hinter dem er seine eigene Welt mit Motiven bevölkern konnte, die ihn interessierten
– vor allem Frauen, nackt oder bekleidet.

„Ich nannte es ‚das System mit seinen eigenen Waffen schlagen‘.“
Indem sich Newton bei allen Aufträgen ein gewisses Maß an Eigenständigkeit
zusichern ließ, konnte er zugleich stets auch seine eigenen Arbeiten realisieren. „Ich
habe es immer verstanden, die Ressourcen meiner Auftraggeber für meine Zwecke
zu nutzen, bei Werbeaufnahmen wie bei Modefotos. Ich nannte es ‚das System mit
seinen eigenen Waffen schlagen‘. Mein Trick bestand darin, dass ich bei jedem Termin
ein paar Stunden für meine persönlichen Arbeiten abzweigte. Natürlich zeigte ich den
Auftraggebern auch diese Bilder, aber meistens veröffentlichten sie lieber die norma-
len Fotos als meine persönlichen Arbeiten … auf diese Weise baute ich mein privates
Archiv auf.“[8]
In *White Women*[9], dem ersten Buch mit seinen Arbeiten, das ihm den Beinamen
„The King of Kink“ (König der kleinen Perversion) einbrachte, veröffentlichte er zwei
seiner Überstundenprojekte. Auf dem „offiziellen“ Foto von Yves Saint Laurents
maskulinem Hosenanzug „Le Smoking“, das 1975 für die *Vogue Paris* nachts auf der
Rue Aubriot im Marais aufgenommen wurde (wo die Newtons damals wohnten),
sieht man das Model bekleidet und allein. Auf dem zweiten Bild aber steht ein zweites
Model daneben – nackt bis auf einen Hut mit Schleier von Paulette. In einer weiteren
doppelten Modeaufnahme fotografierte er das blonde Model Roselyne von hinten,
wie es die Freitreppe eines Schlosses in einem schwarzen, von Karl Lagerfeld entwor-
fenen Chloé-Abendkleid hinaufschreitet, das in der *Vogue Paris* 1975 als „von der Taille
abwärts geschlitzt“ beschrieben wird. In Newtons zweitem Bild ist das Hinterteil
der Frau entblößt.
Das Einverständnis der Models, sich nackt oder in Unterwäsche, aber immer in
High Heels ablichten zu lassen, spielte vermutlich eine große Rolle. Ab den 1970er-
Jahren galt es als Ehre, als eine „Helmut-Newton-Frau“ ausgewählt zu werden. Lange
nach Newtons Tod interviewte Gero von Boehm für seinen Dokumentarfilm *The Bad
and the Beautiful* aus dem Jahr 2020 Charlotte Rampling, Isabella Rossellini, Grace
Jones, Hanna Schygulla und mehrere Models, die für ihn posiert hatten. Rampling
gab zu Protokoll, das Nacktfoto, das Newton 1974 von ihr machte, habe ihr „enorme

A Cure for a Black Eye,
American *Vogue*, Paris, 1974
Model: Jerry Hall

innere Kraft gegeben…Ohne diese Fotos wäre meine ganze Karriere anders verlaufen." Rossellini meinte, Newton habe mit voller Absicht den männlichen Blick auf Frauen in westlichen Gesellschaften abgebildet. Sie selbst habe sich wissentlich daran beteiligt, diesen Blick vor seiner Kamera zu inszenieren. Grace Jones frotzelte, er sei eben „ein bisschen pervers, aber das bin ich auch". Newton machte seine Sichtweise deutlich, als er sagte, er „liebe Frauen"; worauf Susan Sontag in einer Kunstsendung im französischen Fernsehen bissig entgegnete: „Das sagen viele frauenfeindliche Männer."

Newton wiederum führte stets June, die eine eigene Karriere als Fotografin machte, als seine wichtigste Mitverschworene an. „June und ich grübelten über neuen Bildideen, mit denen wir die Leserinnen und Leser der Magazine zu verblüffen hofften."[10] Dass die „Journalisten immer fragen, ob ich mit meinen Models geschlafen habe und ob June nicht eifersüchtig sei", ärgerte ihn.[11] Das Bild *Self Portrait with Wife and Models, Paris 1981*, auf dem June ihm dabei zusieht, wie er nackte Frauen fotografiert, war vermutlich seine Antwort auf diese Frage – und eine weitere Provokation. Der Titel ihres gemeinsamen Buches *Us and Them* könnte leicht als Beleg dafür gelesen

> **„Mit den Puppen konnte er so weit gehen, wie er wollte. Einmal kettete er eines seiner bevorzugten üppigen ‚Models' mitten in einem exklusiven Pariser Wohnviertel nackt an ein Geländer."**

werden, wie nah sich die Newtons in ihrer Ehe standen, wie sehr sie unter einer Decke steckten, wie viel professionellen Respekt sie voreinander hatten und wie sie sich selbst wohl als Einheit gegen den Rest der Welt betrachteten.[12] Ihre offenherzigen, witzigen und manchmal geradezu rührenden Fotos, die sie voneinander zu Hause und bei der Arbeit machten, stehen neben ihren Porträts von *les autres*: von Prinzessin Caroline von Monaco, Catherine Deneuve, Karl Lagerfeld, Gianni Versace, Charlotte Rampling und Brassaï, um nur einige zu nennen.

June – das macht die Autobiografie deutlich – war die Einzige, die die Landschaften und die Vorstellungen von Frauen in seinem Kopf gänzlich verstand; sie wusste genau, woher seine Neigung zu kraftvollen, verrucht-verspielten Narrativen stammte. Egal, wen und wo er fotografierte, ob in Paris, Berlin, New York, Los Angeles oder Monte Carlo: Newtons Œuvre drehte sich jahrzehntelang eigentlich nur um einen einzigen Schauplatz.

Seine Liebe zu Berlin und zur Welt seiner Kindheit war unverbrüchlich. Häufig kehrte er in die Stadt zurück, um hier mehrdeutige Fotos zu machen, in denen gleichermaßen Nostalgie und eine implizite Anklage steckten. Als er 1979 für den Relaunch der deutschen *Vogue* fotografieren sollte, reinszenierte er Situationen seiner Jugend – June hatte eine Rückkehr an die Orte vorgeschlagen, wo er sich als Junge

aufgehalten hatte. Schon 1963 hatte er mit seiner direkt an der Berliner Mauer foto-
grafierten *Mata Hari*-Spionagestory für die *Vogue Paris* für einen politischen Eklat im
Kalten Krieg gesorgt. Und für die bekannte Fotoserie von Frauen unter anderem in
orthopädischen Korsetts, zu finden in dem Buch *Sleepless Nights*[13] fotografierte er in
dem Berliner Bordell Pension Florian die deutsche Moderedakteurin Jenny Capitain –
nackt bis auf den Gips am Bein und die Manschette um den Hals

Newton befasste sich intensiv mit der Neuformulierung seiner vielschichtigen
Beziehung zu den Besonderheiten der deutschen Kultur, die sein Referenzrahmen war.
Genau deswegen lösten der von ihm fotografierte Typ Frau, seine stilisierte Beleuch-
tungstechnik und seine aus extremen Winkeln gefassten Bildausschnitte bei so vielen
Unbehagen aus. „Damals war ich umgeben von der Bildsprache des Nationalsozialismus, wie jeder in Deutschland, und in einem von der Fotografie besessenen Jungen
wie mir hinterließ das einen unauslöschlichen Eindruck."[14] Seine Verehrung für die
Filmemacher der 1920er- und 1930er-Jahre blieb bestehen – als Inspiration für seine
Fotoserie von Frauen in medizinischen Korsetts und Halsmanschetten nannte er
die Filme Erich von Stroheims. In seinem Interview mit der *New York Times* sagte er
2003: „Die Fotografie damals war sehr, sehr gut. Auch die russische Fotografie war
interessant." Zwischen dem Ende des Ersten Weltkriegs und dem Aufstieg des Nationalsozialismus erlebte die deutsche Filmindustrie eine Blütezeit. Auch sogenannte Auf-
klärungsfilme, Pornografie und düstere Thriller boomten. Newton erinnerte sich, als
Kind heimlich in Kinos geschlichen zu sein. Es war das Berlin von Brecht und Bauhaus, der Cafés und Cabarets, ein liberaler, avantgardistischer Magnet für freigeistige
Kreative und Besucher aus ganz Europa und Amerika. Die Drehbuchautorin Anita Loos
sagte, dass sich „in Berlin jede Nachtschwärmerin am Ende als Mann entpuppen
könnte" – und umgekehrt. Jahrzehnte später erklärte Newton, es seien die Ganzkörper-
fahndungsplakate der Baader-Meinhof-Gruppe in einer deutschen Polizeidienststelle
gewesen, die ihn zu seiner monumentalen Serie *Big Nudes* inspiriert hätten. „Im Hin-
blick auf meine *Big Nudes* haben mir in Deutschland einige vorgeworfen, faschistische
Bilder zu machen. Meine Antwort darauf war: Diesen Vorwurf erkenne ich an. Sie
waren ein Rückfall in meine Jugend."[15]

**„Wenn ich gefragt werde: ‚Welche Menschen fotografieren Sie gerne?', lautet meine
Antwort: ‚Die, die ich liebe, die ich bewundere und die ich hasse.'"**

Newton hegte sein Leben lang tiefes Misstrauen gegenüber allem, was für ihn den
Beigeschmack von autoritärer Kontrolle hatte, egal ob von rechts oder von links. „Der
Begriff ‚Political Correctness' hat mich immer abgeschreckt, weil er mich an Orwells
Gedankenpolizei und faschistische Gewaltherrschaft erinnert", schrieb er in seiner
Einleitung zum *SUMO*. Eine neue kreative Spielwiese erschloss er sich in den 1990er-
Jahren mit seinen Porträtfotos für *Vanity Fair* und das Magazin *The New Yorker*. Von

den Vorgaben der Modemagazine fühlte er sich zunehmend eingeengt, gegen die Forderungen der Promi-Manager in Hollywood sträubte er sich ebenfalls. Ab den 1970er-Jahren hatten vor allem Salonlöwinnen, Filmstars und Prinzessinnen jeglichen Alters gern für ihn posiert. Mit vielen von ihnen verband ihn eine langjährige Freundschaft. In seinen späteren Jahren jedoch richtete er die Kamera auf Männer – es entstand eine Galerie von Reichen und Mächtigen, Politikern und Playboys. Auch das Rechtswesen nahm er wieder ins Visier und fotografierte einen Richter, einen Kriminalbeamten und den Anwalt Rudy Giuliani, damals Bürgermeister von New York.

Helmut Newton erkannte, welche vielversprechenden Möglichkeiten er hatte, wenn er den detailreichen Witz, mit dem er Berühmte fotografierte, auch auf die Berüchtigten anwendete. Zu seiner großen Genugtuung trieb er den rechtsextremen französischen Politiker Jean-Marie Le Pen zur Weißglut, indem er ihn, der Eingebung des Augenblicks folgend, dazu überredete, mit den beiden Dobermännern zu posieren, die er in Le Pens Garten entdeckt hatte. Das Bild sorgte für Furore, weil die Presse es mit einem bekannten Foto von Hitler verglich. Leni Riefenstahl, die Regisseurin der Propagandafilme über den Nürnberger Reichsparteitag 1934 und Hitlers Olympische Spiele 1936, umwarb er so lange, bis sie sich als gealterte Frau von ihm fotografieren ließ. Die beiden schlossen eine seltsame Freundschaft, die er in seiner Autobiografie so beschrieb: „Das nahmen mir viele übel, darunter auch June, die nie verstanden hat, dass ein Jude eine solche Beziehung zu einer Person mit einer derart dubiosen politischen Vergangenheit haben kann." Eines seiner Porträts von ihr allerdings zeigt Riefenstahl, gewinnend lächelnd und mit der Filmkamera im Schoß, in einem Moment, in dem sich ein Streifen Film um ihre Handgelenke geschlungen hat. Eine bleibende Aussage.

Die erotischen Vorlieben und Fetische, denen Newton mit seinem Werk nachging – die großen, statuesken Frauen, die Pools und Interieurs, in denen er sie inszenierte, die Charaktere, die er gern fotografierte –, sind auf die eine oder andere Weise eine lebenslange Verarbeitung, Überwindung und Sublimation jener Faszination und jenes Widerwillens, die er gegenüber dem empfand, was ihn prägte. So wurde er zu dem nonkonformistischen, zynischen und lakonischen Menschen, dessen Visionen einige der wichtigsten und provokantesten Bilder hervorgebracht haben, anhand derer sich die Mode der zweiten Hälfte des 20. Jahrhunderts betrachten lässt. Letzten Endes wird genau dieser Aspekt seines umfangreichen Werks noch lange für Erstaunen, Begeisterung und Entsetzen sorgen.

Pages 40/41
American *Vogue*, Rudi Gernreich, Miami, 1975
Models: Lisa Taylor and Jerry Hall

Nova, **Paris, 1973**
Model: Willy van Rooy

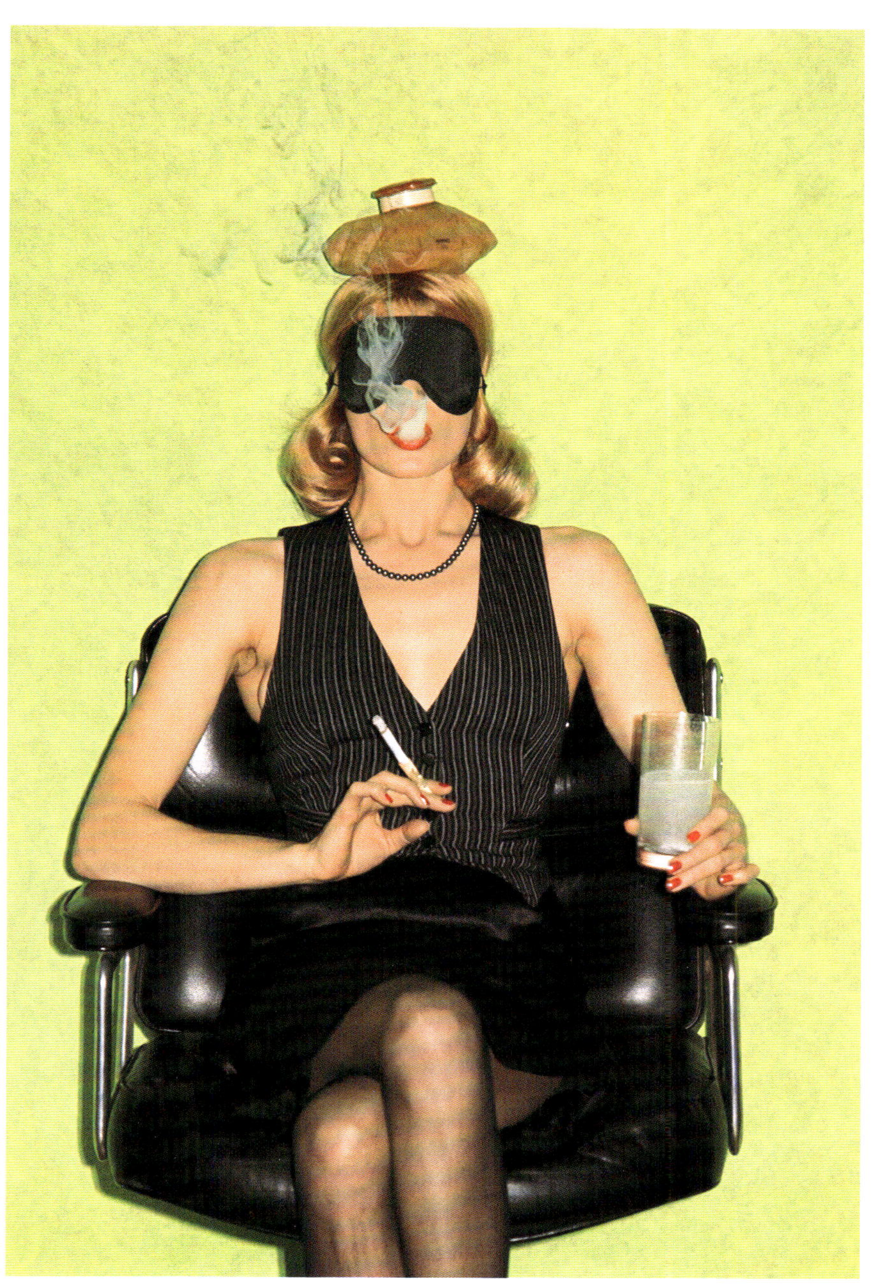

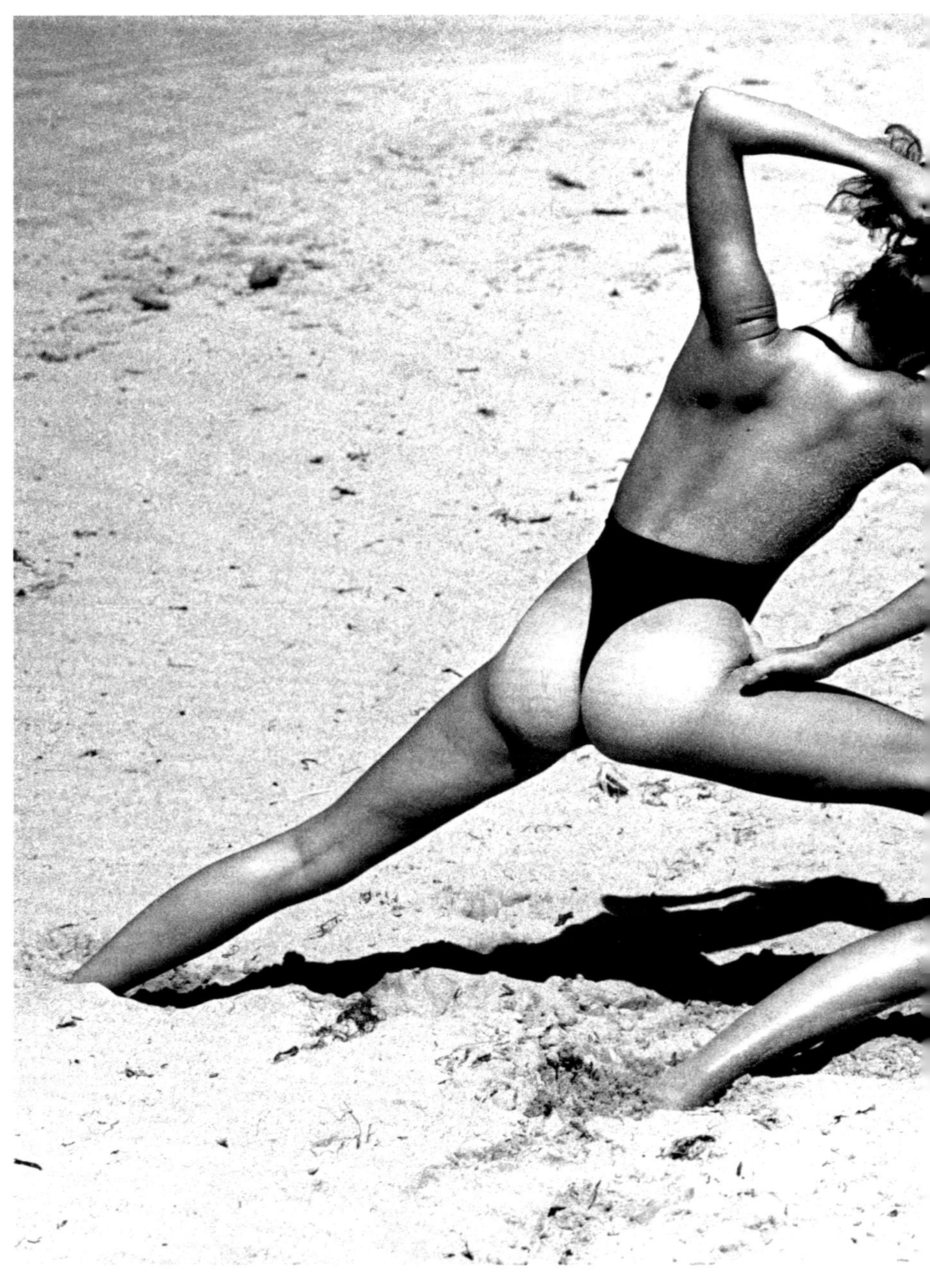

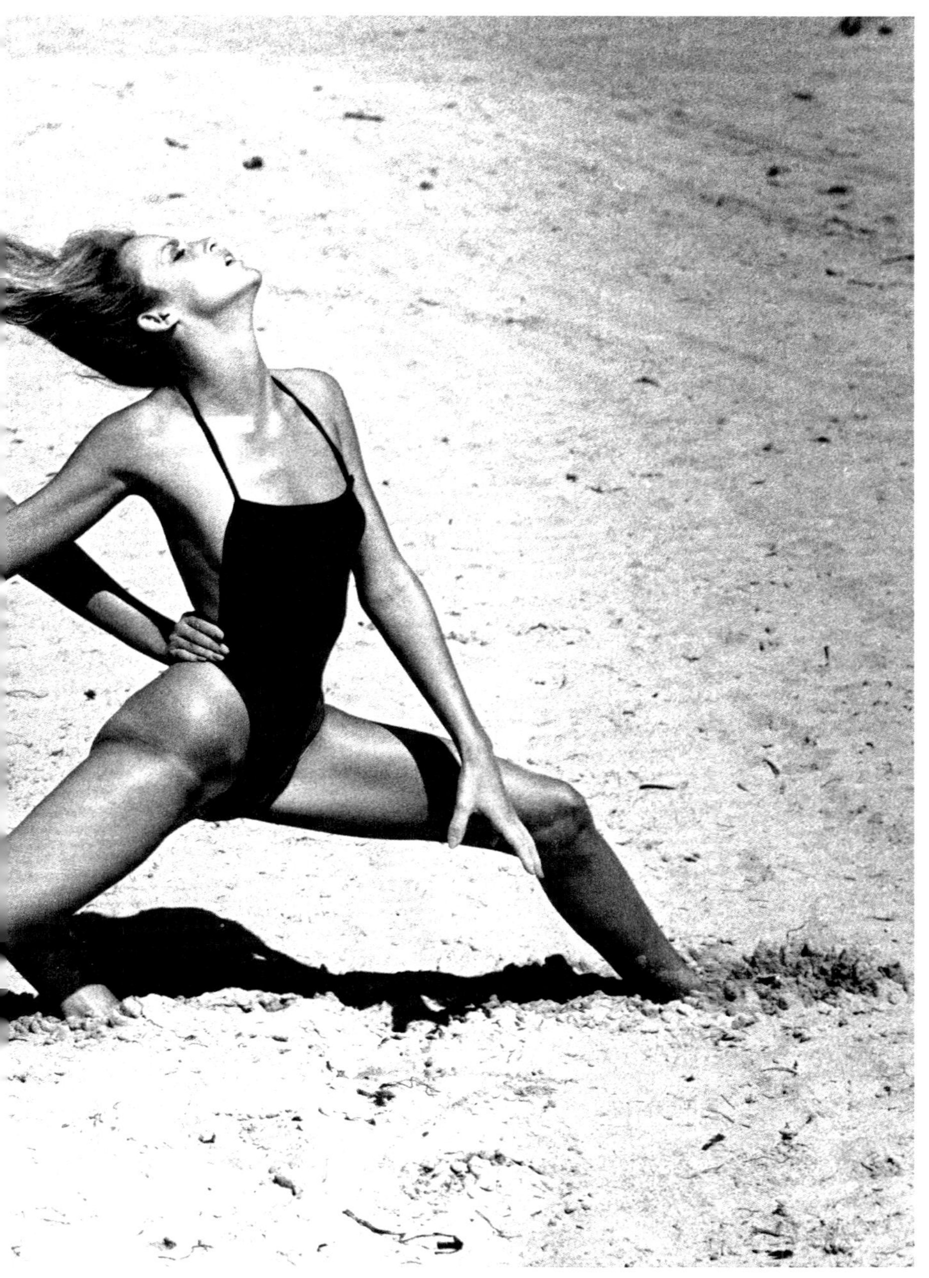

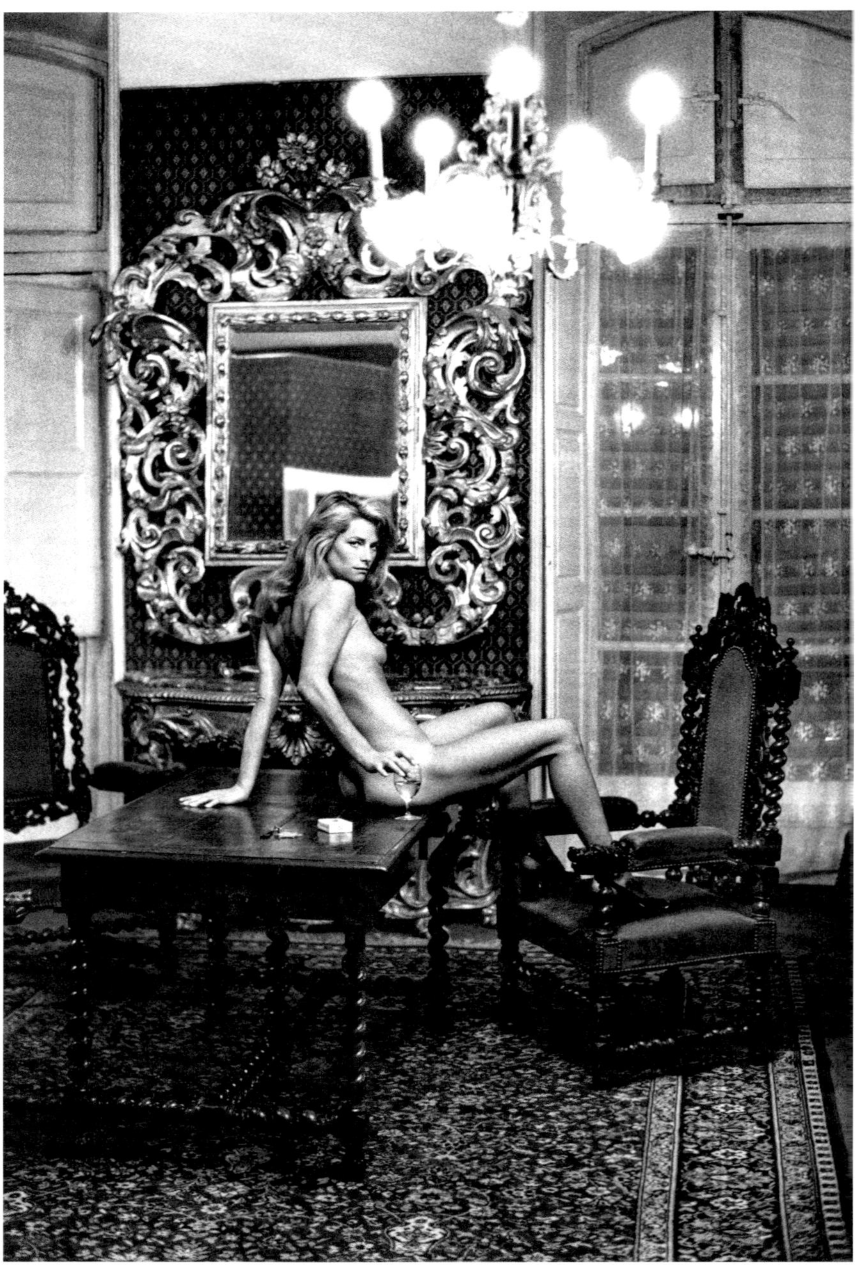

Équilibriste entre chic et illicite

Par Sarah Mower

« Lorsque le *Vogue* américain est sorti en kiosques à l'été 1975, avec *The Story of Ohhh…* dans ses pages, la critique s'est déchaînée. Je venais de me faire un nom. Je n'ai plus jamais regardé en arrière. »

Mai 1975 : le *Vogue* américain publie 12 pages d'un shooting de mode réalisé par Helmut Newton. Le photographe savoure, sans gêne aucune, le scandale que ses images déclenchent. Sa réaction d'alors est un bon point de départ pour sonder la personnalité de l'homme, le situer dans l'histoire de la mode et de la photographie. L'un des clichés est de ceux qui, dira-t-on, façonnent une époque. On y voit le modèle Lisa Taylor, habillée d'une tunique et d'une jupe Calvin Klein, assise, jambes écartées, sur un canapé d'extérieur. Elle alpague du regard un homme torse nu qui passe par là. Celui-ci est vu de trois-quarts dos, la tête hors cadre. La scène peut être interprétée, sans équivoque, comme une expression du désir féminin. L'angle de la prise de vue et la pose du mannequin sont du jamais-vu dans les pages d'un magazine pour femmes.

Dans le documentaire *Helmut by June*, réalisé par son épouse en 1995, le photographe explique comment il a tordu le cou aux conventions et repensé la scénographie de la mode : « Le cliché parfait doit évoquer une image tout droit sortie d'un film, d'un souvenir personnel ou de l'appareil d'un paparazzi. Tout sauf une photo de mode. »

Cette photographie de Lisa Taylor, Helmut Newton semble davantage l'avoir prise à l'avant-poste d'une révolution sociale. Mise en scène avec la complicité de Polly Allen Mellen, rédactrice en chef progressiste des pages mode de *Vogue*, l'image incarne pour beaucoup la glamourisation d'une puissance nouvellement acquise dans une Amérique en pleine libération sexuelle, dont la femme est le porte-drapeau. La contraception vient d'être légalisée et, deux ans plus tôt, la Cour suprême a rendu un verdict en faveur de l'avortement sous certaines conditions. Mais ce qui choque les âmes conservatrices exposées à *The Story of Ohhh…* se trouve ailleurs, dans leur analyse de ces scènes estivales, imaginées autour de trois protagonistes : « J'ai été accusé de dépeindre une certaine bestialité et d'encourager le sexe entre deux femmes et un homme », se souvient Helmut Newton, avec une satisfaction non feinte, dans son autobiographie[1].

Le grand public y découvre deux femmes en bikini et robe du soir, un homme avec son chien – les thèmes récurrents de la piscine, de l'indolence sybarite, de la tension sexuelle, parfois avec une présence canine, n'ont pas échappé à ceux qui connaissent l'œuvre d'Helmut Newton. Grace Mirabella, rédactrice en chef, reçoit une avalanche de courriers rageurs, *Vogue* est retiré de la vente en Floride : rien d'autre qu'une aubaine dans sa carrière, dira le photographe. « Je venais de me faire un nom. Je n'ai plus jamais regardé en arrière. »

L'œuvre d'Helmut Newton, de shootings professionnels en travaux personnels, est vaste. Et le photographe s'est toujours enorgueilli, félicité même, de flirter avec l'ambiguïté, le sous-entendu et la satire sociale. Son travail met en scène le regard posé sur les femmes et la mode dans la seconde moitié du XXe siècle, autant qu'il en témoigne et l'épingle. Il signe l'épilogue d'une culture occidentale à géométrie variable quant aux débats sur le libre arbitre des femmes, la pornographie, ce qui est vu ou donné à voir, et dans quel contexte. L'ordre moral, politique et de genre est, raconte-t-on alors, en passe d'être foulé aux pieds par la « société permissive » d'après-guerre, dont Helmut Newton est un membre actif. Son travail ne cesse cependant de soulever la même question : qu'est-ce qui est donc autorisé ou non dans le champ social ? Nul doute qu'il se délecterait de savoir que la controverse continue d'agiter les spectateurs, confrontés à cette même question, mais à une autre époque, avec d'autres cartes en main.

Son travail est aussi, à bien des égards, l'autobiographie en filigrane d'un juif de Berlin ayant subi la montée du nazisme. Une série d'actes discrets mais subversifs, sophistiqués, comme une revanche, mâtinée de ce qu'Helmut Newton appelait son « méchant humour berlinois ». Dans les années 1980, il est célèbre, riche et courtisé par le gotha. Il fait installer ses archives au sein de la Helmut Newton Foundation, dans un bâtiment en face de la gare de Bahnhof Zoo. C'est de là qu'il avait fui Berlin en 1938.

Page 42
Charlotte Rampling, Hotel Nord-Pinus, Arles, 1973
In the documentary *The Bad and the Beautiful* by Gero von Boehm, Charlotte Rampling talked about the confidence and career-enhancing effect of being photographed nude by Newton in 1973. The background was the interior of the Hotel Nord-Pinus in Arles. Rampling, who was to star with Dirk Bogarde in *The Night Porter*, the controversial movie directed by Liliana Cavani, was a subject Newton subsequently photographed over a number of years.

Opposite
Winnie off the Coast of Cannes, 1975
Model: Winnie Hollman

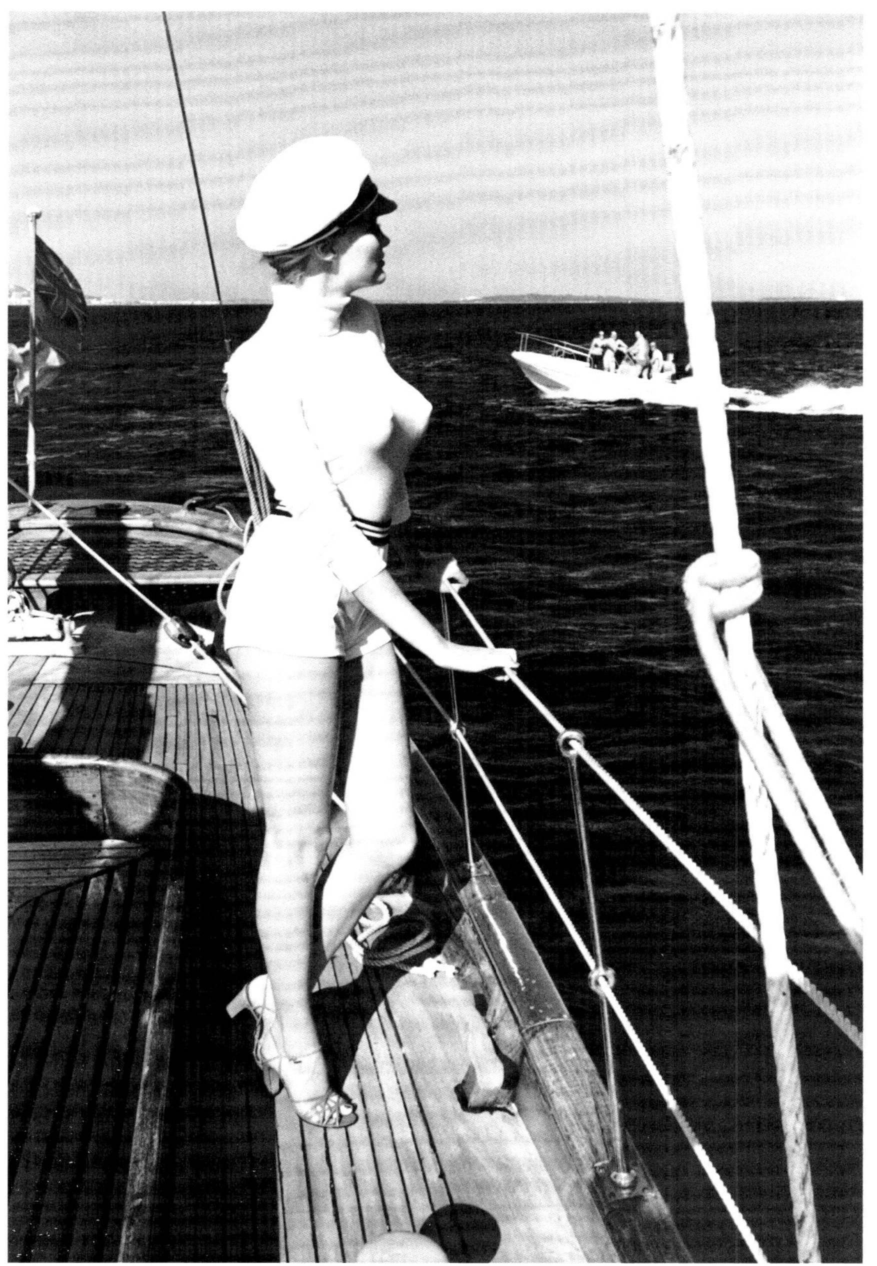

Helmut Neustädter est né à Berlin en 1920. Sa sensibilité s'est forgée au contact des arts conventionnels et de la décadence de la rue, dans une république de Weimar en déclin, une culture dissolue, empreinte d'un mauvais présage. Le jeune Helmut, issu d'une classe privilégiée, vit une jeunesse joyeuse, baignée d'une obsession pour le sexe et la photographie. L'arrivée au pouvoir des nazis détruit tout. En 1938, il s'enfuit seul, en bateau, pour Singapour. Sa mère a pris tous les risques pour lui obtenir un billet. Il a 18 ans quand il monte dans un train, armé de deux appareils photo comme des promesses de carrière, et salue une famille qu'il ne reverra plus. Deux ans passent, il est transféré en Australie et incarcéré en tant qu'ennemi alle-mand. Il finira par rejoindre l'armée australienne. Puis c'est le retour à la vie civile, son installation en tant que photographe, en 1946. Il prend le nom d'Helmut Newton, rencontre la comédienne June Browne suite à une annonce passée pour trouver un modèle. Ils se marient à Melbourne en 1948.

« **Le photographe peut aller aussi loin qu'il lui plaît, en enchaînant l'un de ses "modèles" favoris, au corps nu et voluptueux, à une grille au cœur des quartiers chics de Paris.** »

Son autobiographie établit la psycho-géographie dessinée en lui par son éducation berlinoise – avant ces écrits, il ne s'était confié qu'à son épouse June. « Mes parents m'ont offert une belle jeunesse. » Max, son père, est fabricant de boucles et boutons. Sa famille vit dans le confort de l'ancien monde, entourée de domestiques. Sa mère, Claire, lit *Vogue*. Helmut Newton se souvient d'un premier émoi érotique « à l'âge de trois ou quatre ans », lorsqu'il voit sa nounou à moitié dévêtue. Ici commence sa course effrénée d'un fantasme sexuel à l'autre. Sa fascina-tion pour la prostitution ? Il la doit à Erna la Rouge, une dominatrice reine du trottoir, que son grand frère Hans lui montre alors qu'il n'a que sept ans. À Berlin, plongé dans la tourmente économique et l'hyperinflation, les femmes sont de plus en plus nombreuses à vendre leur corps.

L'œuvre d'Helmut Newton ne montre que ça : une vie bourgeoise dans laquelle il expose ce qui se passe, dans son imaginaire, derrière les portes closes. « J'ai toujours été fasciné par les hôtels et les chambres d'hôtels. Avec mes parents, j'ai séjourné dans de grands établissements à travers l'Europe. Ils demeurent pour moi parés d'un certain mystère. Ils ont souvent servi de décor à mes shootings de mode. Comme d'autres hôtels, plus petits ou moins recommandables[2]. »

Gâté et, de son propre aveu également, peu intéressé par l'école, le jeune Helmut devient un champion amateur de natation. Il court les filles autour des piscines à cie

ouvert et des lacs de Berlin, n'échappant pas au culte allemand du corps et de la
santé qui prévaut à l'époque. Son unique ambition est de devenir photographe :
« À 12 ans, je me suis rendu dans un magasin d'articles à petits prix et y ai acheté un
appareil photo avec mon argent de poche. » Il a pour référence les photographies
d'avant-gardistes tels que Martin Munkácsi, László Moholy-Nagy et Erich Salomon,
publiés dans des hebdomadaires grand public. Un temps, il nourrit le rêve d'une
carrière de photoreporter pour la presse du crime et du sordide. Il est fasciné par le
travail des paparazzi, s'imagine sur des scènes de crime, prend des postures fidèles
de photographe en herbe. Les scènes de crimes sexuels ont souvent sa préférence
(*Murder Scene, Cannes 1975*, sous une lumière diurne crue, de nuit et dans une salle
de bains d'hôtel, en est un exemple). Il se plaît à choquer, à repousser les limites.
Jamais il n'arrêtera.

Sa mère exauce son rêve le jour où elle l'envoie en apprentissage auprès d'Yva, la
photographe moderniste Else Neuländer-Simon, que tout le monde s'arrache. Celle
qui le nourrit de son savoir sur les appareils photo, l'éclairage, la chambre noire, les
poses, est l'une des femmes puissantes qui influencera sa trajectoire de vie. « Yva
faisait de la photographie de mode, des portraits de danseurs de ballet, de comé-
diens et comédiennes. Nous avons réalisé un bon nombre de catalogues de sous-
vêtements. Je ne m'en lassais pas. Ces jours ont été les plus heureux de ma vie berlinoise… J'aurais pu baiser le sol qu'elle foulait. » Ses héros, Munkácsi, Moholy-Nagy,
Salomon et Yva, juifs eux aussi, appartiennent à la vague artistique progressiste qui
déferle sur l'Europe dans les années 1920 et 1930. Loin de Berlin, Helmut Newton
sera dévasté d'apprendre la mort d'Yva en camp de concentration. « J'ai toujours fait
de mon mieux pour garder sa mémoire vivante. »

Dans le milieu des années 1970, sa renommée de photographe de mode n'est plus
à faire en Europe : son nom figure dans le *Vogue Paris*, *Nova*, *Queen* et le *Vogue*
anglais. Le livre *Pages from the Glossies: Facsimiles 1956–1998*[3] ne compte pas moins
de 524 pages dédiées à son travail pour la presse magazine. Ils sont pourtant une
petite poignée à la direction artistique et rédaction en chef des rubriques mode
(Willy Landels pour *Queen*, Caroline Baker pour *Nova*, Francine Crescent et Jacques
Faure pour *Vogue Paris* et, plus tard, Anna Wintour pour *Vogue* outre-Atlantique) à
offrir une tribune aux visions méticuleuses mais périlleuses du photographe.
« Qui d'autre aurait publié ces nus, ces photos de mode folles, chargées en tension
sexuelle ? » déclara-t-il au sujet de Francine Crescent[4]. Lorsqu'il immortalise, pour
la haute couture, des femmes vêtues de pied en cap, son talent pour le double jeu
demeure bien présent. Son cliché baptisé *Chez Yves Saint Laurent* (American *Vogue*,
1977) met en scène des modèles habillés par le grand créateur, dans un salon
parisien très chic. Impossible pourtant de ne pas y voir le reflet d'un fastueux
bordel parisien.

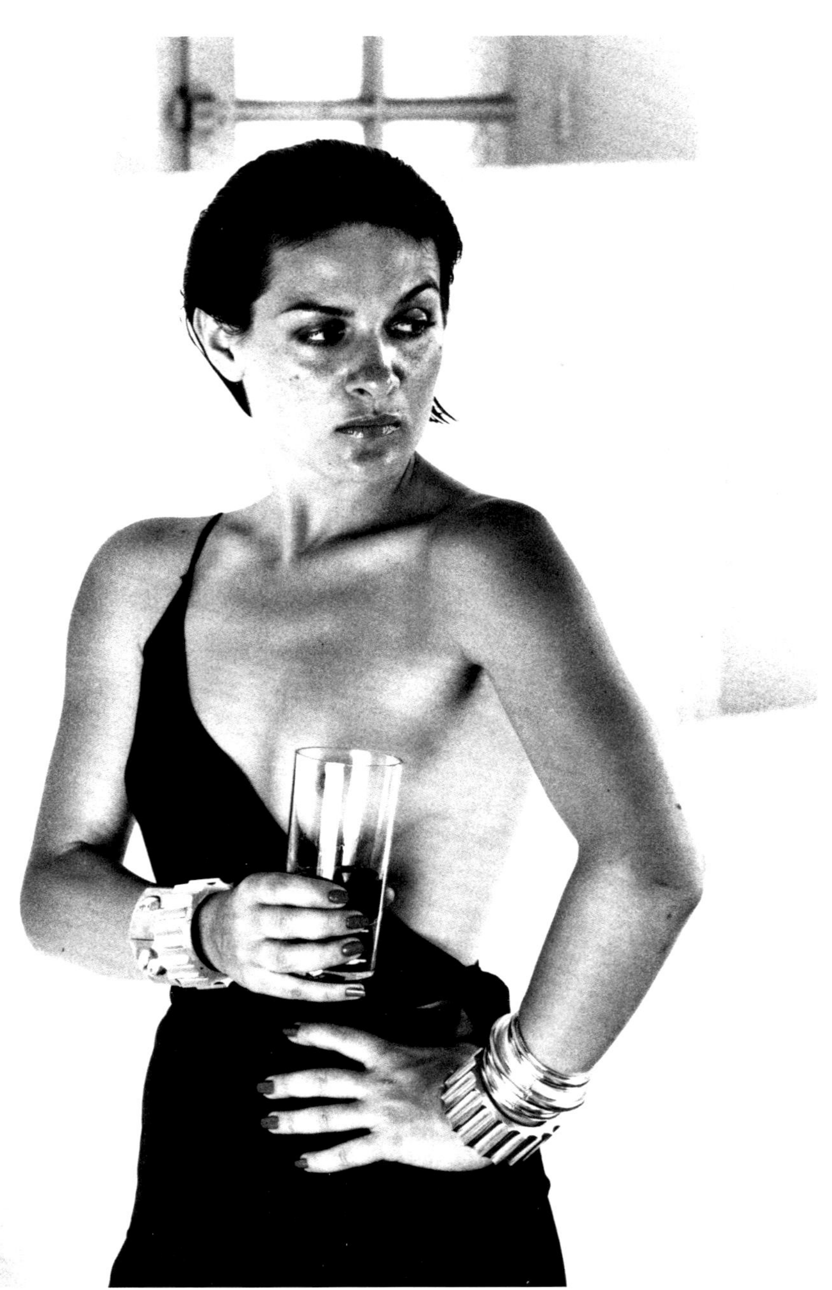

Provoquer l'ire et le désir : voici les clés d'un succès pensé dès ses débuts. « Il faut être à la hauteur, même d'une mauvaise réputation », lâche-t-il un jour en riant à son compatriote et ami Karl Lagerfeld[5]. Helmut Newton se présente comme un « flingue à louer », protège son indépendance et ses finances pour vivre confortablement avec June (qui se lancera à son tour dans la photo, en 1970, sous le nom d'Alice Springs). Helmut Newton veut à tout instant être sûr de savoir s'y prendre pour croquer. Sa carrière fleurit durant les décennies consuméristes d'après-guerre, qui voient aussi naître l'idée de « femmes puissantes » et libérées. L'argent rentre, les portes de la haute société et des voitures de luxe s'ouvrent pour lui. Et surtout, il jouit d'une liberté de vivre et de travailler comme il l'entend. Paris et Ramatuelle, où il vit dans les années 1960 et 1970, Monte-Carlo ensuite et le Chateau Marmont à Los Angeles, en hiver : il fait de ces destinations huppées les décors de ses shootings, n'hésitant pas à mettre aussi à nu, parfois, la brutalité de leur face cachée. À Monaco, il déniche les coins sombres qui l'intéressent : murs en béton, chantiers, la falaise que longe la corniche, et son propre garage souterrain. Et toujours ce travail d'équilibriste qui l'anime puissamment, cette fine ligne entre l'illicite et ce qui est alors considéré comme chic, qu'il franchit délibérément quand l'envie lui prend.

« Un flingue à louer »

Pour préparer ses idées et références, Helmut Newton rédige des notes détaillées. Mais il insiste rapidement sur la liberté de travailler vite et sans intermédiaire. « J'ai toujours été un loup solitaire, assisté par une seule personne, si besoin. » Un modèle, parfois deux, la rédactrice en chef mode ou la styliste, quelqu'un pour la coiffure et le maquillage. Personne d'autre n'est autorisé sur le shooting. Et la règle vaut aussi bien pour les publicités que les commandes des rédactions. Son équipement tient dans une sacoche de photographe, avec peut-être une ou deux petites lumières. Et il en est fier. Il arme, mitraille, ne consomme que quelques pellicules sur une journée entière de travail. Ce professionnalisme de l'immédiat, il le doit, confie-t-il, à la photographe qui a accompagné ses 16 ans et ses ambitions : Yva. « Ma technique n'a pas vraiment évolué depuis mon adolescence, dans les années 1930. Je ne possède pas de flash de studio, je travaille peu en studio », peut-on lire dans son autobiographie.

Helmut Newton est le photographe du dehors, pas du décor : l'instantané d'un lieu le fascine. Il en fera son empreinte. « Mon imagination avait besoin de la réalité, du terrain. J'ai aussi compris qu'être photographe de mode était l'unique moyen pour moi de façonner l'univers que je voulais, de demander aux modèles d'incarner un certain type de femmes[6]. » Ses clichés les plus célèbres ont souvent été pris de nuit,

Paloma Picasso,
Vogue Paris, Saint-Tropez, 1973

dans les rues, avec l'éclairage disponible sur place, parfois une autre source lumi-
neuse pour révéler des détails (il mentionnera l'influence des clichés de Brassaï dans
Paris de nuit). Il travaille en couleurs, programme ses shootings lorsque le soleil est
au zénith pour obtenir les contrastes inimitables qui caractérisent son œuvre. Une
prise de risque technique qu'il ose sans crainte, avec aplomb, même. Pourtant, avec
la photographie argentique, rien n'était jamais acquis d'avance. À cette époque,
sa charge de travail est énorme, les budgets de production toujours plus bas et les
magazines impatients.

Helmut Newton est dans son élément. (Il avoue que sa capacité de concentration
est limitée et expliquera à son ami Gero von Boehm, réalisateur de films et documen-
taires, qu'il manquerait de patience pour transposer son univers dans un film.) Il a
le goût de ce qui est pris sur le vif – même si tout a été minutieusement pensé.

> « Le photographe a Berlin, cette ville qui l'a vu grandir, chevillé au corps et au cœur. Il y retourne souvent, en revient avec des clichés semant le doute, empreints de nostalgie autant que d'accusations voilées. »

Ses premières prises (celles qui permettent de valider la composition de la photo), qu'il réalise sur Polaroid, lui paraissent souvent plus chargées en électricité que le cliché final. Deux expositions et un livre[7] ont été consacrés à cet aspect de son travail.

Helmut Newton n'a jamais eu besoin, ou envie, de voyager loin. Il excelle dans l'art de construire des scènes dans des lieux qui lui sont familiers, parfois à deux pas de chez lui. Le *Vogue Paris* lui demande d'être là au moment où les maisons parisiennes dévoilent leurs nouvelles collections à la presse, en pleine nuit ? Il utilise des mannequins de vitrine et non des modèles. Pratique, certes, facétieux, peut-être. Mais surtout un miroir de l'objétisation de la femme par les hommes. Et l'ouverture d'un nouveau champ des possibles pour le photographe, comme mettre en scène des mannequins des deux sexes dans des poses explicites et des décors luxueux. Le photographe peut aller aussi loin qu'il lui plaît, en enchaînant l'un de ses « modèles » favoris, au corps nu et voluptueux, à une grille au cœur des quartiers chics de Paris.

Pouvoir compter sur Helmut Newton pour livrer des résultats d'un glamour absolu pour un budget tout à fait abordable : voilà qui ne cesse de séduire ses clients pendant des décennies. Cependant, le photographe veille à y trouver son compte, toujours. Il entretient un rapport ambivalent, calculé, face à cette presse magazine qui est son gagne-pain. Profession : photographe de mode, mais il s'en sert surtout pour nourrir le royaume dont il est le maître, le peupler des sujets qui l'intéressent – principalement les femmes, habillées ou dévêtues.

« J'appelle ça "battre le système". »

Si Helmut Newton impose à ses clients de pouvoir travailler dans la plus grande intimité, c'est aussi afin de pouvoir créer pour lui-même. « J'ai toujours su tirer profit des ressources de mes clients – dans la publicité ou les magazines. J'appelle ça "battre le système". Je me gardais une ou deux heures sur le temps prévu pour mes propres recherches. Je montrais bien entendu les rendus de ces sessions aux clients, mais les photos étaient d'une telle nature qu'ils préféraient se cantonner aux versions premières. C'est ainsi que j'ai construit mes archives personnelles au fil des ans[8]. »

Il a dévoilé les résultats de deux de ces sessions privées dans *White Women* (*Femmes secrètes*)[9]. Premier ouvrage dédié à son travail de photographe, il lui vaut le surnom de « King of Kink » (« le roi du vice »). Sur la photo « officielle » du célèbre smoking Yves Saint Laurent, prise de nuit en 1975 sur les pavés de la rue Aubriot, dans le Marais (où Helmut Newton vivait à l'époque), on ne voit que le modèle. Sur la seconde, elle est rejointe par une femme, habillée d'un simple chapeau à voilette de chez Paulette. Dans un autre shooting de mode à tiroir, il photographie un modèle, la blonde Roselyne, de derrière, sur les marches d'un grand escalier de château. Elle porte une robe du soir signée Karl Lagerfeld pour Chloé, « fendue depuis la taille », dit la légende du *Vogue Paris* de 1975. Sur le cliché jumeau, les fesses du modèle sont exposées.

Le consentement des femmes à être photographiées en sous-vêtements ou dans le plus simple appareil – mais en talons hauts, toujours – n'est pas étranger au travail du photographe. Dès les années 1970, être choisie pour incarner une « femme Helmut Newton » est un honneur.

En 2020, longtemps après la mort du photographe, Gero von Boehm s'est penché sur le sujet dans son documentaire *The Bad and the Beautiful* (*Helmut Newton : l'effronté*). Il y mène des entretiens avec Charlotte Rampling, Isabella Rossellini, Grace Jones, Hanna Schygulla et d'autres ayant posé pour lui. L'actrice Charlotte Rampling explique que le nu qu'Helmut Newton a réalisé d'elle en 1974 lui a donné « une immense force intérieure... Sans ces photographies, [ma] carrière aurait été bien différente. » Pour Isabella Rossellini, Helmut Newton choisissait délibérément de montrer les femmes à travers le regard des hommes dans la société occidentale. Et elle a délibérément choisi d'y prendre part face à son objectif. Grace Jones : « Il était un peu pervers, mais moi aussi. » Le photographe a toujours argué que son travail montrait à quel point il « ador[ait] les femmes ». Un constat que Susan Sontag commentera d'un « Énormément d'hommes misogynes disent ça » dans une émission culturelle de la télévision française [« Apostrophes » de Bernard Pivot, 1979, VdT].

Helmut Newton a dit de June, son épouse (elle-même photographe), qu'elle était sa complice, qu'ils conspiraient de concert : « Nous imaginions comment surprendre à chaque fois dans les pages des magazines[10]. » Il s'agace des journalistes qui ne cessent de lui demander s'il couche avec ses modèles, si June est jalouse[11]. Peut-on voir une réponse à ces questions, et une provocation de plus, dans *Self Portrait with Wife and Models, Paris 1981*, une photographie dans laquelle son épouse le regarde en train de photographier des femmes nues ? Le titre de leur livre à quatre mains, *Us and Them*[12] (« Nous et eux ») en dit long sur le lien et la complicité qui les unissent, le respect qu'ils ont chacun pour le travail de l'autre, et leur sentiment mutuel de faire bloc face au reste du monde. Les portraits qu'ils ont réalisés l'un de l'autre, sans fard, drôles et parfois poignants, chez eux ou au travail, apparaissent au milieu d'autres, *des autres* : la princesse Caroline de Monaco, Catherine Deneuve, Karl Lagerfeld, Gianni Versace, Charlotte Rampling et Brassaï…

Helmut Newton l'affirme sans détour lorsqu'il publie son autobiographie : June est la seule à pleinement comprendre les paysages et les images qu'il porte en lui. Son épouse connaît les racines de son appétence pour les visuels puissants, le jeu et le feu brûlant. Quels qu'aient été les lieux (Paris, Berlin, New York, Los Angeles ou Monte Carlo) et sujets de ses photographies, l'œuvre d'Helmut Newton puise sa source en un seul et même lieu.

Le photographe a Berlin, cette ville qui l'a vu grandir, chevillé au corps et au cœur. Il y retourne souvent, en revient avec des clichés semant le doute, empreints de nostalgie autant que d'accusations voilées. En 1979, invité à réaliser un shooting pour le nouveau lancement du *Vogue* allemand, Helmut Newton redonne vie à des scènes de sa jeunesse – June lui a soufflé de retourner sur les lieux où il traînait jadis ses guêtres. En 1963, il avait provoqué un incident diplomatique en pleine guerre froide avec un reportage photo réalisé devant le Mur autour du personnage de *Mata Hari* pour *Vogue Paris*. Parmi les clichés sulfureux publiés dans *Sleepless Nights* (*Nuits blanches*)[13], citons celui où Jenny Capitain, rédactrice en chef mode allemande, pose nue, seulement « vêtue » d'une minerve et d'un plâtre à la jambe. La photo a été prise dans une chambre de la pension Florian, célèbre maison close berlinoise.

Helmut Newton cherche à exposer la relation si contrastée qu'il entretient avec ce qui constitue le terreau de la culture allemande (donc ses propres références). C'est peut-être pour cela que le type de femmes qu'il photographie, ses techniques d'éclairage, les angles toujours extrêmes de ses prises de vue mettent tant de monde mal à l'aise. « Adolescent, j'ai été baigné, comme tout le monde en Allemagne, dans l'imagerie nazie. Cela a laissé une trace indélébile sur le jeune garçon obsédé de photographie que j'étais[14]. » Il admire par ailleurs les cinéastes des années 1920 et 1930 – les films d'Erich von Stroheim lui ont, dira-t-il, inspiré sa série de clichés de femmes portant minerves et corsets médicaux. « La photographie était de haute volée à cette

David Bow e,
Monte Carlo, 1933

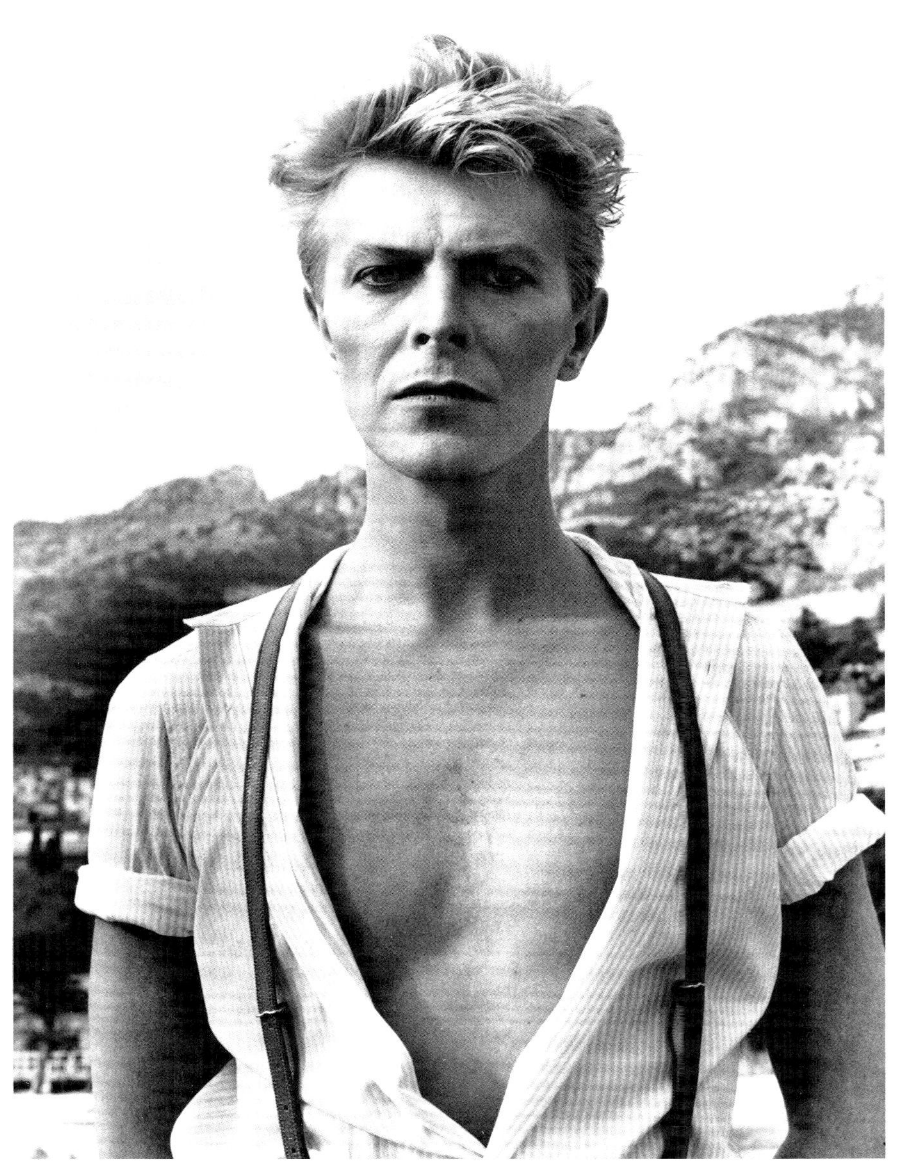

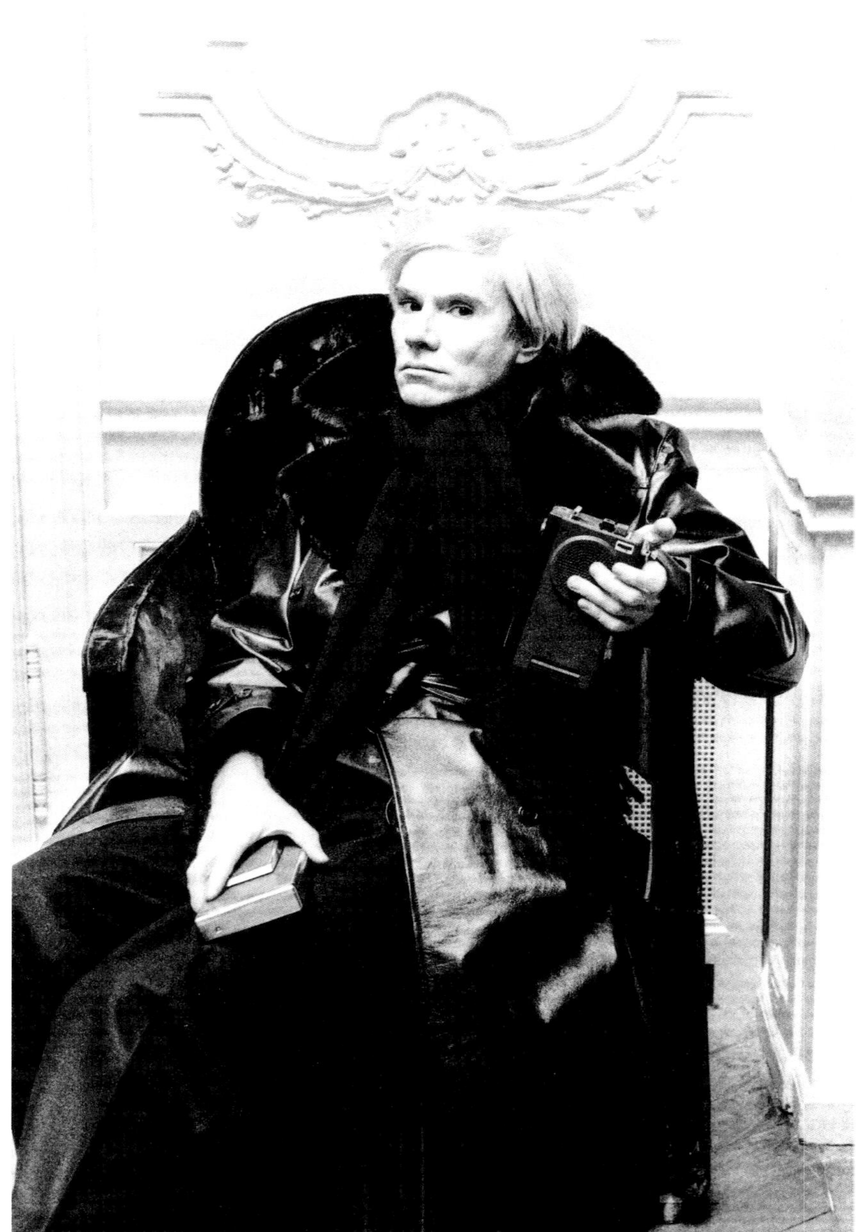

époque. La photo russe était intéressante, aussi », raconte-t-il en 2003 dans un entretien avec le *New York Times*. Entre la fin de la Première Guerre mondiale et la montée du national-socialisme, l'industrie cinématographique allemande est florissante – y compris dans le domaine de l'« éducation sexuelle », de la pornographie et des films noirs. Helmut Newton se souvient de ses entrées en douce dans les cinémas durant son enfance. C'est le Berlin de Bertolt Brecht, du Bauhaus, des cafés et des cabarets, qui attire les âmes libres, progressistes et avant-gardistes d'Europe et des États-Unis. Comme l'a un jour souligné la scénariste américaine Anita Loos : « Le soir à Berlin, une femme peut aussi bien être un homme. » Et vice versa. Longtemps après, il racontera avoir imaginé son monumental *Big Nudes* en souvenir de photos grandeur nature de la bande à Baader aperçues dans un commissariat de police. « Après la publication de ces photos, j'ai été accusé par certaines personnes en Allemagne de produire des visuels à caractère fasciste. Je l'ai admis. C'était un flash-back sur ma jeunesse[15]. »

« À la question "Qui aimez-vous photographier ?", je réponds "Ceux que j'aime, ceux que j'admire et ceux que je hais". »

De gauche ou de droite, peu importe : toute forme d'autoritarisme lui inspire une méfiance viscérale. « Le "politiquement correct" m'a toujours révolté. Cela m'évoque la Police de la Pensée chez Orwell, les régimes fascistes », confie-t-il dans l'introduction de *SUMO*. Dans les années 1990, les portraits qu'il réalise pour *Vanity Fair* et *The New Yorker* lui ouvrent de nouvelles perspectives de liberté créatrice. Les magazines de mode et les contraintes qu'ils imposent, les agents hollywoodiens et leurs exigences le lassent. Les femmes du beau monde, les stars du cinéma et les princesses – avec qui le photographe entretiendra souvent une longue amitié – ont bien volontiers posé pour lui à partir des années 1970. Il tourne à présent son objectif vers les hommes, composant une galerie de personnalités politiques, de play-boys, de figures riches et puissantes. La loi et ses représentants aussi : un juge, un détective, l'avocat Rudy Giuliani, alors maire de New York.

Et, pour la première fois de sa carrière, il saisit l'occasion d'en égratigner certains. Il savoure. Helmut Newton déclenche ainsi la colère de Jean-Marie Le Pen après l'avoir persuadé de poser avec ses dobermans, aperçus par le photographe dans le jardin : la presse n'hésitera pas à comparer le cliché à celui, célèbre d'Adolf Hitler avec son chien. À force de flatteries, il convainc Leni Riefenstahl, ancienne cinéaste au service de la propagande hitlérienne (elle a couvert le congrès de Nuremberg en 1934 et les jeux Olympiques de Berlin de 1936) de passer devant l'objectif.

Andy Warhol,
Paris, 1974

Une étrange amitié le lie à cette femme : « Je me prends des rafales de critiques,
y compris de June, qui, comme d'autres, ne comprend pas comment un juif peut
avoir ce type de relation avec une personne au passé politique plus que trouble. »
L'un des portraits qu'il réalise de Leni Riefenstahl la montre souriante, caméra
d'époque sur les genoux. À y regarder de plus près, on remarque le ruban noir d'une
pellicule autour des poignets de la vieille dame, ainsi menottée. L'intention du photographe ne fait alors plus aucun doute.

Les motifs et fétiches sexuels qu'Helmut Newton a explorés d'un shooting à
l'autre, les corps féminins sculpturaux qu'il a mis en scène au bord des piscines et
dans des appartements, les personnages qu'il s'est plu à représenter et photographier
ont probablement été pour lui un moyen de gérer, dépasser, sublimer ce qui le
composait, toutes ces choses pour lesquelles il avait un mélange d'attirance et de
répulsion. De là est né l'homme anticonformiste, cynique, laconique, dont le regard
et l'imaginaire ont produit une œuvre vaste et controversée. Celle-là même qui a
marqué, défini peut-être, la mode dans la seconde moitié du xxe siècle. Nul doute
que le travail d'Helmut Newton continuera longtemps d'étonner, d'enchanter et
de choquer.

16th Arrondissement,
Vogue Paris, Paris, 1975
Newton's work for _Vogue Paris_ between 1961 and
1983 was the golden era in which he made some
of the most lastingly important photographs in
twentieth-century fashion. As Paris witnessed
the ascendance of Yves Saint Laurent and Karl
Lagerfeld at Chloé, Newton placed haute couture
and prêt-à-porter clothes in locations and scenarios which hinted provocatively at the secret lives
of the bourgeoisie. The composition of this photograph, showing an evening dress from the 1975
Chloé collection, typically leaves the narrative up
to the viewer's imagination. The address in the
16th arrondissement was Karl Lagerfeld's apartment, where the designer invited Newton to fulfil
several shoots.

Sources
1 Helmut Newton, _Autobiography_, Doubleday,
2003. 2 Helmut Newton, _White Women_, Quartet
Books, 1976. 3 Helmut Newton, _Pages from the
Glossies: Facsimiles 1956–1998_, edited by June
Newton and Walter Keller, Scalo, 1998 (TASCHEN
reprint 2015). 4 Helmut Newton, _SUMO_,
TASCHEN, 1999. 5 Quoted by the designer in his
introduction to _Helmut Newton_, Pantheon Books,
Centre national de la photographie, Paris, 1987.
6 Newton, _SUMO_. 7 Helmut Newton, _Helmut
Newton: Polaroids_, TASCHEN, 2011. 8 Newton,
Autobiography. 9 Newton, _White Women_.
10 Newton, _Pages from the Glossies_. 11 Sarah
Mower, "The 'King of Kink' Made Naughty
Fashionable", _New York Times_ interview, 2003.
12 Helmut Newton and Alice Springs, _Us and
Them_, Scalo, 1998 (TASCHEN reprint 2016).
13 Helmut Newton, _Sleepless Nights_, Schirmer/
Mosel, 1978. 14 Newton, _SUMO_. 15 Mower,
"The 'King of Kink'".

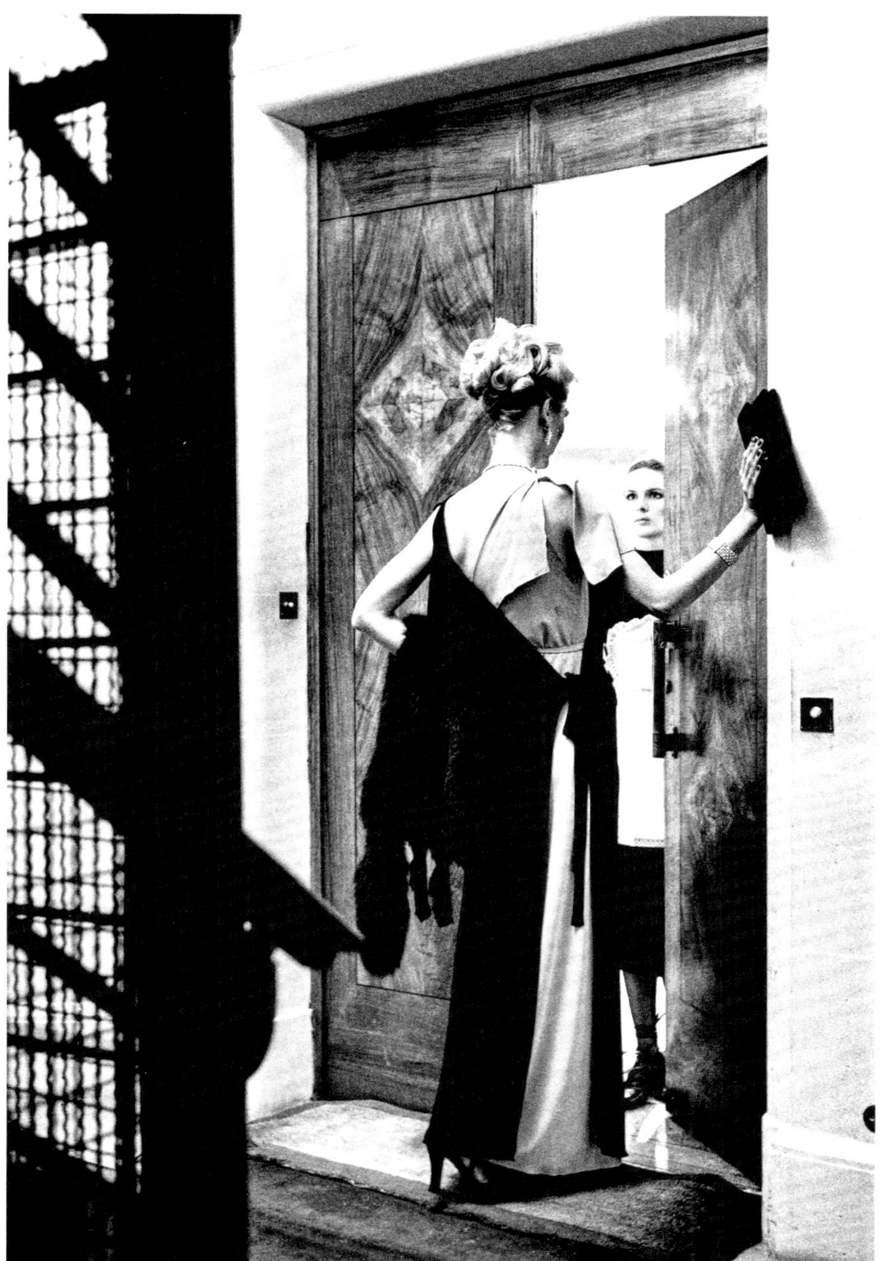

Elsa Peretti as a Bunny,
Vogue Paris, Halston,
New York, 1975

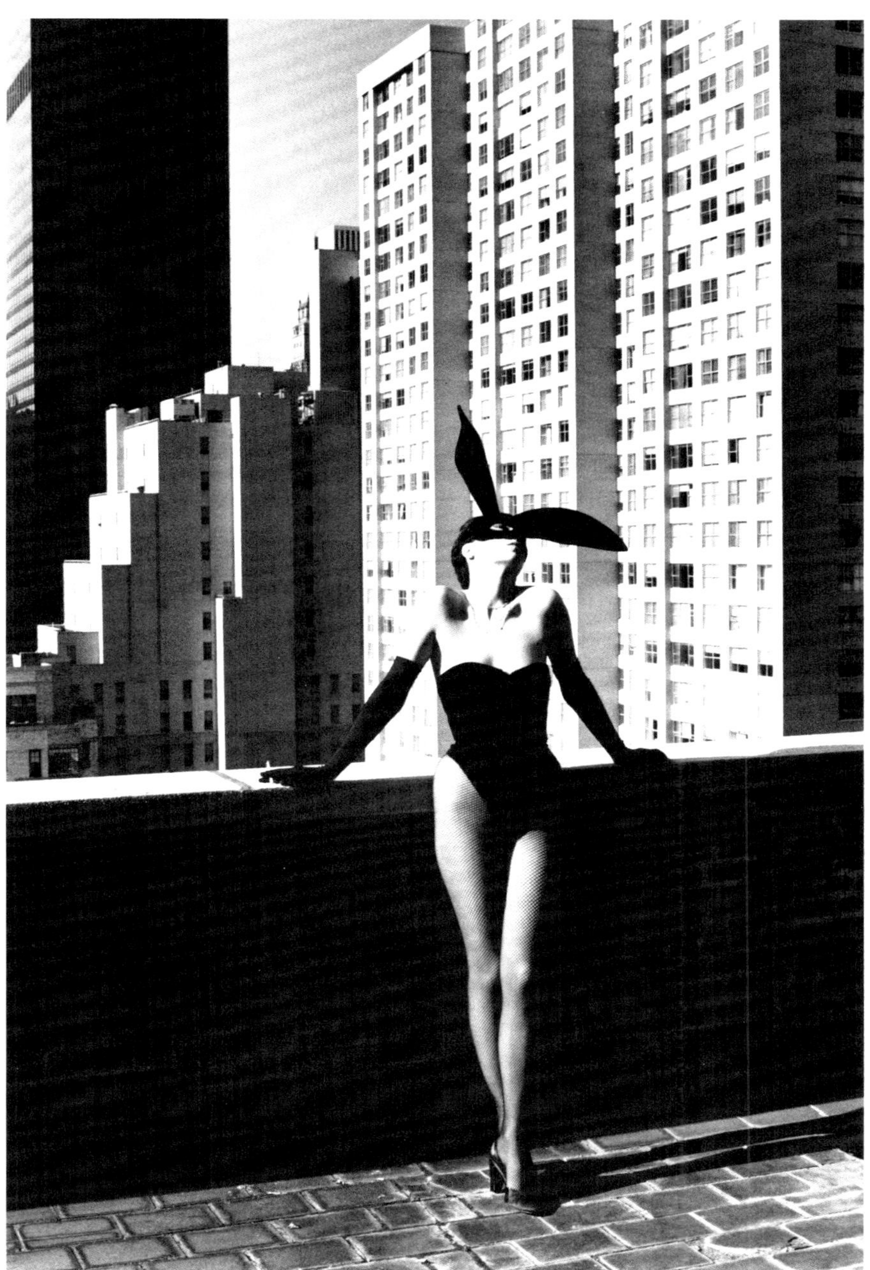

Pages 61–63
Rue Aubriot, *Vogue Paris*,
Yves Saint Laurent, Paris, 1975
Models: Vibeke Knudsen (in suit)
and Eija Vehka Aho
In one of the most celebrated photographs of his
career, Newton defined the pivotal moment of
Yves Saint Laurent's groundbreaking masculine-
feminine seventies fashion for *Vogue Paris*. His
evocation of elegant androgyny is placed on the
street at night, suggestively laced with the mysteri-
ous atmosphere of film noir, and an echo of the
cross-dressing of 1930s Berlin. Using only available
street light, Newton's expertise in shooting at
night – looking for "a certain magic that happens
after dark" – had been inspired by his admiration
of Brassaï's legendary Paris night photography.
Typically, he chose a location very close to where
he lived – he and his wife had an apartment on
rue Aubriot. The second shots which Newton
took for himself that night, in which the model is
joined by a naked woman, cemented the lasting
impact of Newton's notoriety.

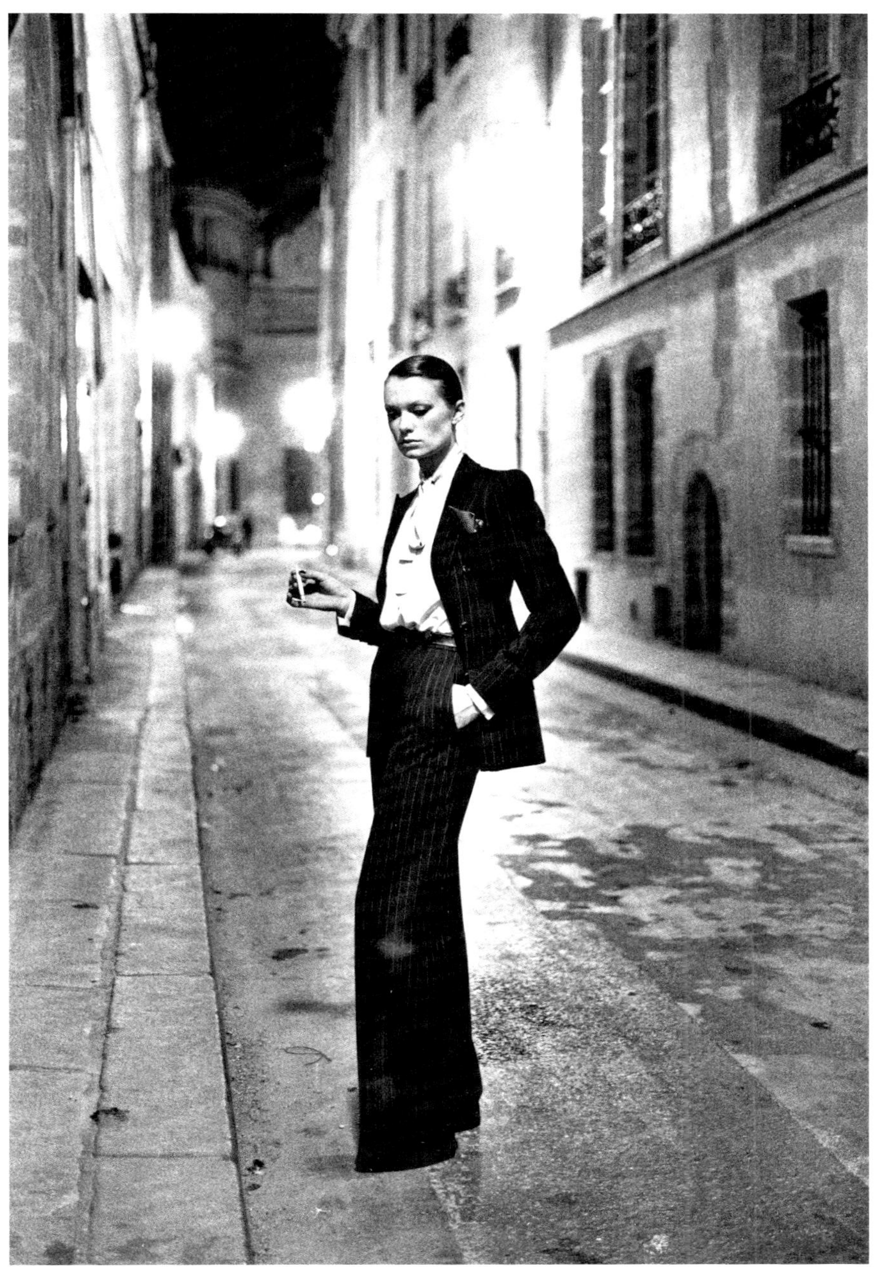

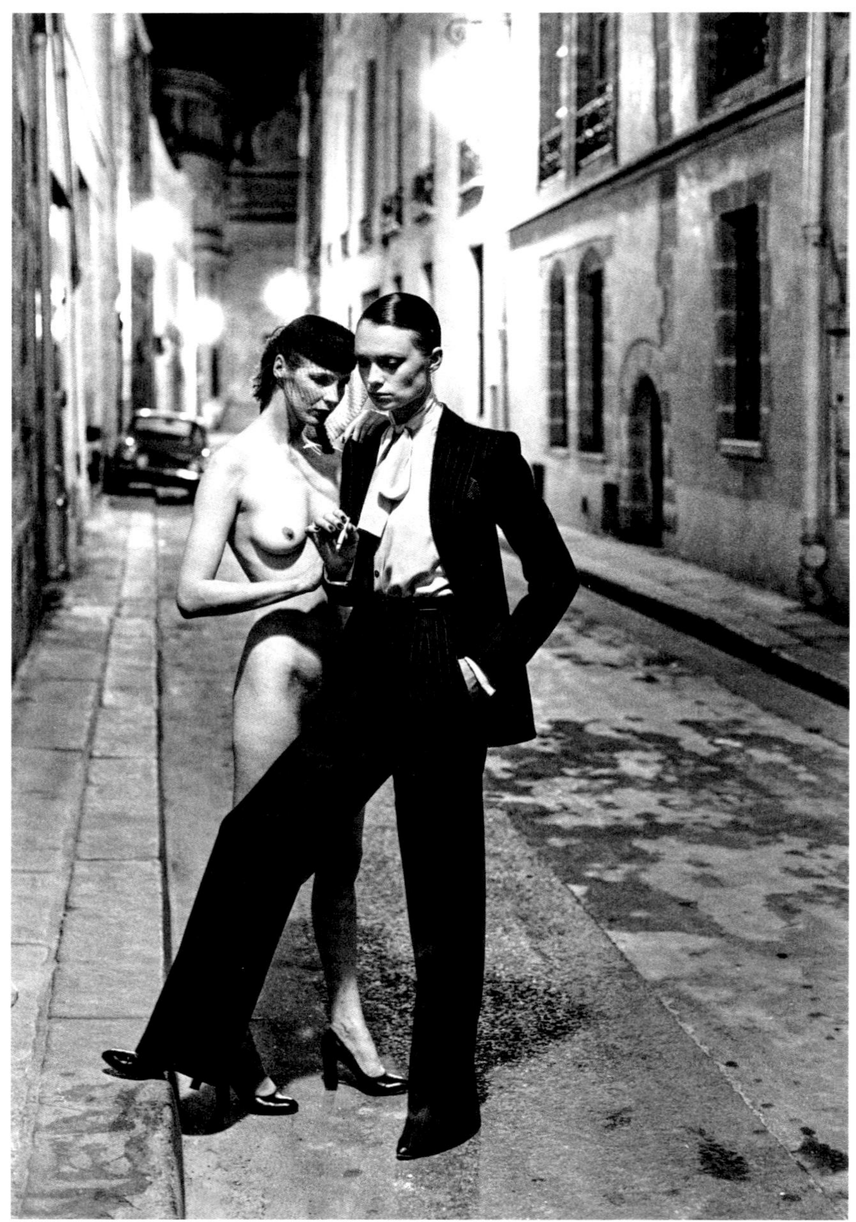

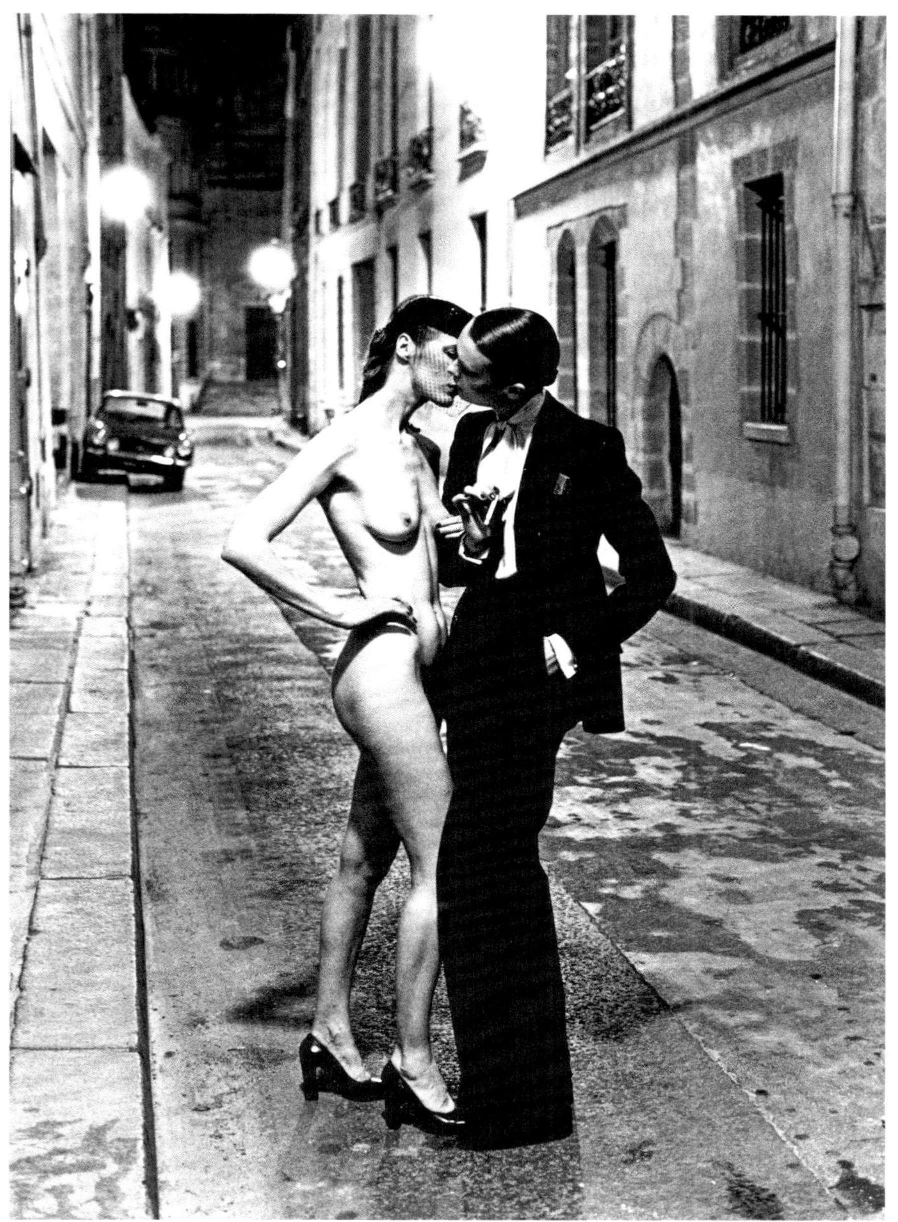

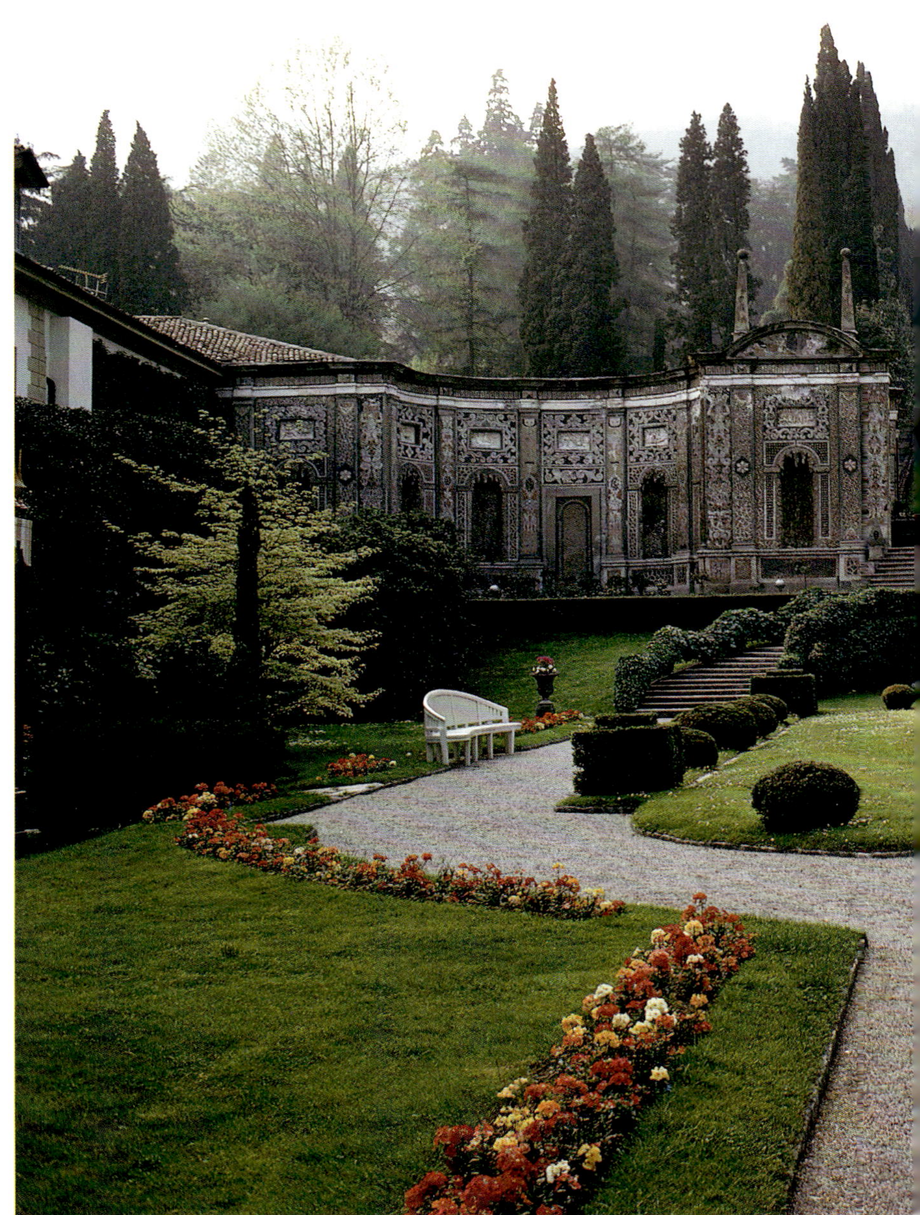

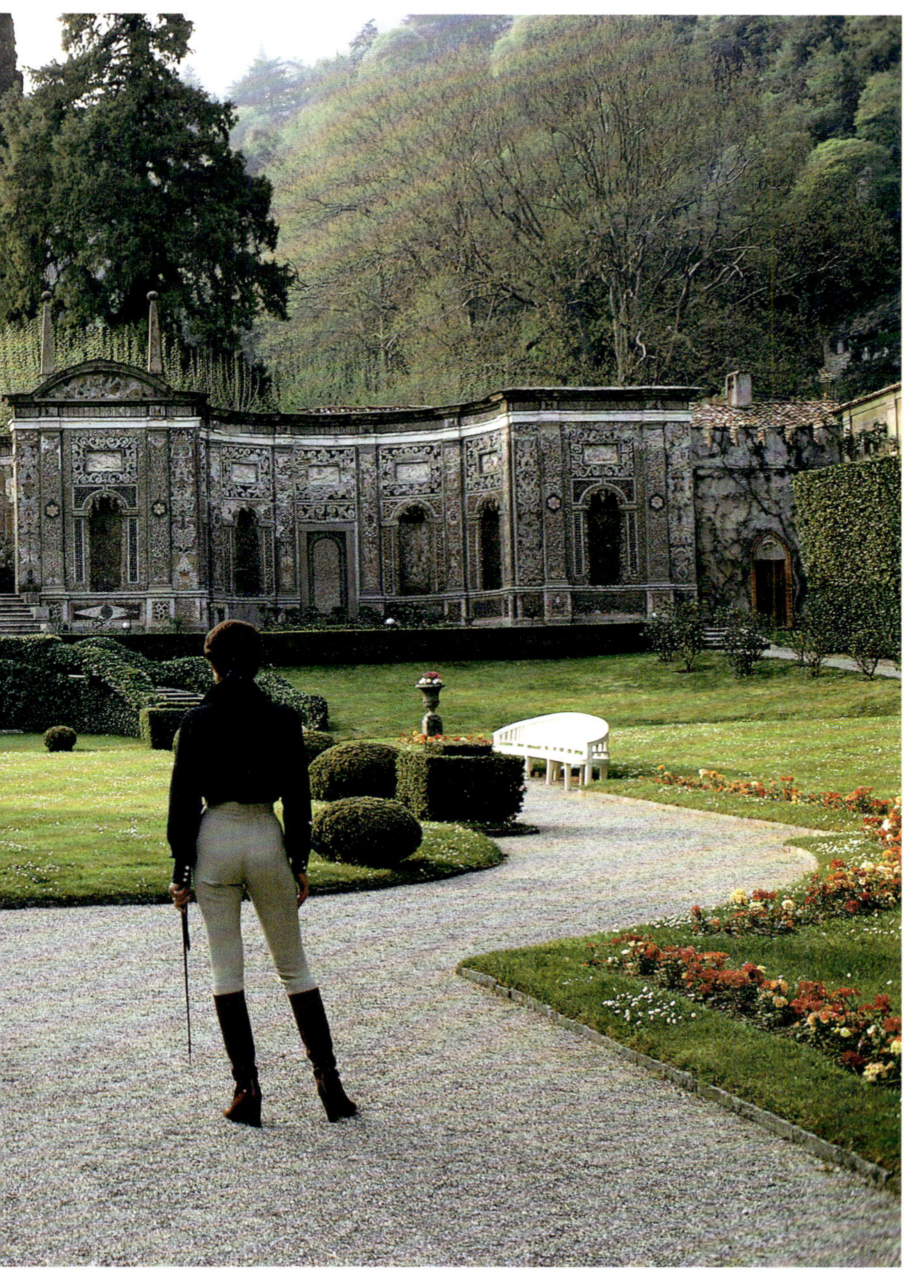

The Story of Ohhh…,
American *Vogue*, Saint-Tropez, 1975

Pages 64/65
Villa d'Este, *Réalités*, Lake Como, 1975
Model: Anne Godet
Newton received a "dream assignment" from
Réalités magazine to photograph the luxurious
Villa d'Este hotel on Lake Como in spring 1975. Not
only were the milieux of grand European hotels
his interest since childhood, but he was also in
need of a few more images for his first book,
White Women. He decided to do two versions,
one for the magazine and one for himself – one
dressed and one nude – while avoiding guests,
tipping barmen and stopping a maid who found
his Polaroids. When *White Women* was published,
the Villa d'Este director banned him forever. Years
later he was invited back to much acclaim.

Pages 68/69
Vibeke Riding Her Husband's Mechanical Bear,
Paris, 1975
Model: Vibeke Knudsen

Pages 70/71
Karl Lagerfeld, Paris, 1976
Newton forged an enduring intellectual friendship
with Karl Lagerfeld as fellow German expatriates
in Paris who shared many references to art, film,
history, photography and fashion. During the take-
off of both their careers in the 1970s – Newton at
Vogue Paris, Lagerfeld at Chloé – he often
photographed the designer, amongst his many
fashion narratives crystallising the social land-
scape. Gesture and backdrop evoke multiple
Newtonian echoes in the moment that Lagerfeld
tosses a bouquet of lilies across the Eiffel Tower.
The imposing presence of the landmark, shot in
black and white, might suggest a link with the
first photograph Newton, aged twelve, made of
the Funkturm radio tower in Berlin.

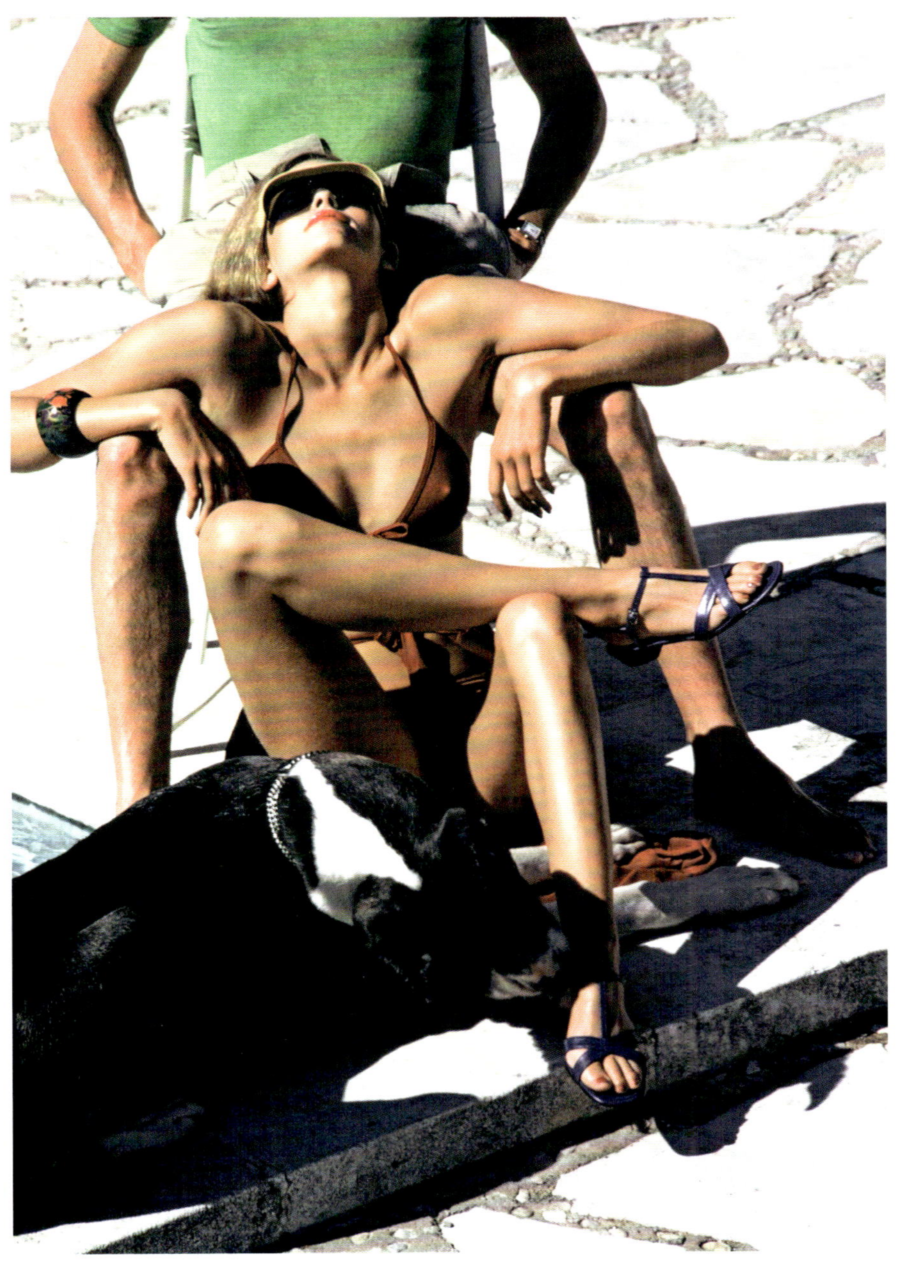

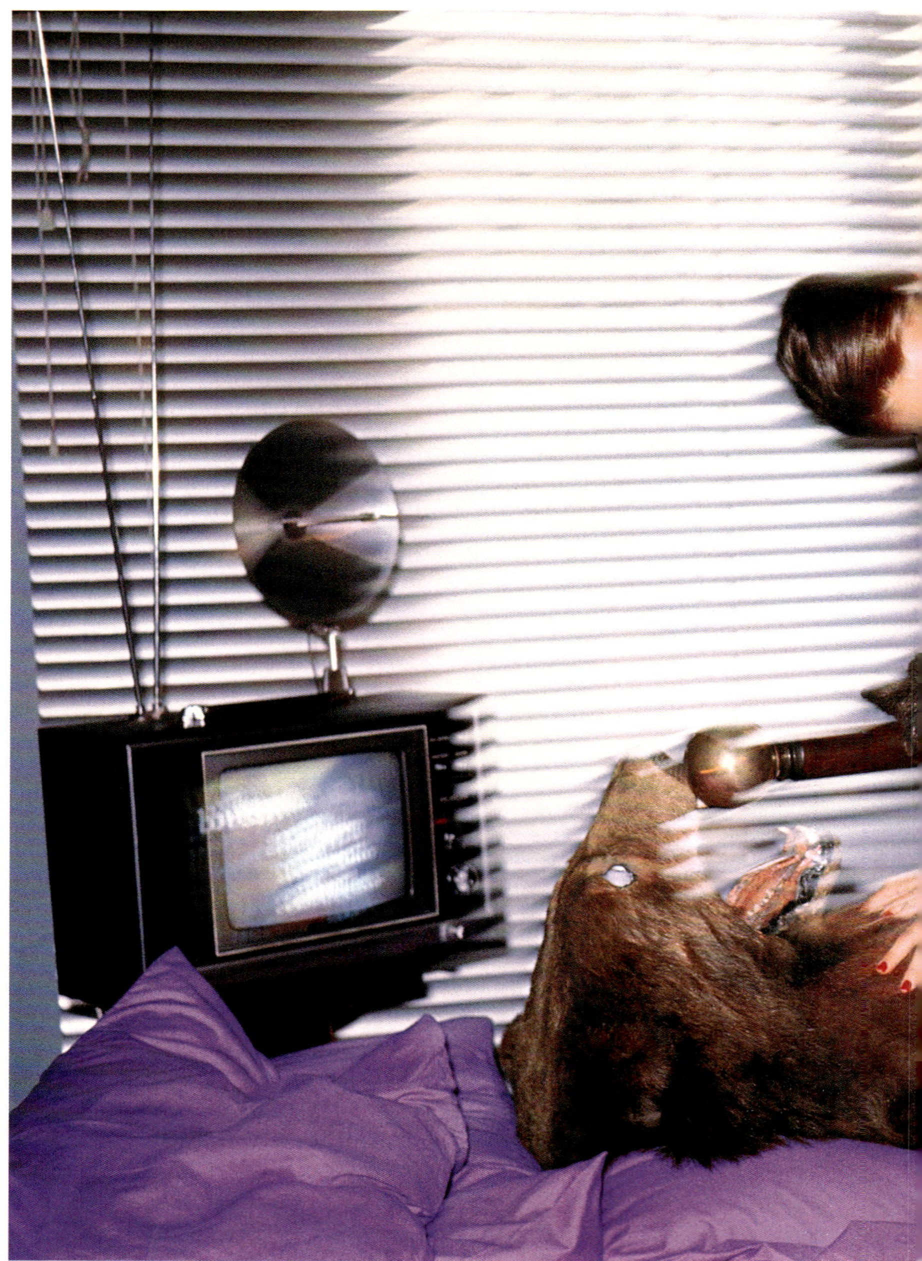

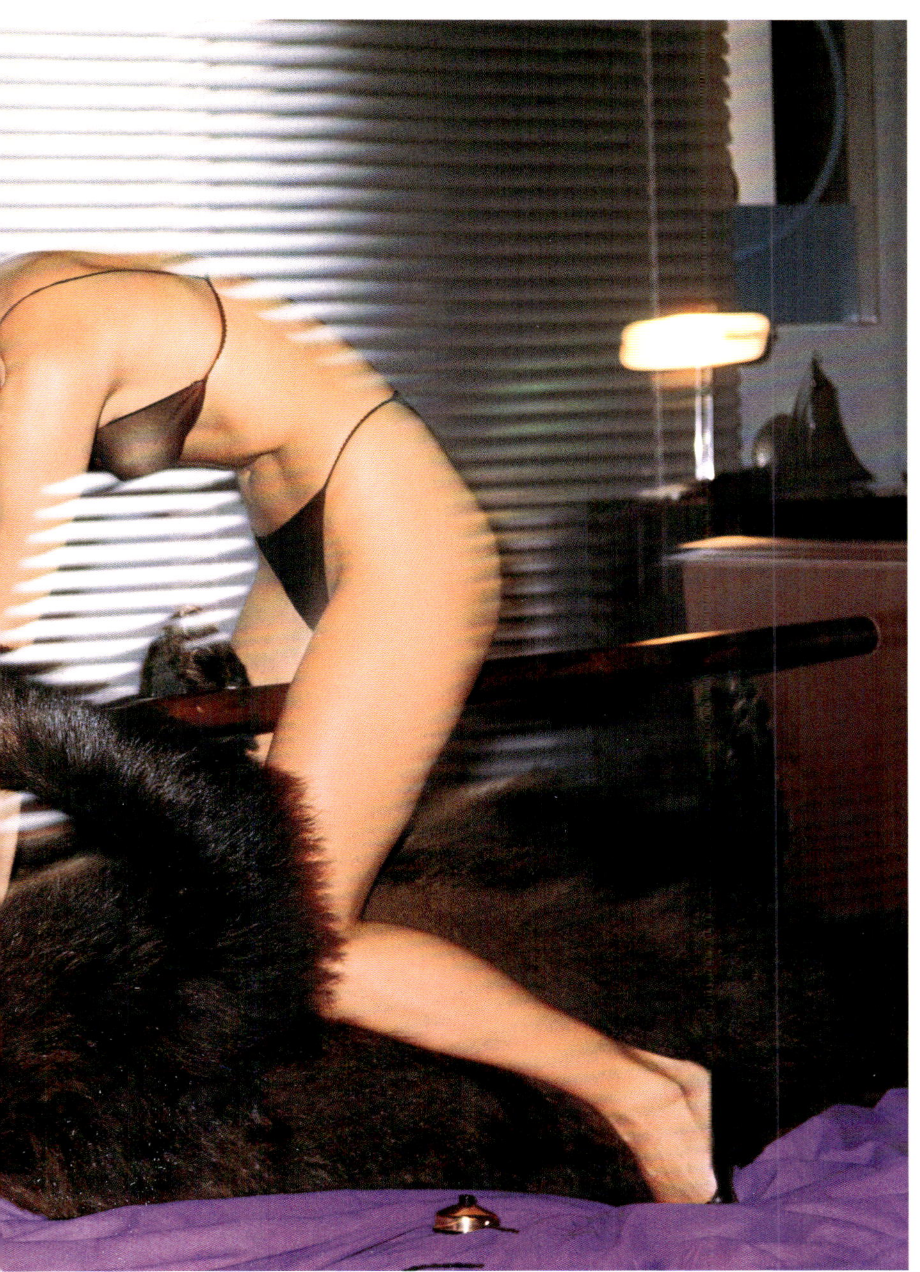

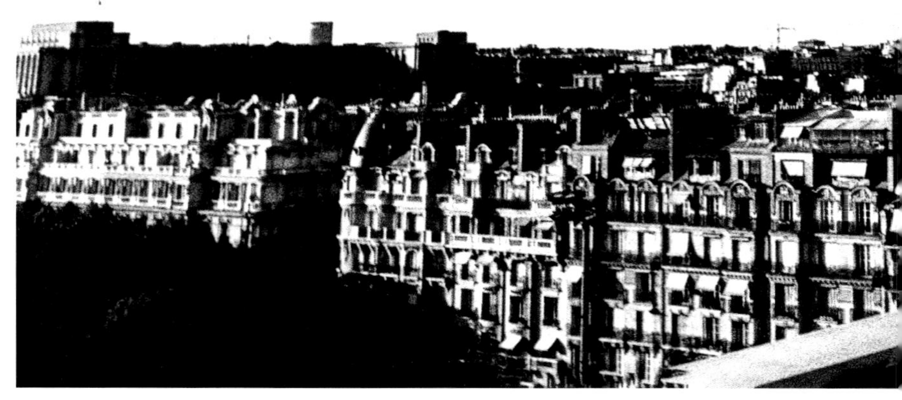

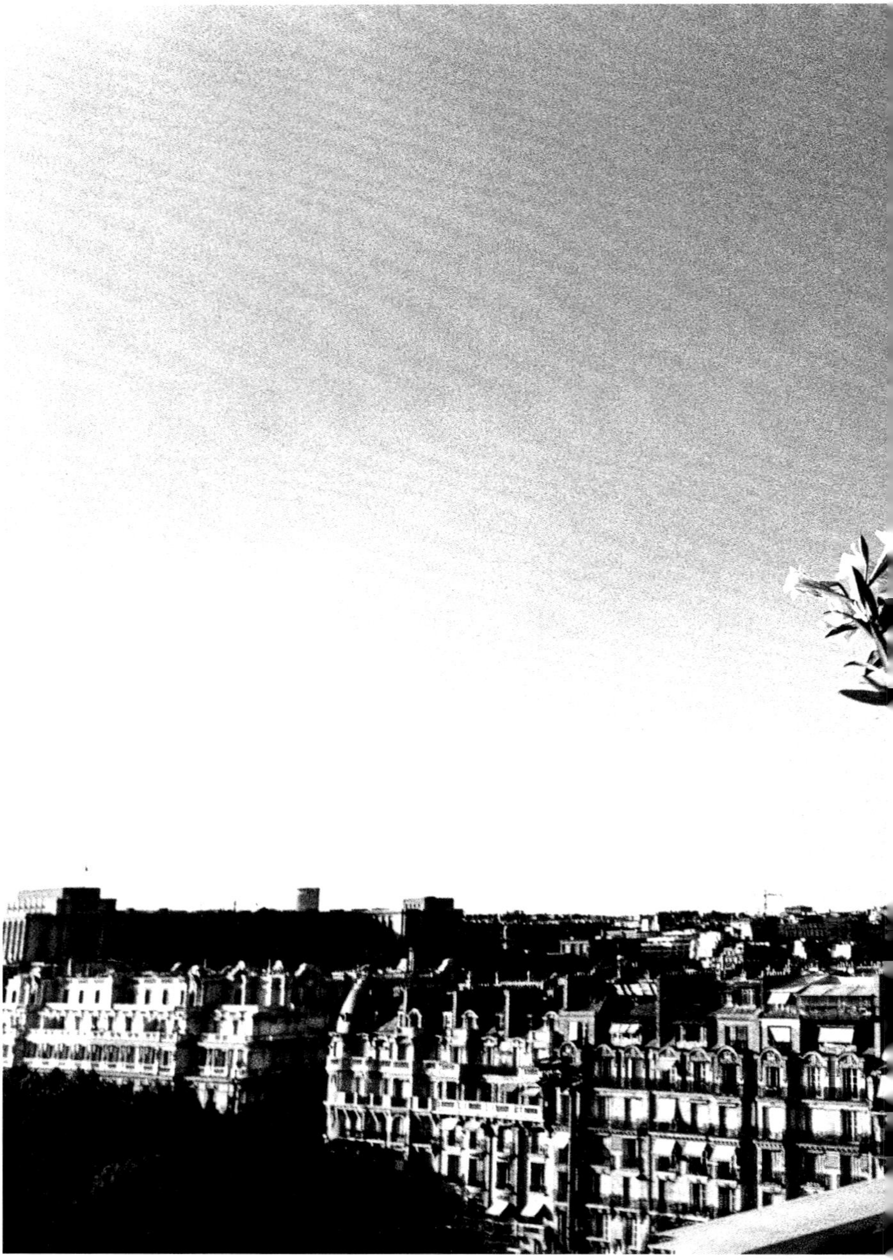

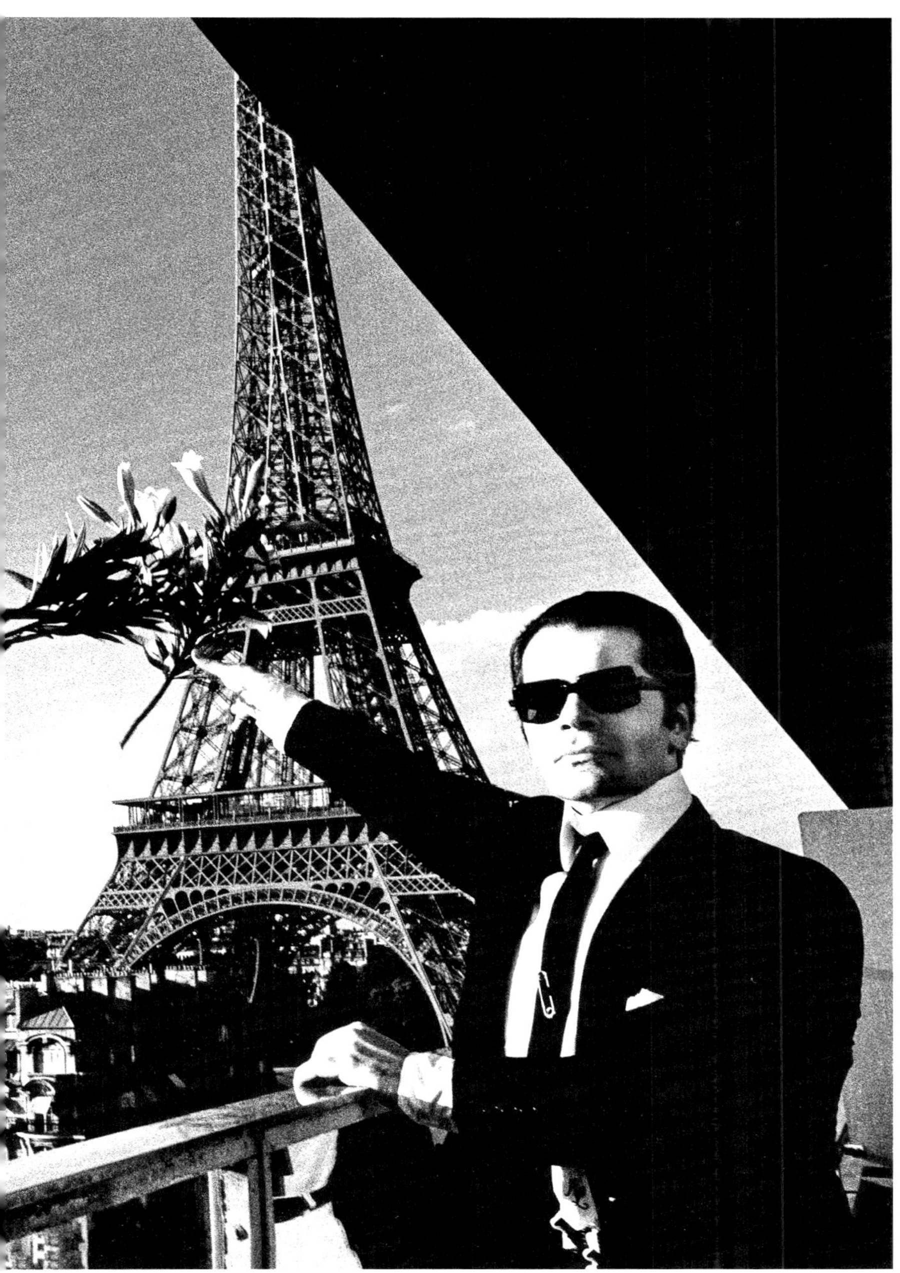

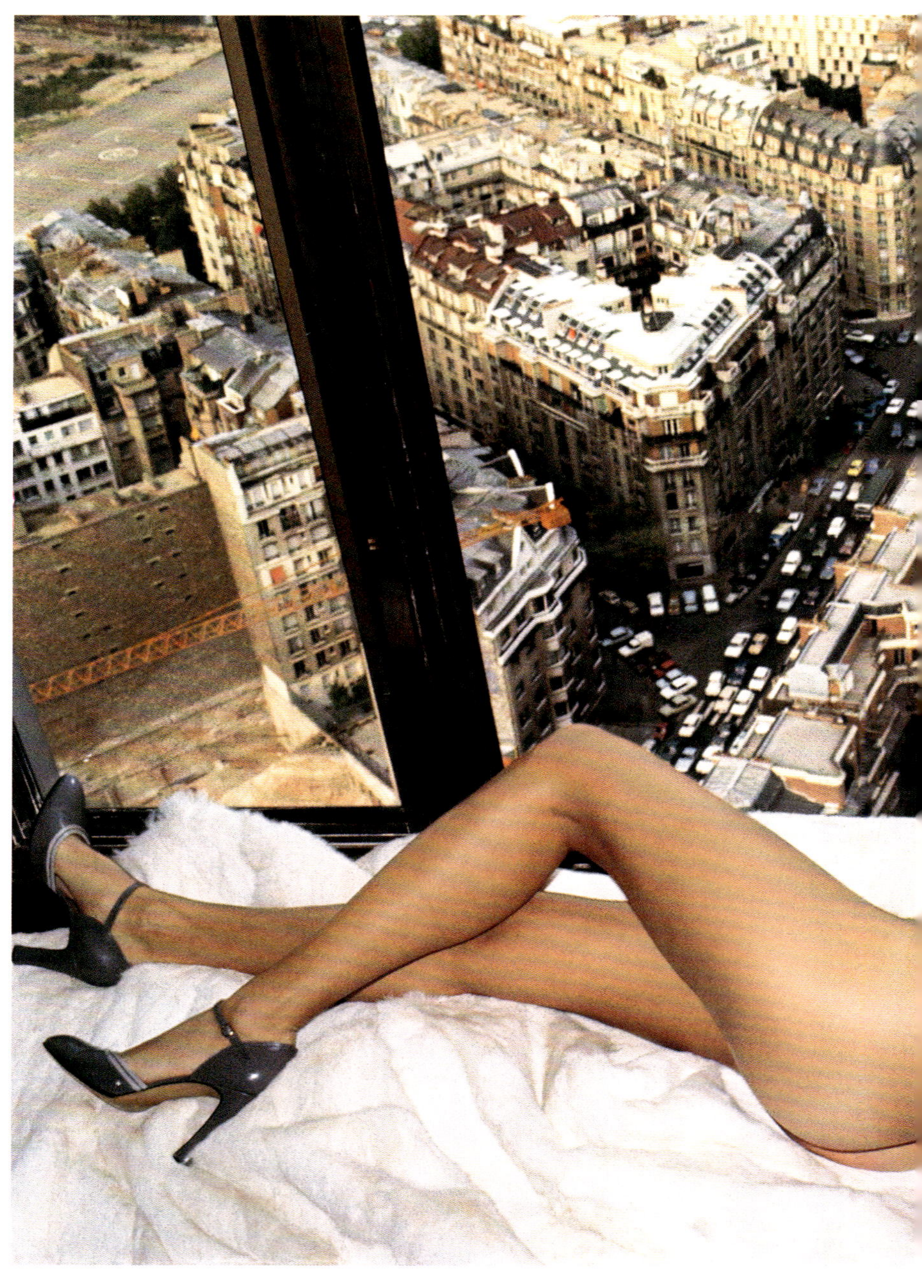

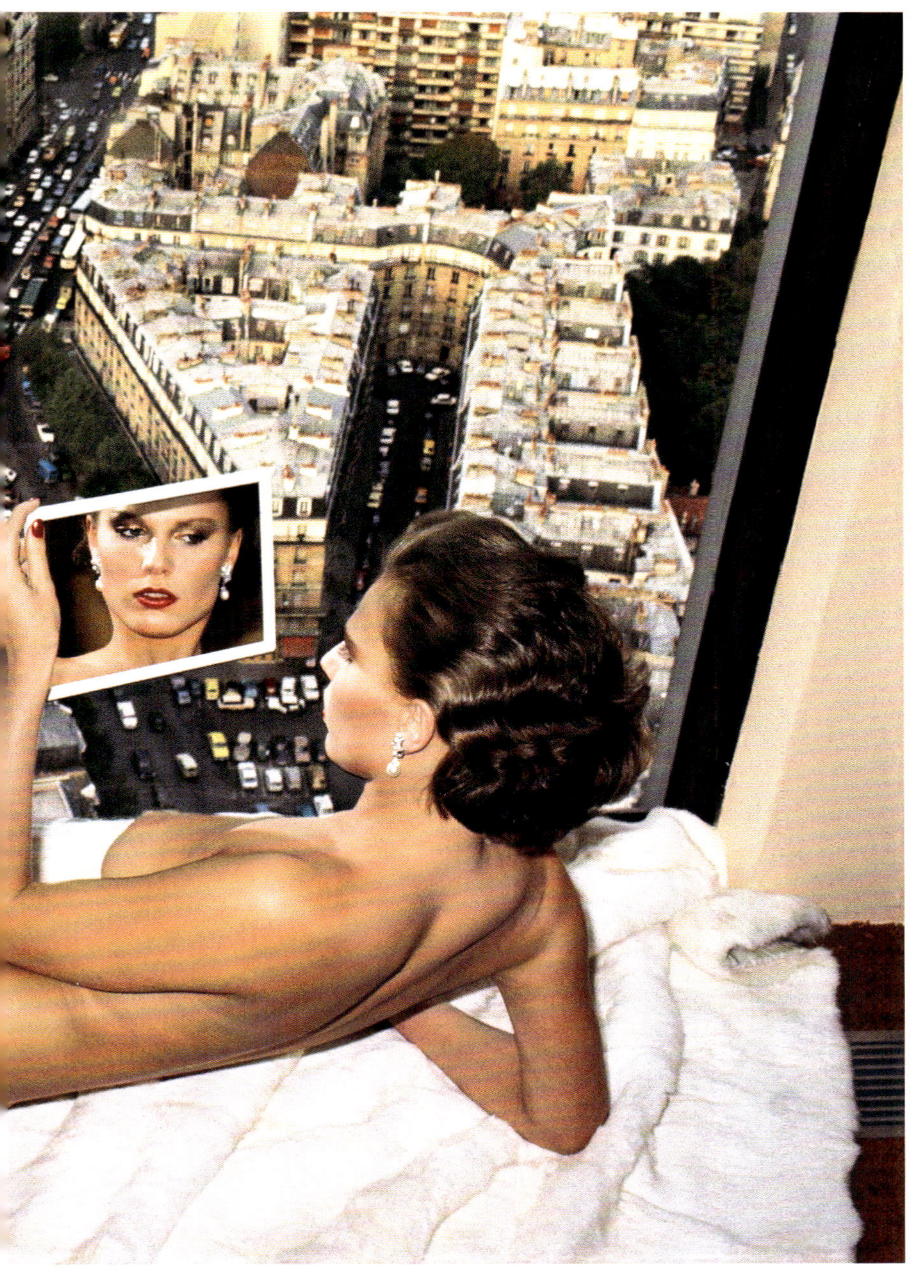

Catherine Deneuve,
Esquire, Paris, 1976

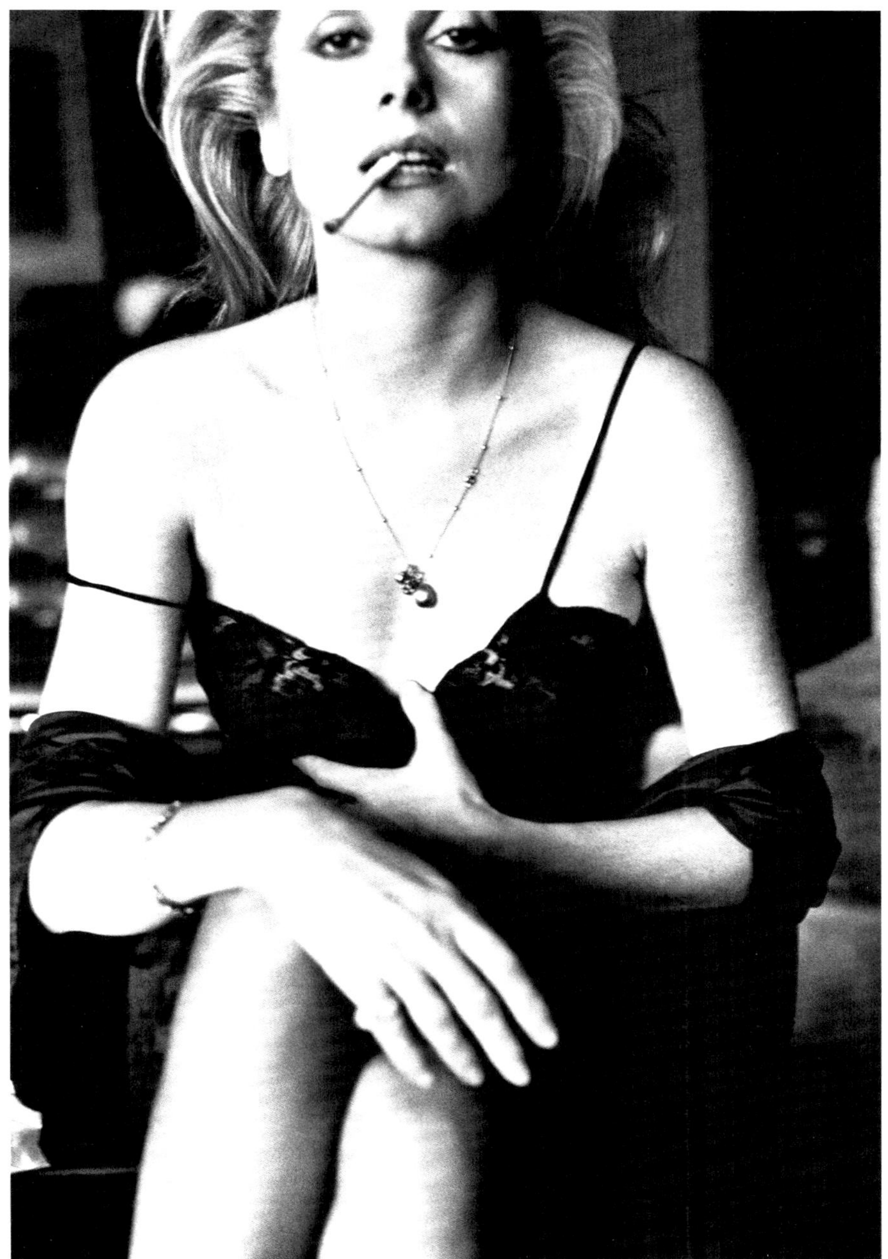

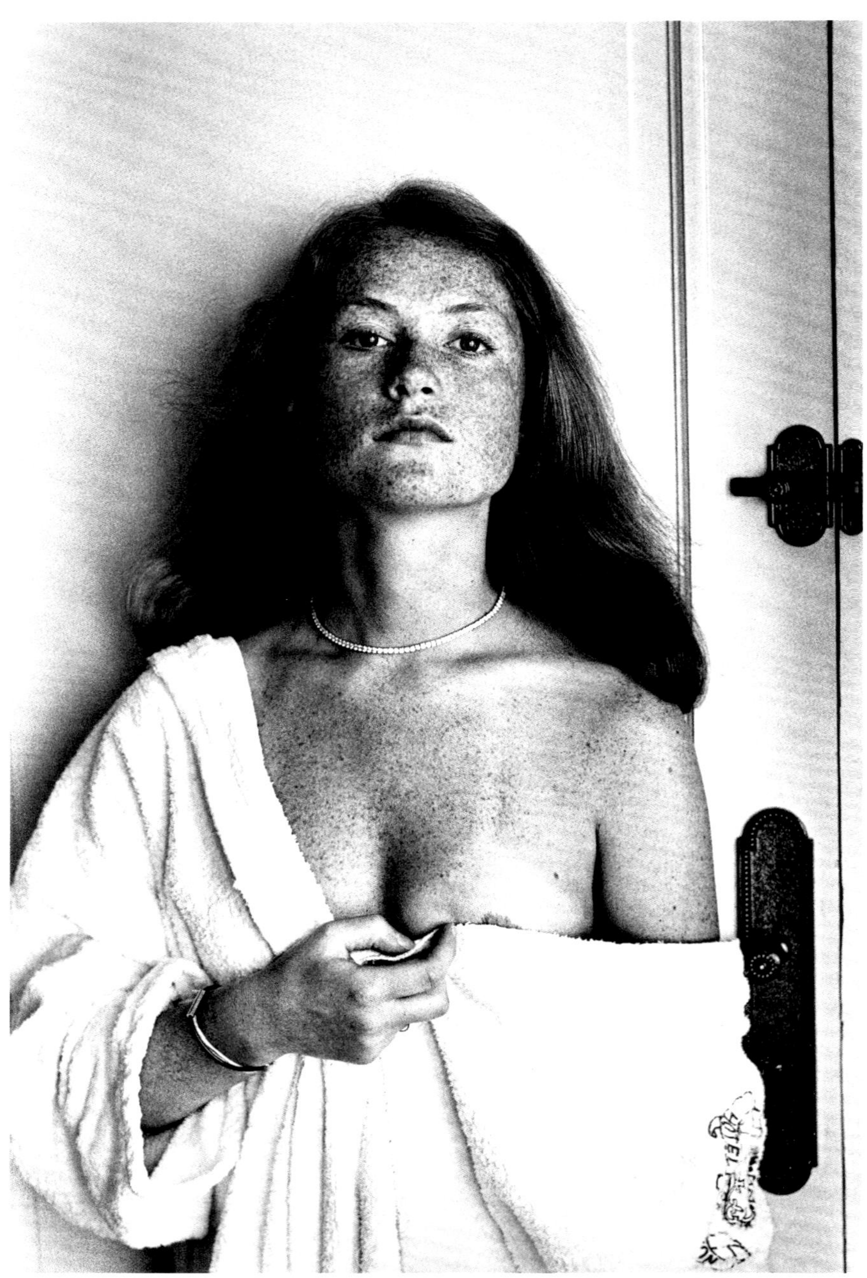

Isabelle Huppert,
Hotel Carlton, Cannes, 1976

Jenny Capitain, Pension Florian, Berlin, 1977
In one of the scandalising series of nude women
in orthopaedic braces, the German fashion editor
Jenny Capitain is photographed at the Pension
Florian, "a house of dubious repute" in Berlin. In
her account, Capitain was spotted by Newton on
a street in Paris – he admired her legs – and was
approached by his wife June, beginning a long
working relationship as an ideal model and as a
friend. When Capitain broke her leg, Newton was
excited to capture one of his abiding erotic fascin-
ations in this portrait. In his autobiography, he
attributed his inspiration to his hero worship of
Erich von Stroheim. The Austrian director and
actor appeared, wearing a neck and back brace,
as a German commandant in Jean Renoir's subversive 1937 *La Grande Illusion*, a film which Nazi
censors tried but failed to eliminate.

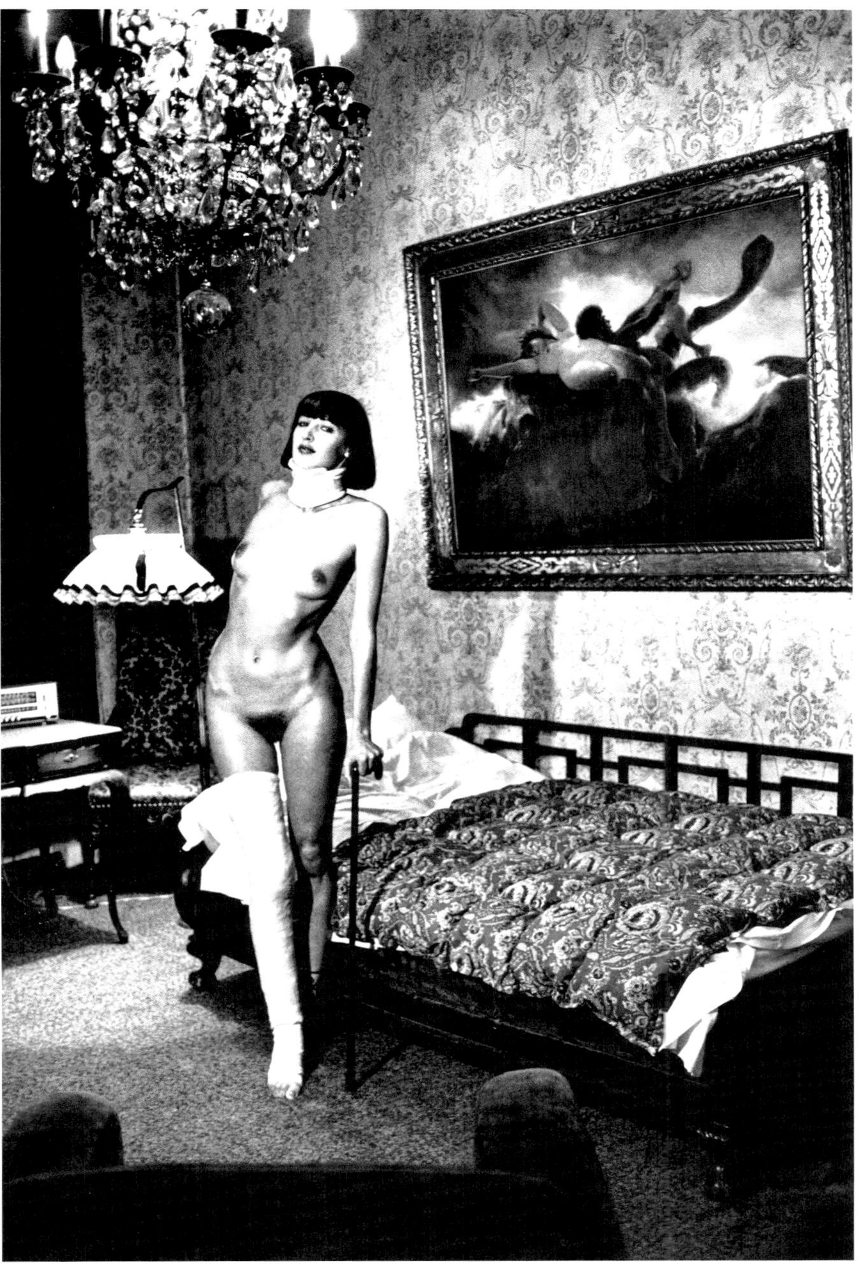

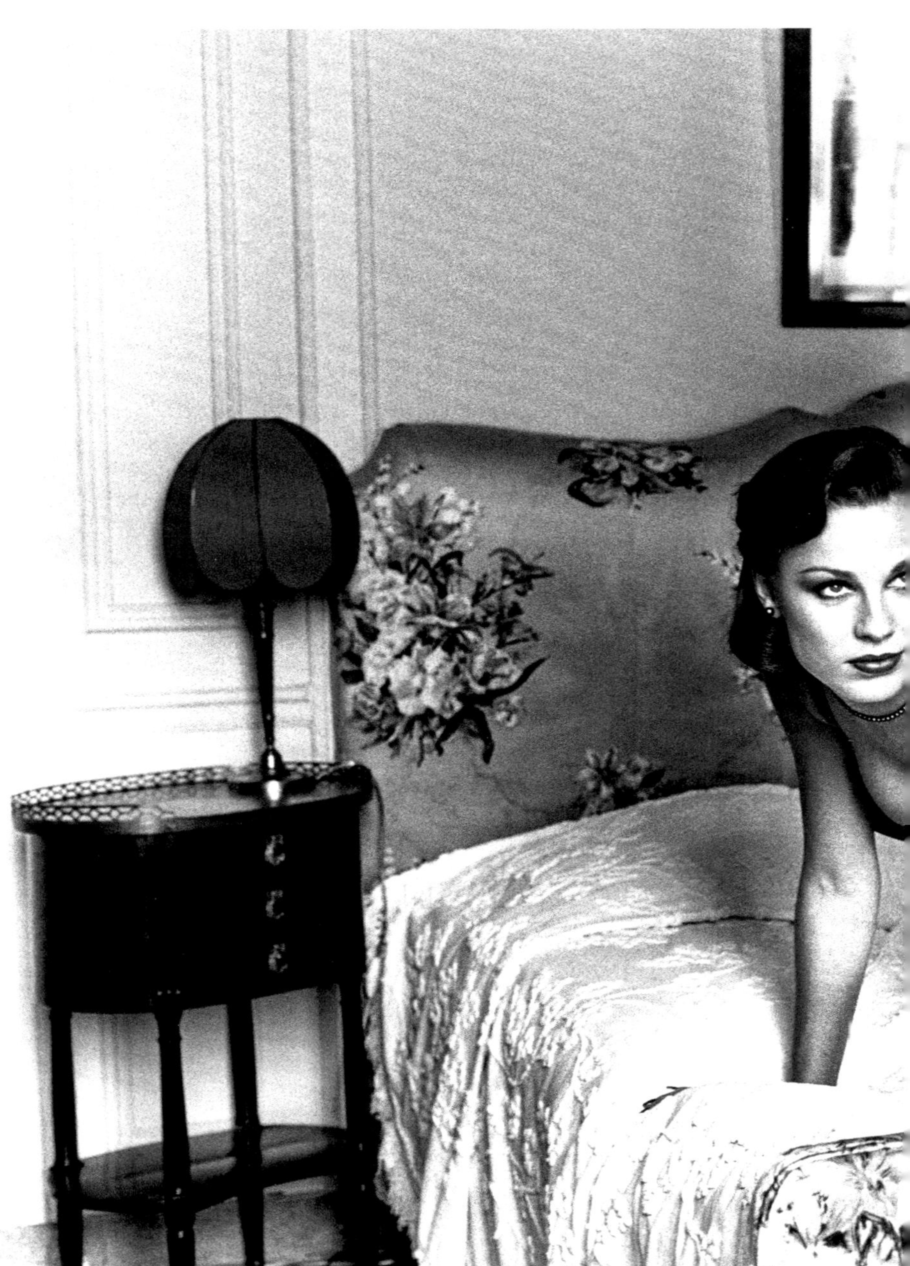

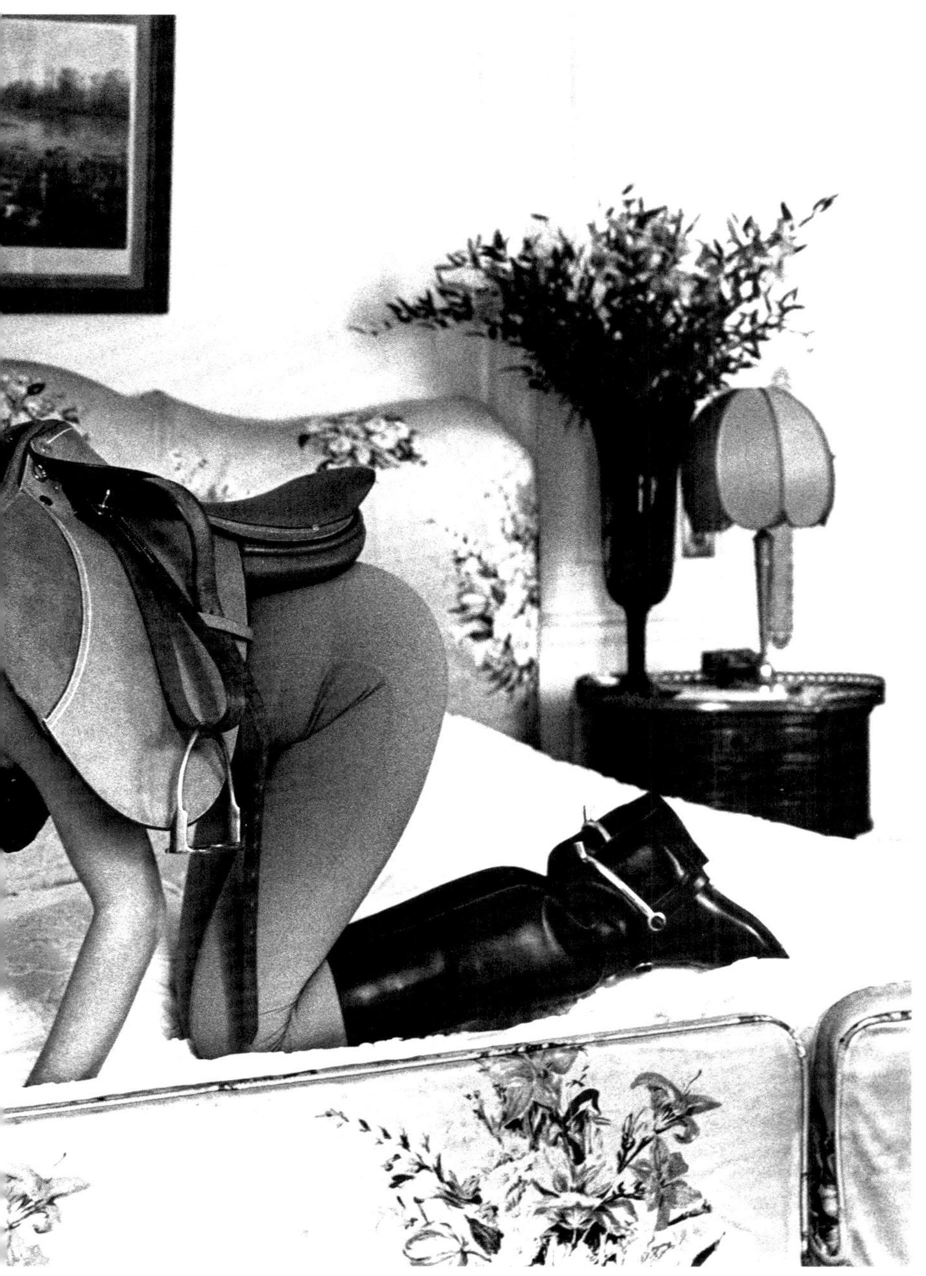

**Nude and Police Dog,
Pentax Calendar,
Saint-Tropez, 1976**

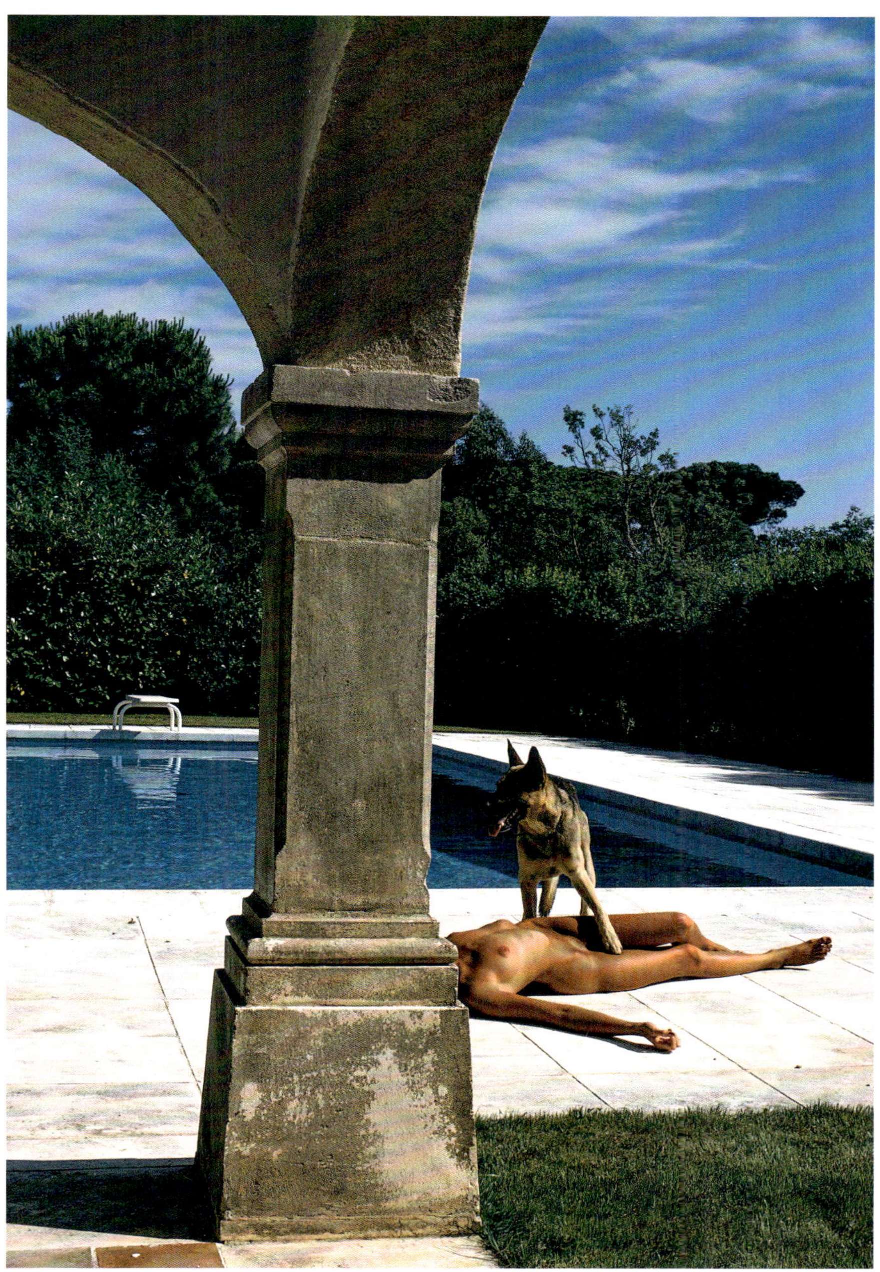

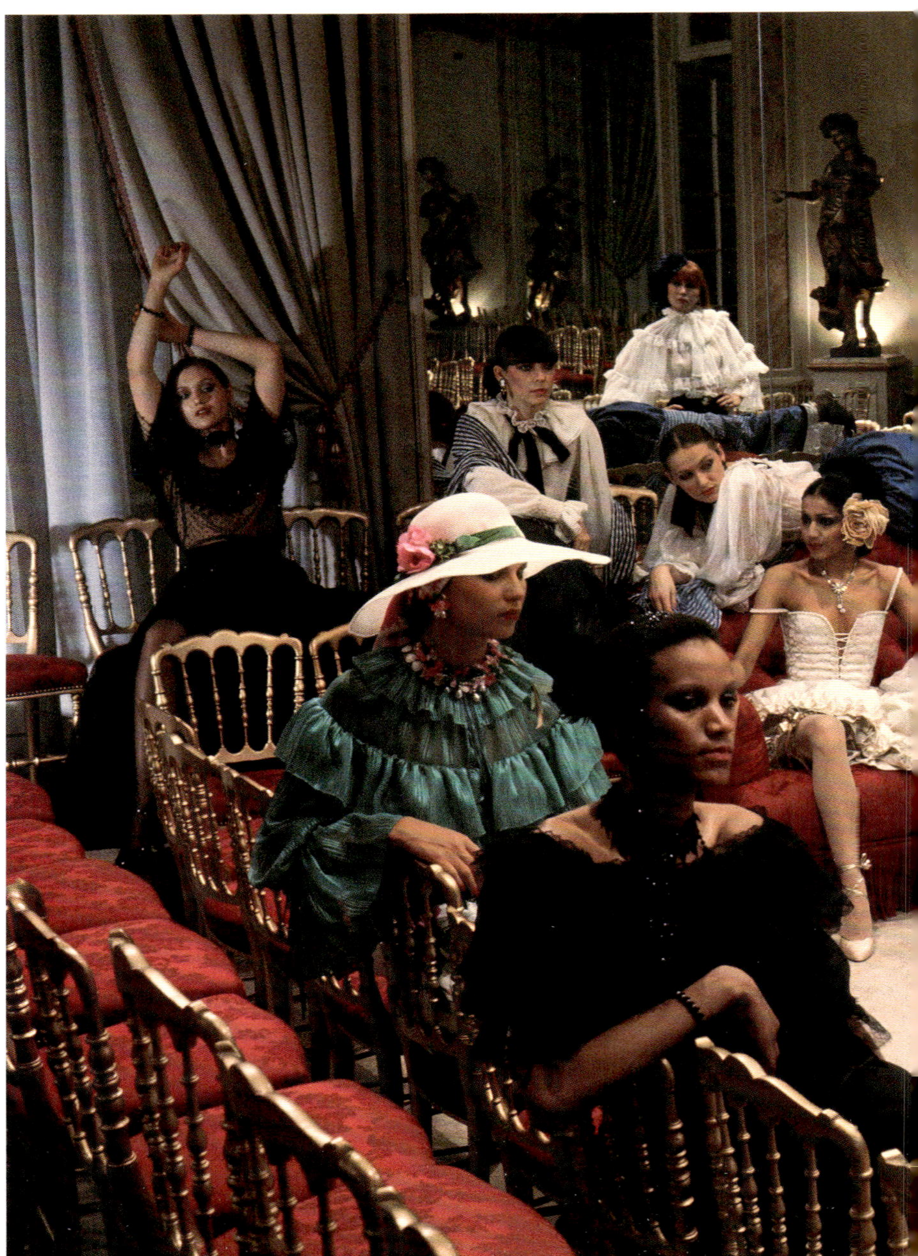

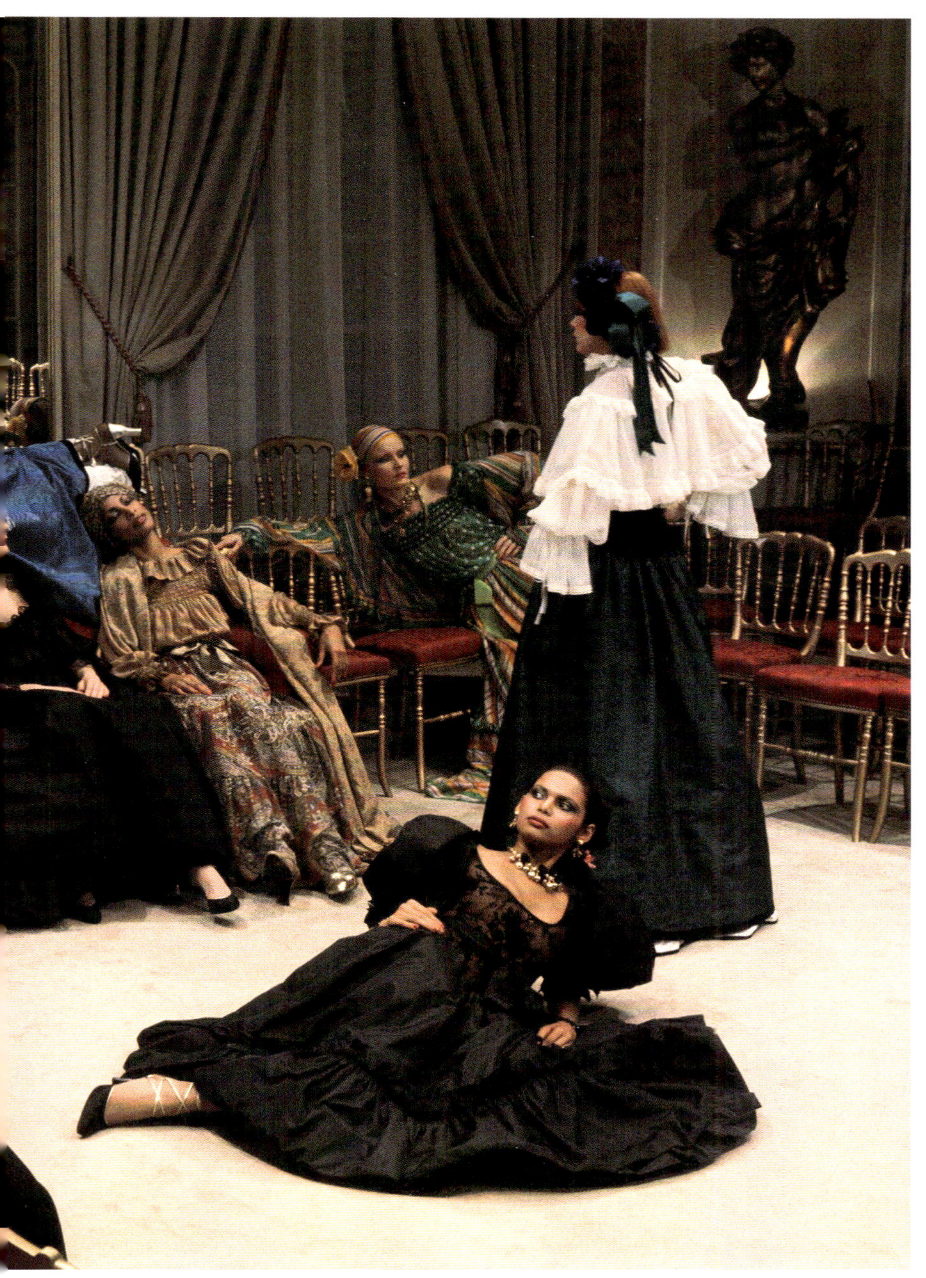

Vogue Paris,
Paris, 1976

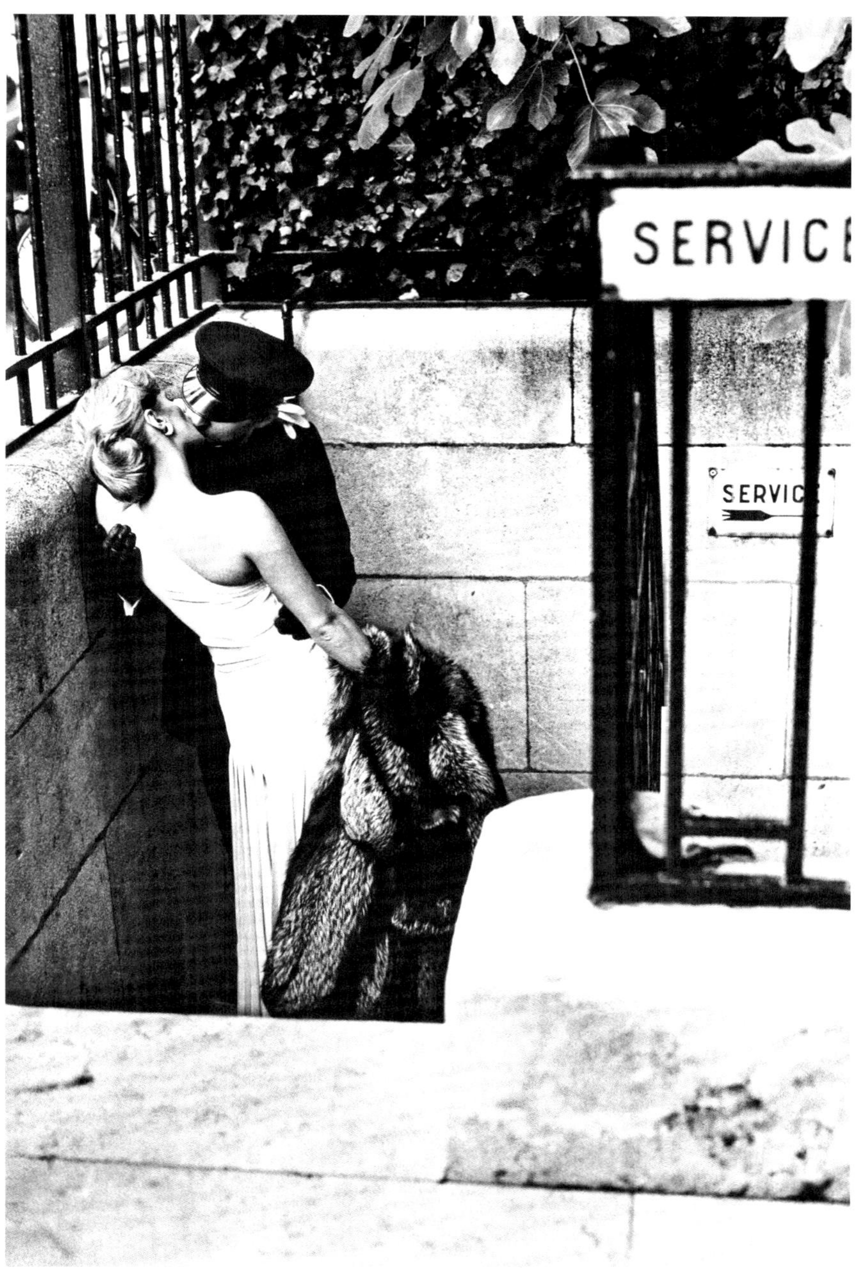
SERVICE
SERVICE

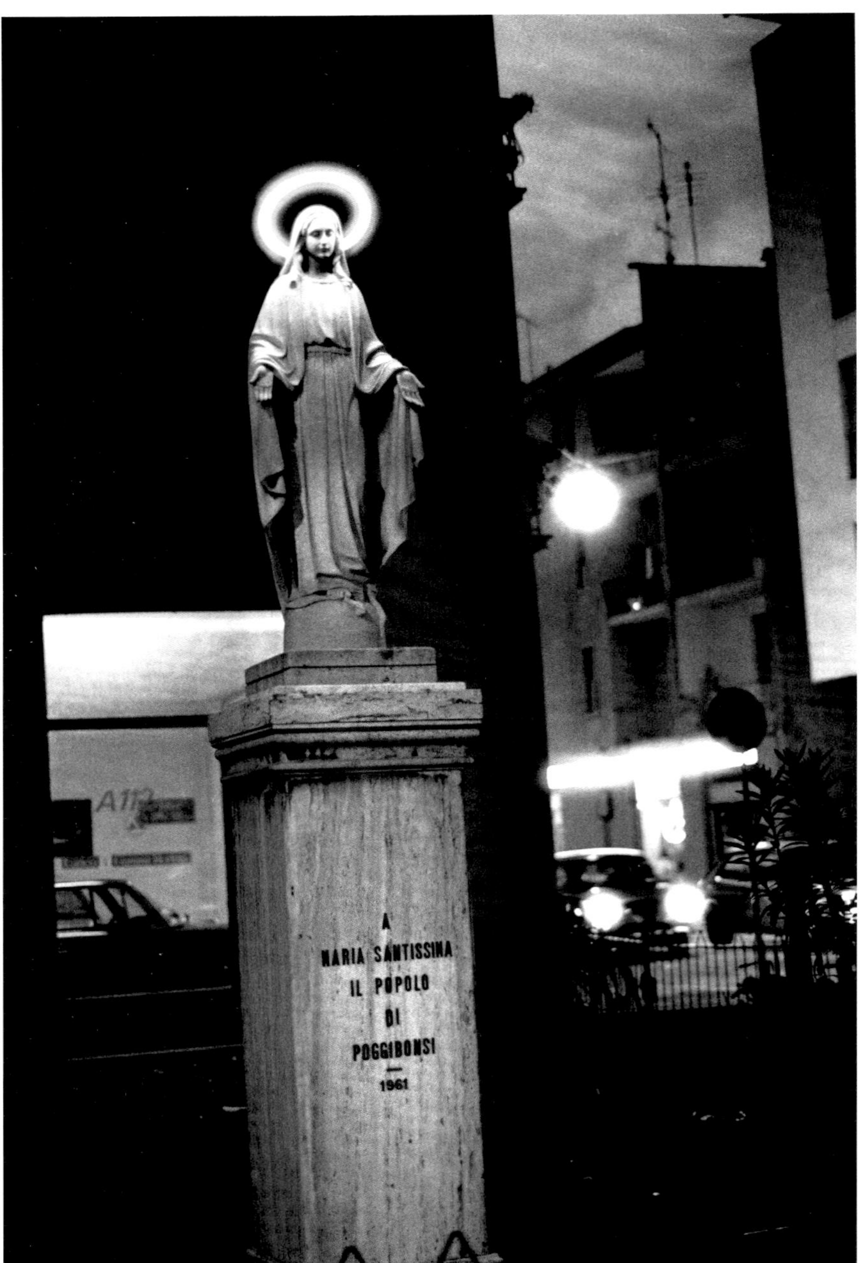
A112

A
MARIA SANTISSIMA
IL POPOLO
DI
POGGIBONSI
1961

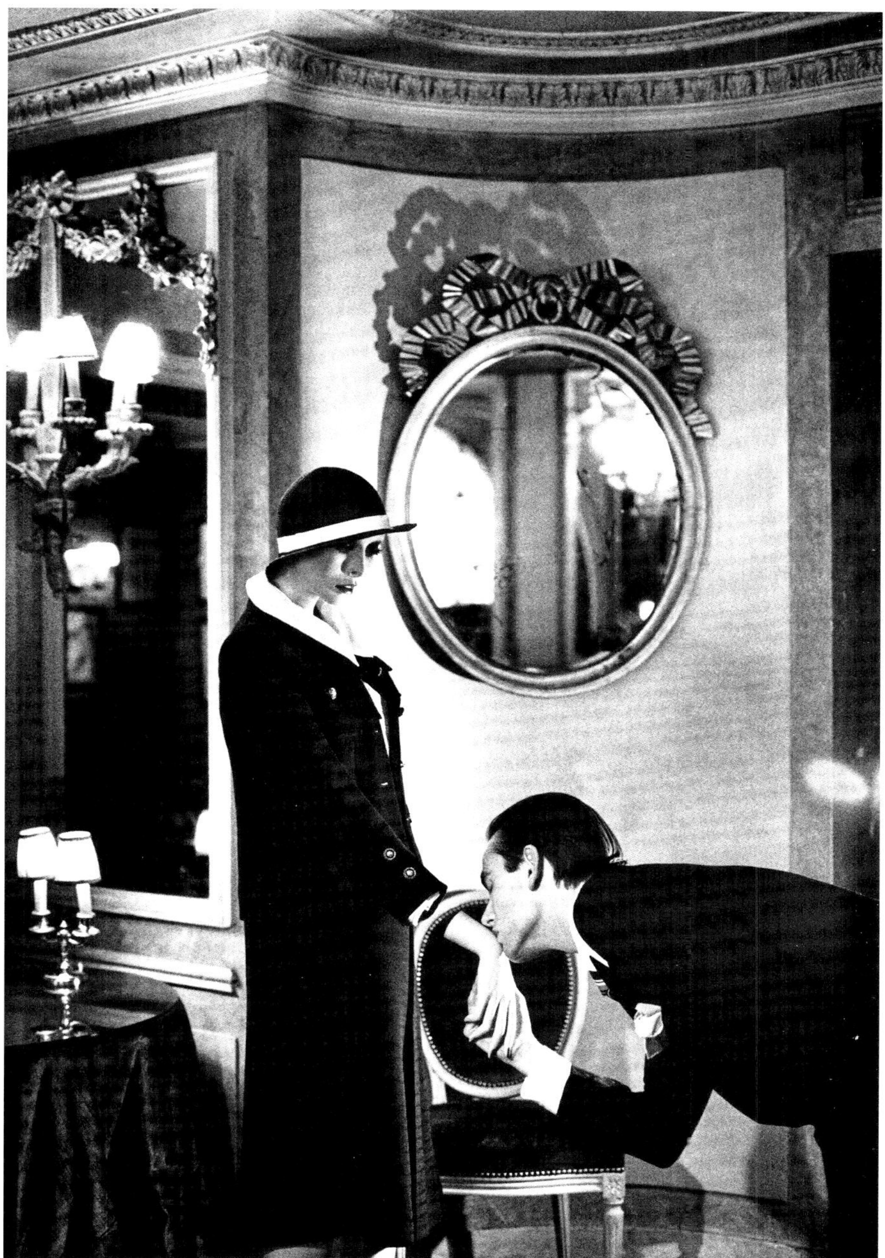

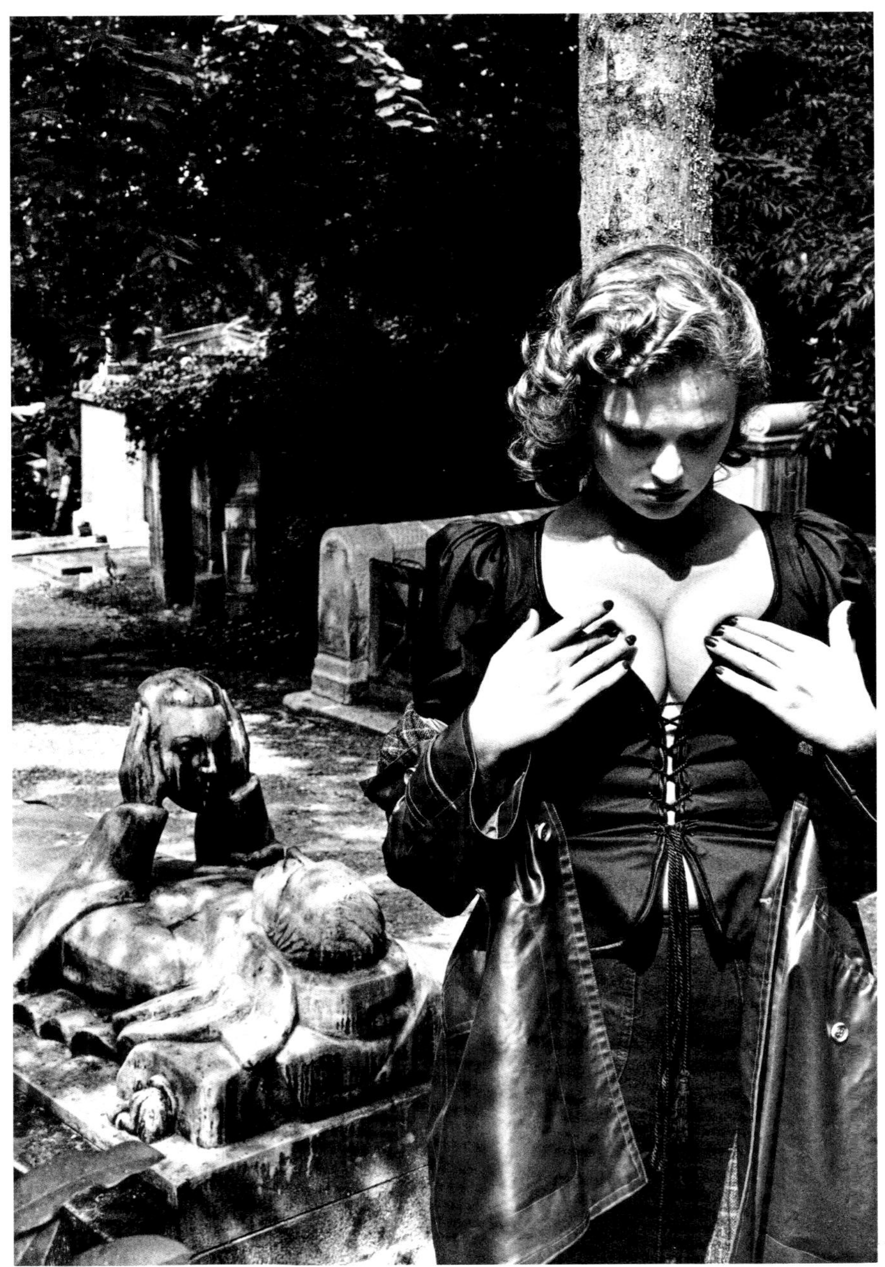

**The Tomb of Talma,
Yves Saint Laurent,
Père Lachaise, Paris, 1977**
Model: Hilde Kristin Sole

Pages 92/93
**Égoïste, Yves Saint Laurent,
Jardin des Tuileries, Paris, 1978**
Model: Loulou de la Falaise

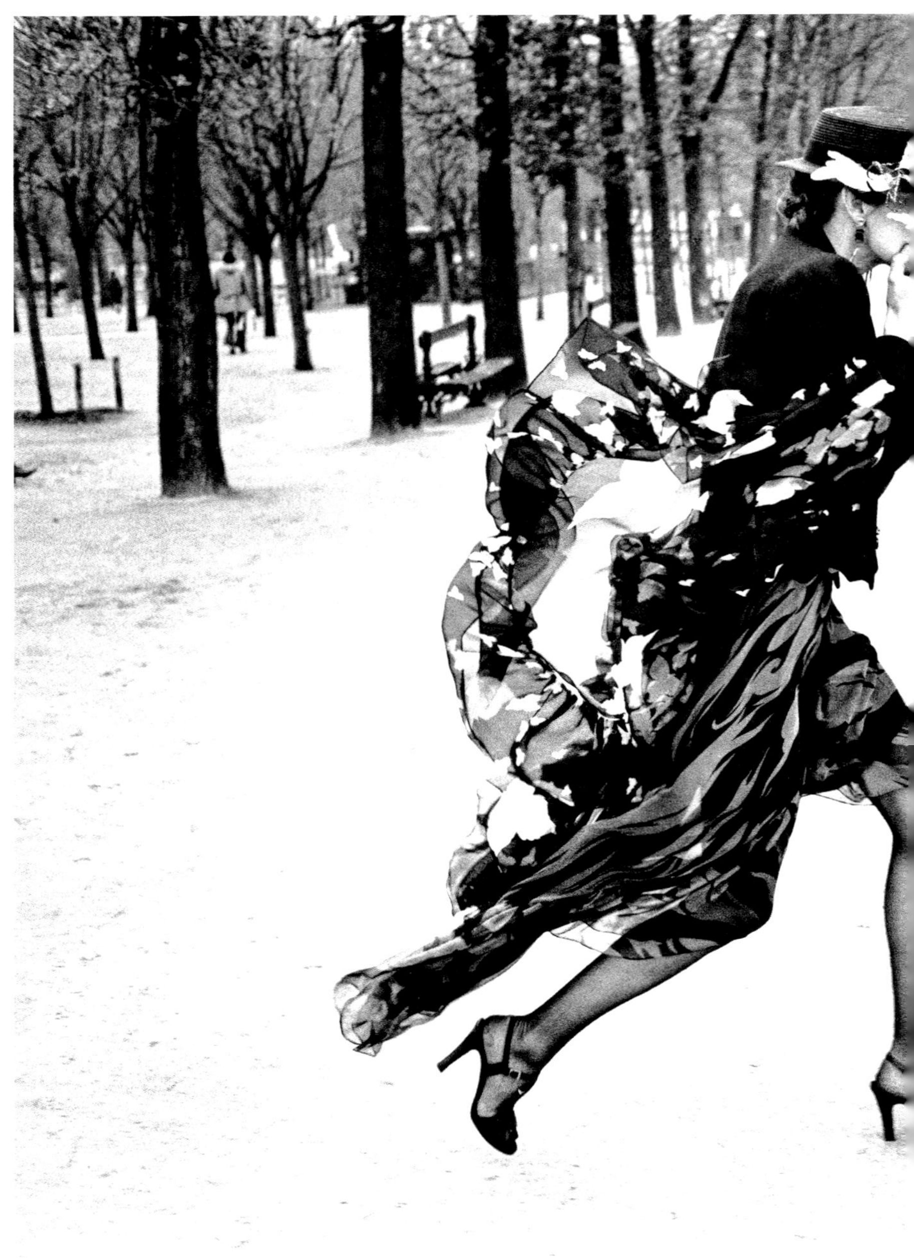

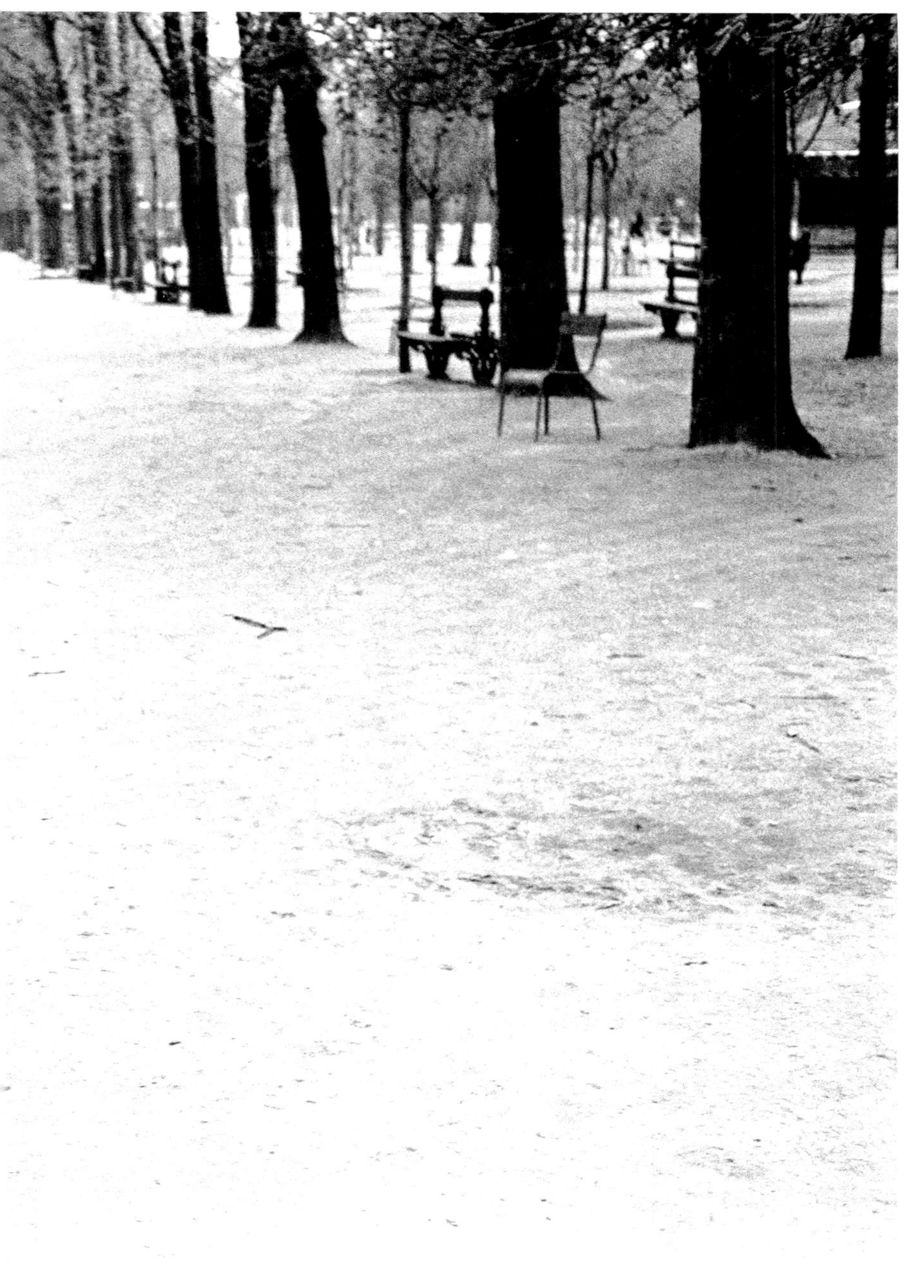

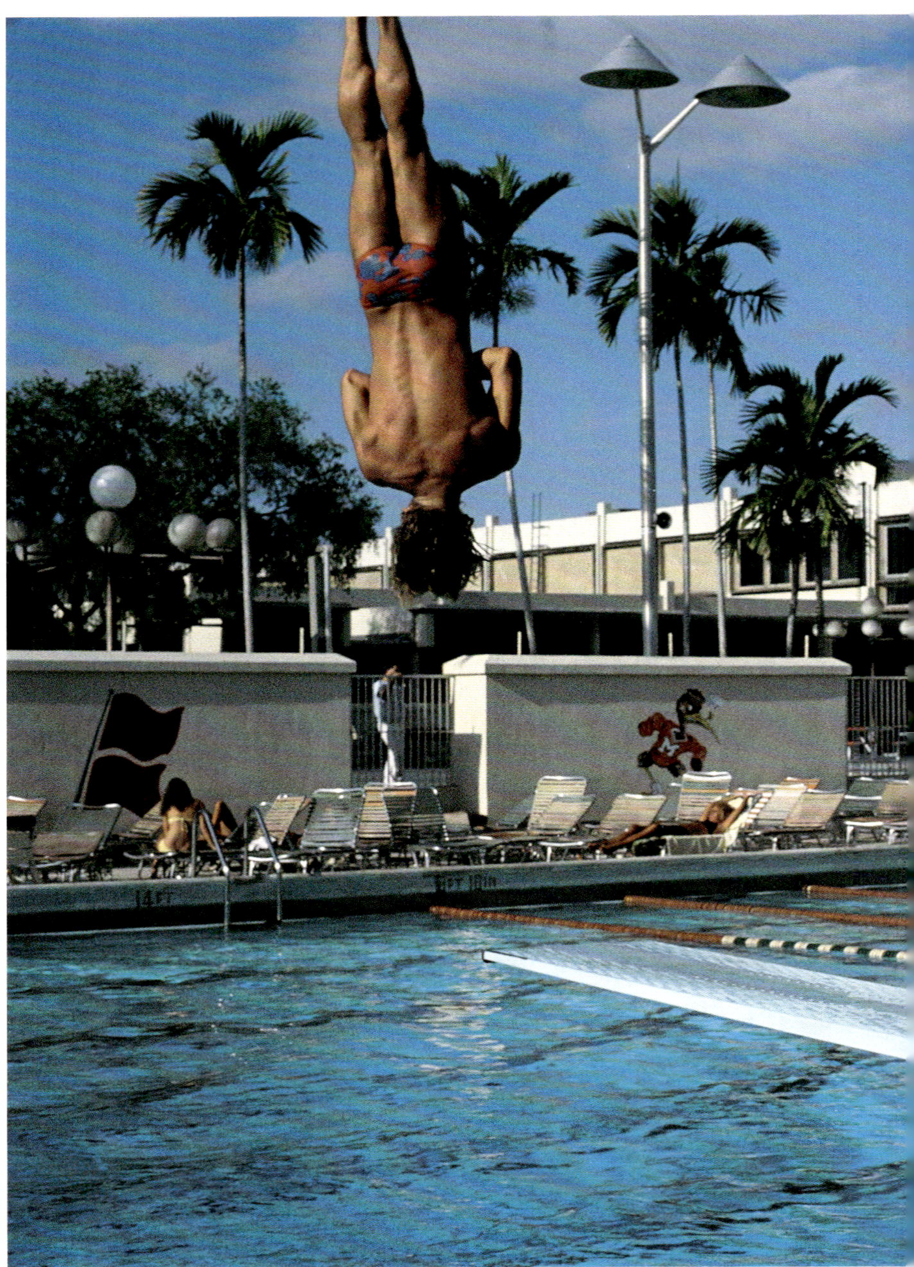

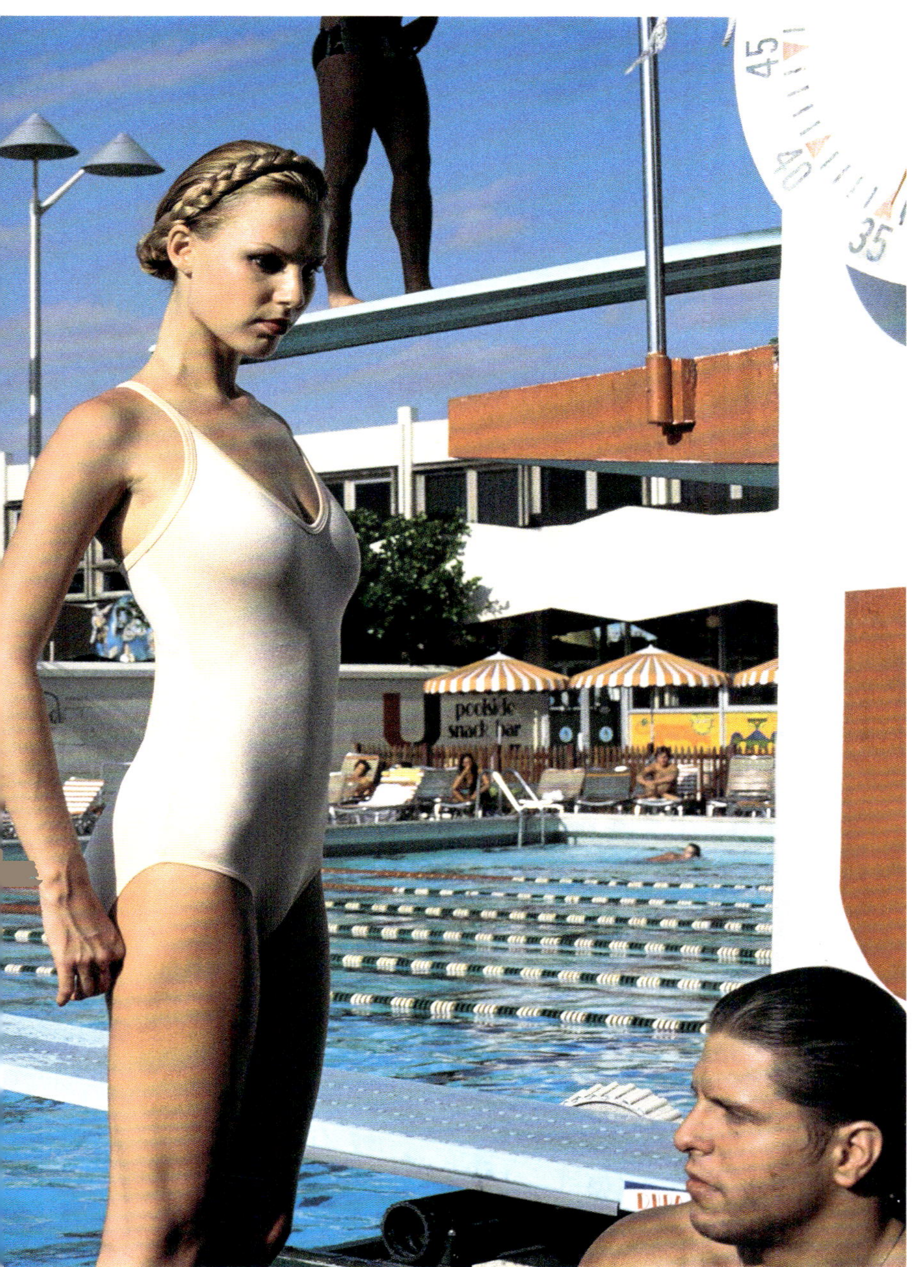
poolside
snack bar
45
40
35

David Hockney,
Piscine Royale,
Paris, 1975

Pages 94/95
The New York Times Magazine,
University of Miami, Florida, 1978
Newton loved swimming pools. He took countless
opportunities to shoot in outdoor pool locations,
making a signature of his technically brilliant
colour photographs taken in midday sunlight.
Whether the pool was in France, Italy, Monaco or
as seen here at the University of Miami in Florida,
the subject matter of places where sport, expen-
sive leisure and near-naked athletic bodies come
together drew out a lifetime of playful social
commentary and nostalgia. A clue is smuggled
into this picture: the girl in the white swimsuit
standing assertively over the man has her blonde
hair plaited into a Germanic Gretel braid. During
his teenage years in the 1930s, Newton was a
keen swimmer, chasing girls at the Berlin Swim
Club and the Halensee lake. "I've loved photographing swimmers ever since," he explained in
his autobiography.

Pages 98/99
Vogue Paris, **Jean Patou and Guy Laroche,**
Piscine Deligny, Paris, 1978

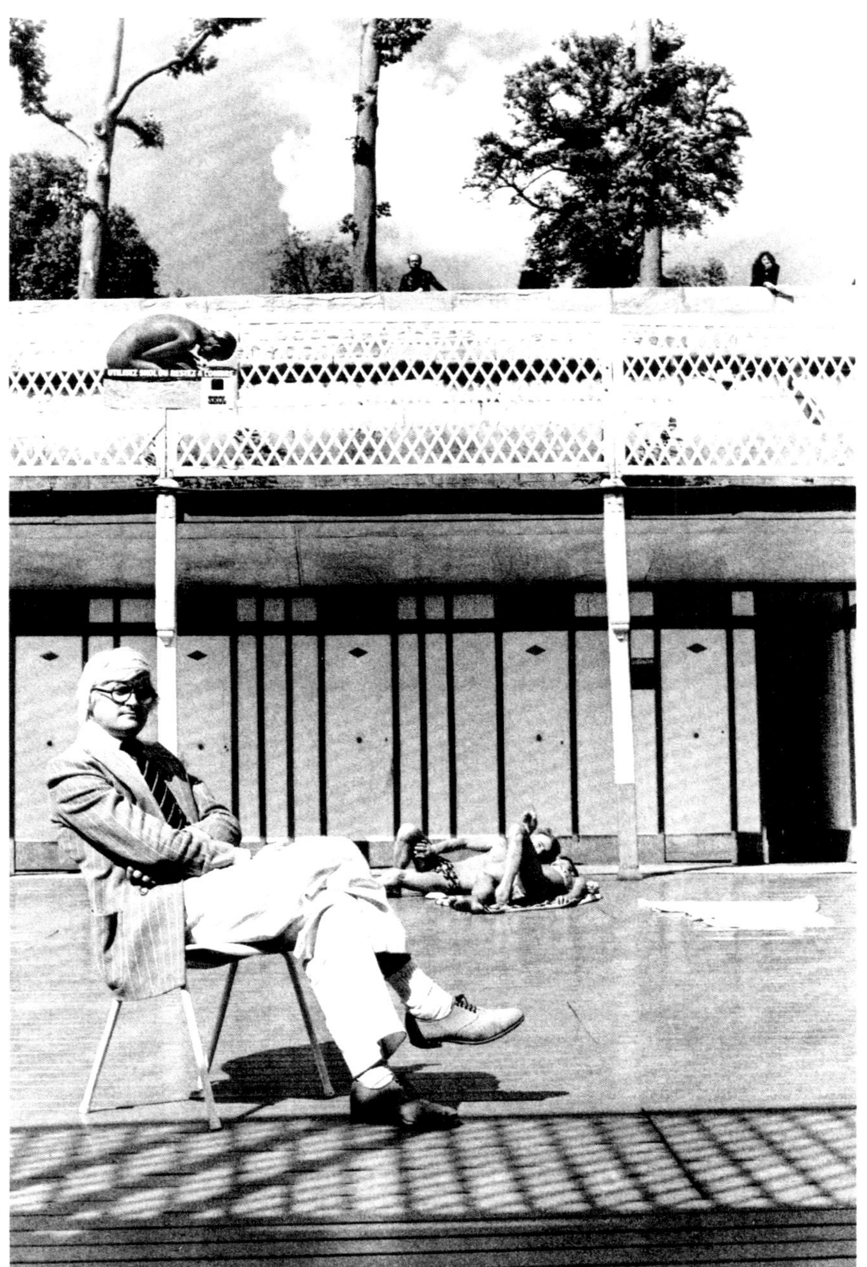

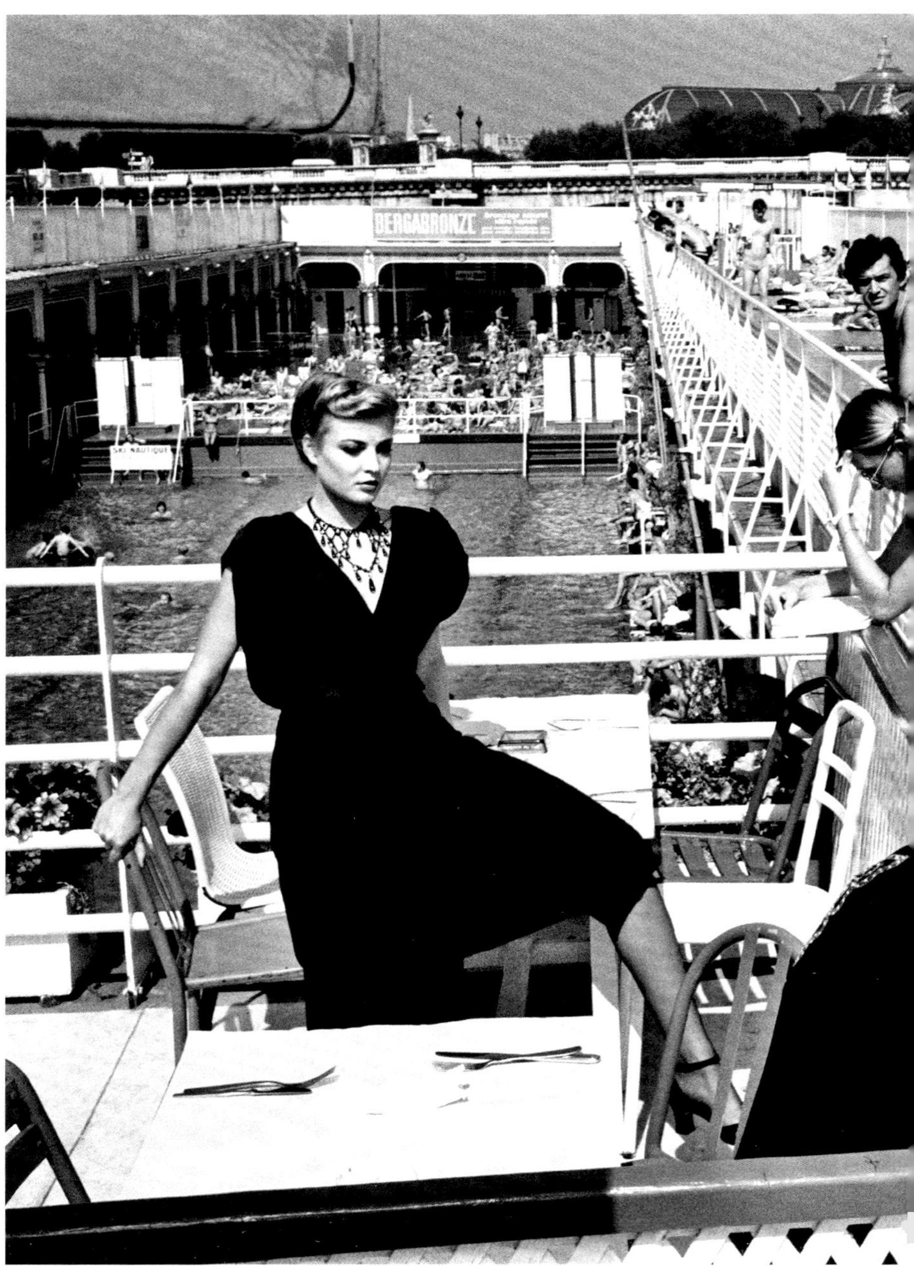
BERGABRONZE
SKI NAUTIQUE

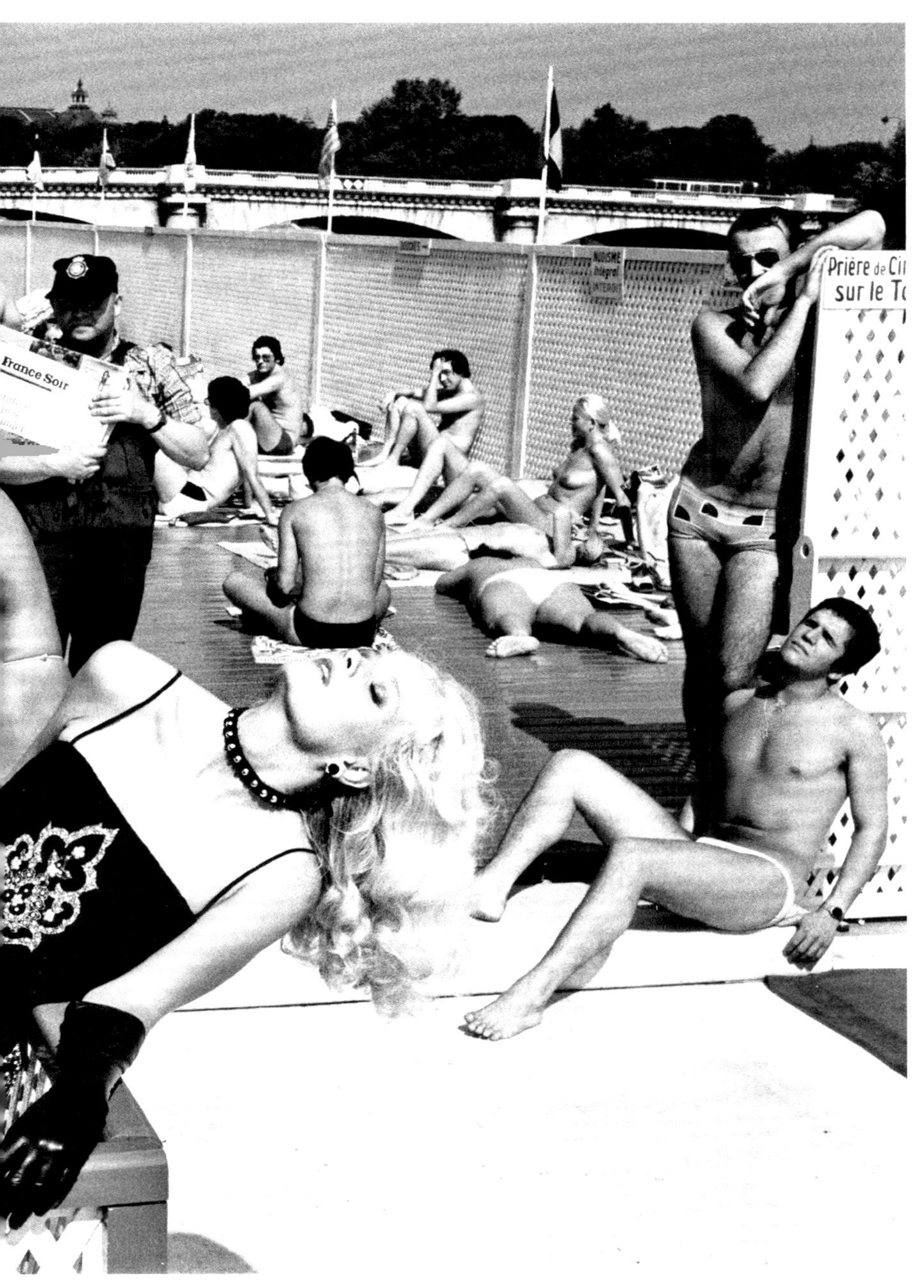

France Soir
NUDISME
intégral
INTERDI
Prière de Ci
sur le To

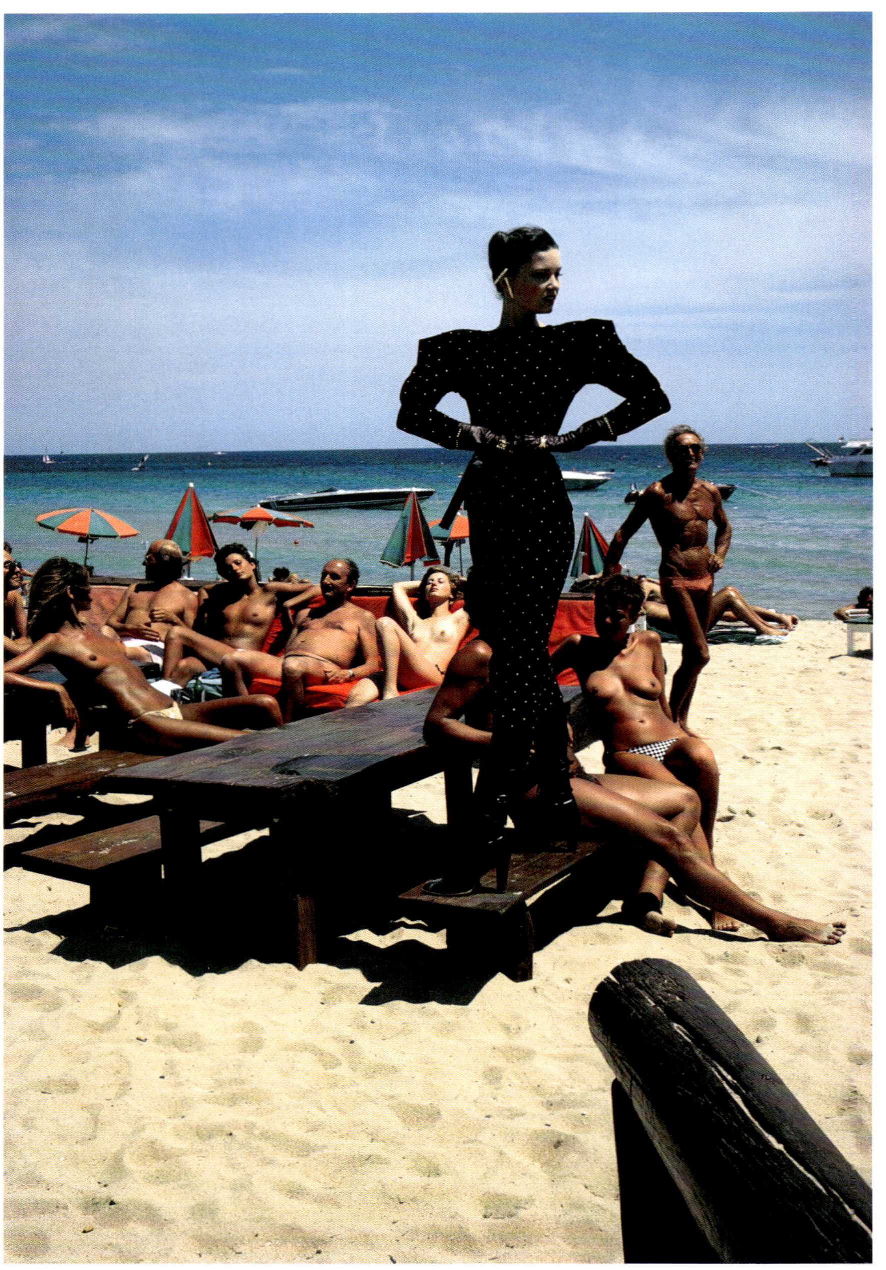

Stern, Thierry Mugler, Saint-Tropez, 1978

"For many years I have been watching the crowds on the Saint-Tropez beaches. There is no better place in the world for a voyeur like me to be constantly amused. It was here in 1969 on the Plage de la Voile Rouge that the girls took off their bras in public for the first time. It was here that the helicopters of the Gendarmerie sprayed indelible paint on the nude sunbathers on the public beaches so they could identify them later and fine them. Every beach has its particular clientele: chic and snobby, whorey and popular, poor or family crowds. There are people from Marseille and Paris, tourists from Los Angeles and Düsseldorf. The scene is so very familiar to me. That's why I've chosen to do the *Stern* pictures here. Often the places that I know intimately hold more mystery for me than an unknown or exotic location. I can already see the photos in my mind. Those great elegant models dressed totally in black, with hats and veils, black-stockinged legs, high-heeled black shoes, black gloves, every inch of their skin covered, amid all these half-naked men and women sunbathing on the beach."

Monte Carlo Beach Club,
American *Vogue*, 1979

Pages 104/105
In the Grunewald,
German *Vogue*, Berlin, 1979

Pages 106/107
Berlin, Berlin!,
German *Vogue*, Berlin, 1979
Newton returned to Berlin to make an extensive
story for German *Vogue*, which had just been
relaunched for the first time since the 1920s. "I
agonised for quite some time on how I should do
my photos. Finally, June came up with a great idea;
why not do all the pictures in the same places I
used to frequent as a boy when I was living there?"
Newton was astonished that so little had changed
since the twenties and thirties: "Even the furniture
in the beer garden, where I photographed the
lederhosen scene, seemed exactly the same. The
scenes around the lakes, with girls in their underwear, reminded me of early days when we went
swimming in the lake and everybody took their
clothes off by the bank. It seemed as if I had
stepped into the past. I was very lucky with the
light – big black clouds hung over the city every
day – it was very intense and sharp, what I call
'black light'." He talked about recreating this
ominous, half-celebratory, half-accusatory series
in *World Without Men*.

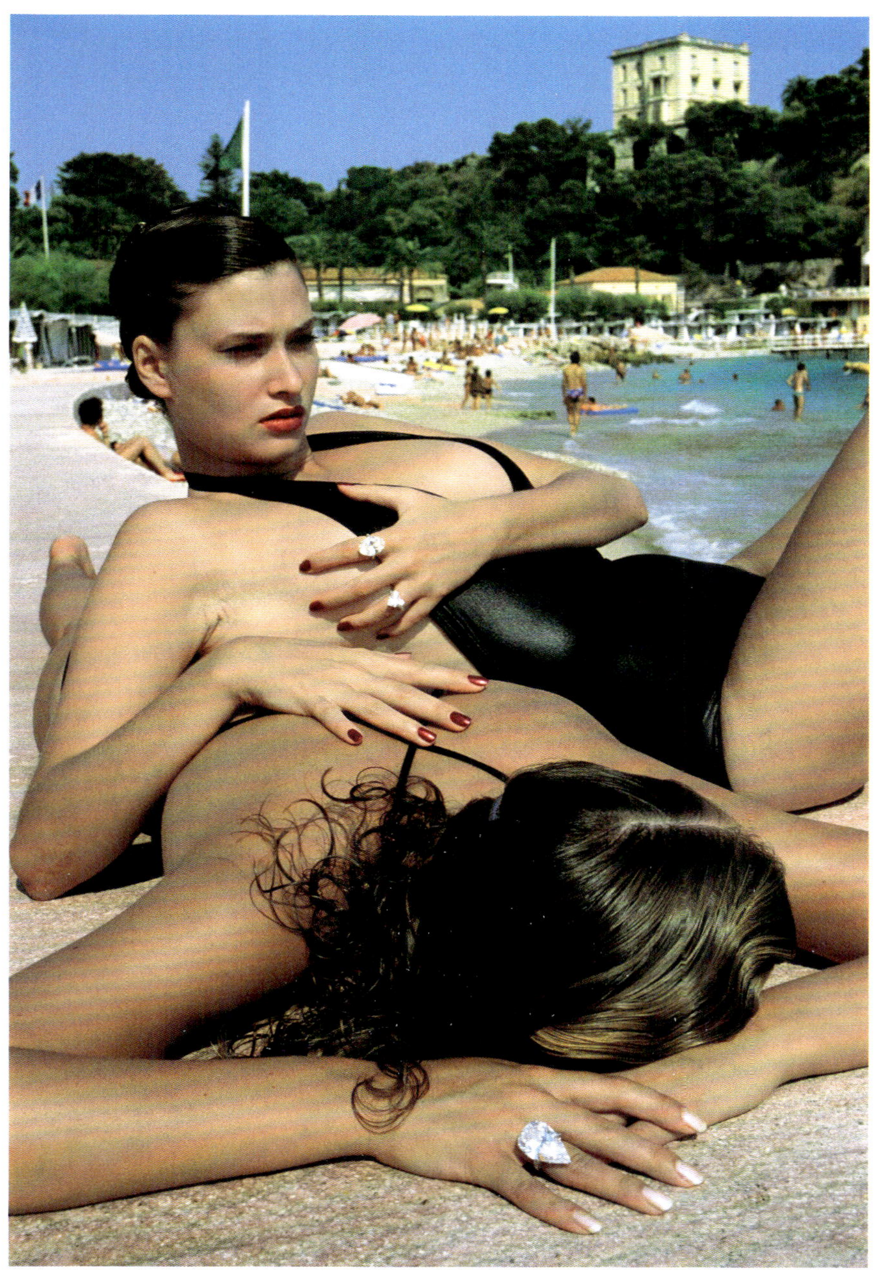

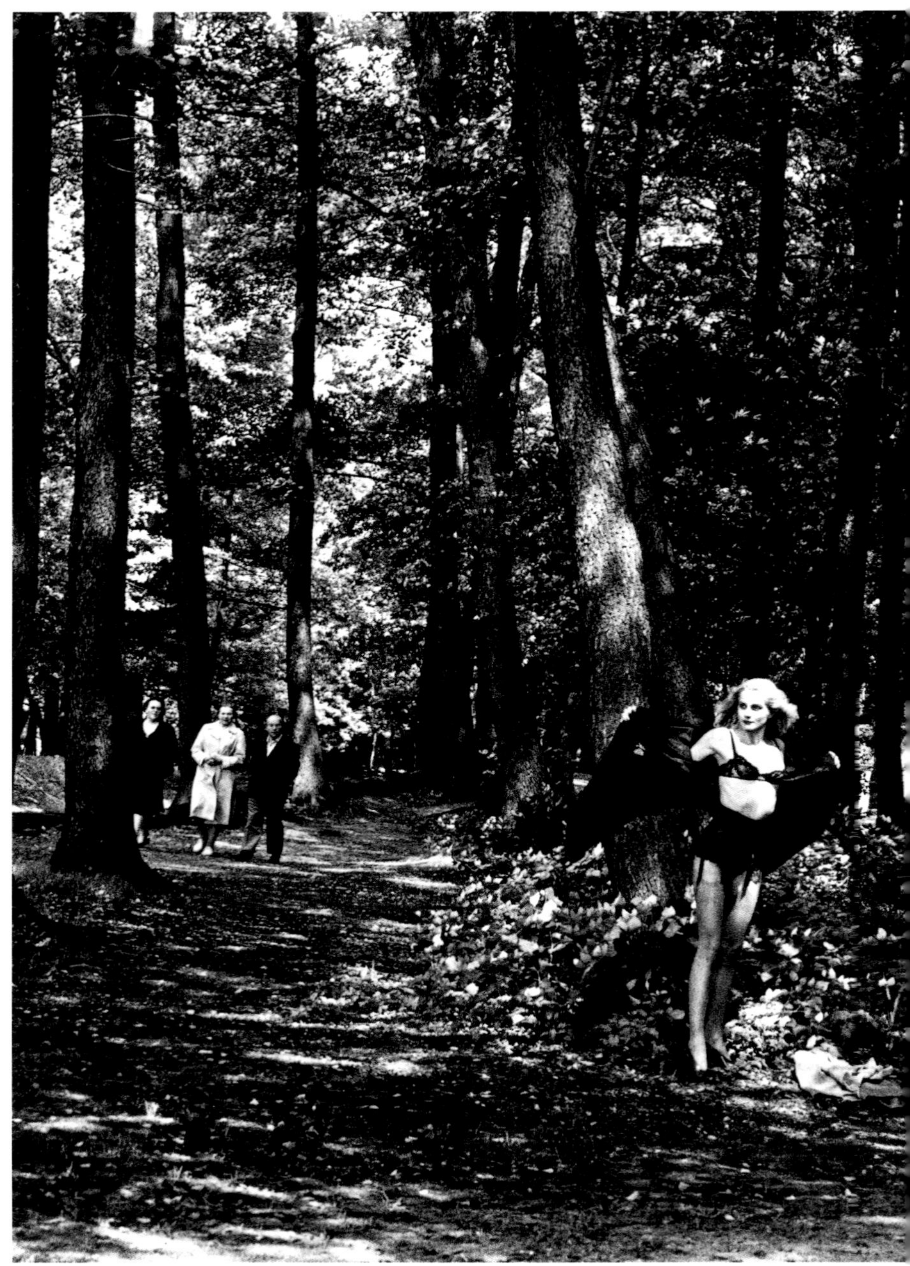

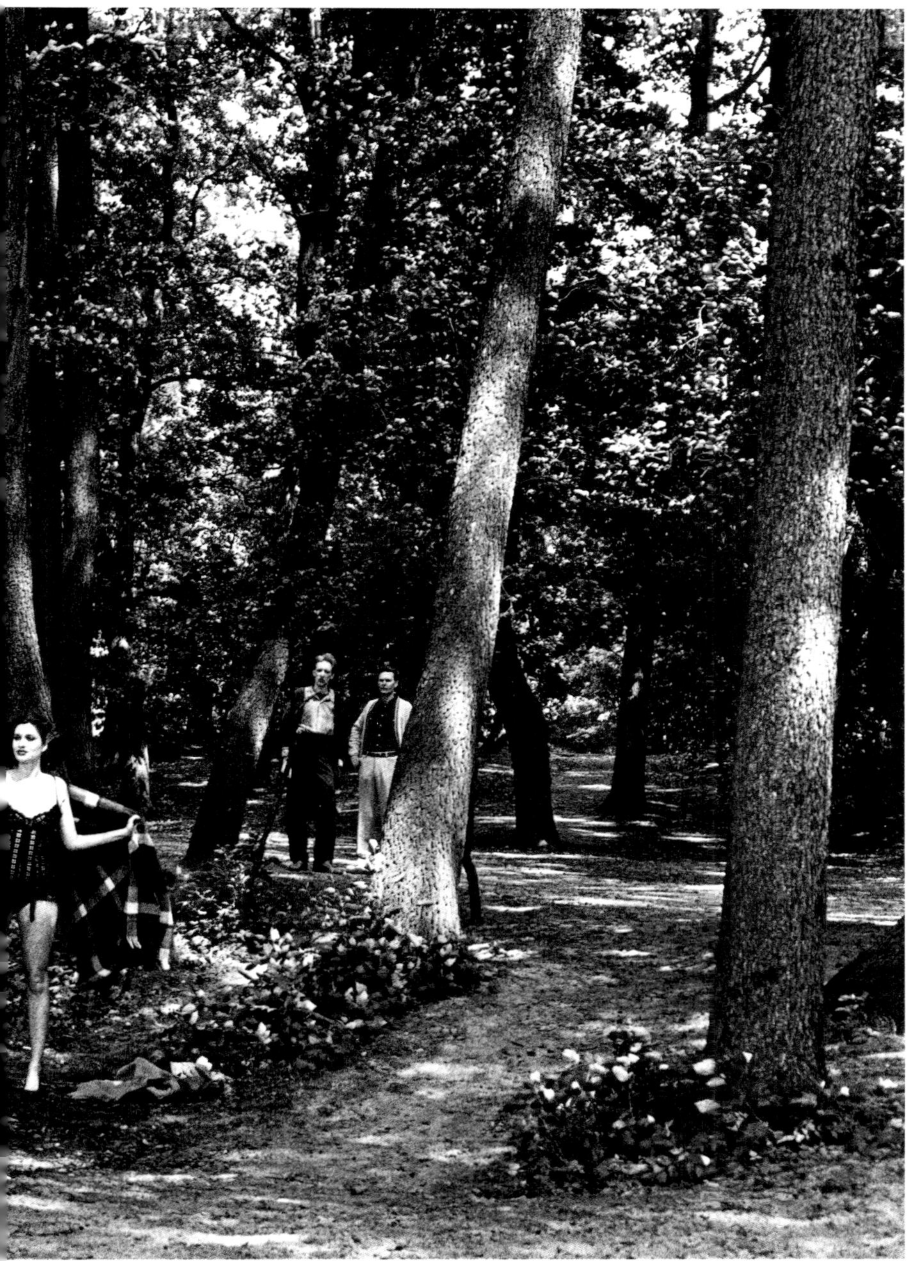

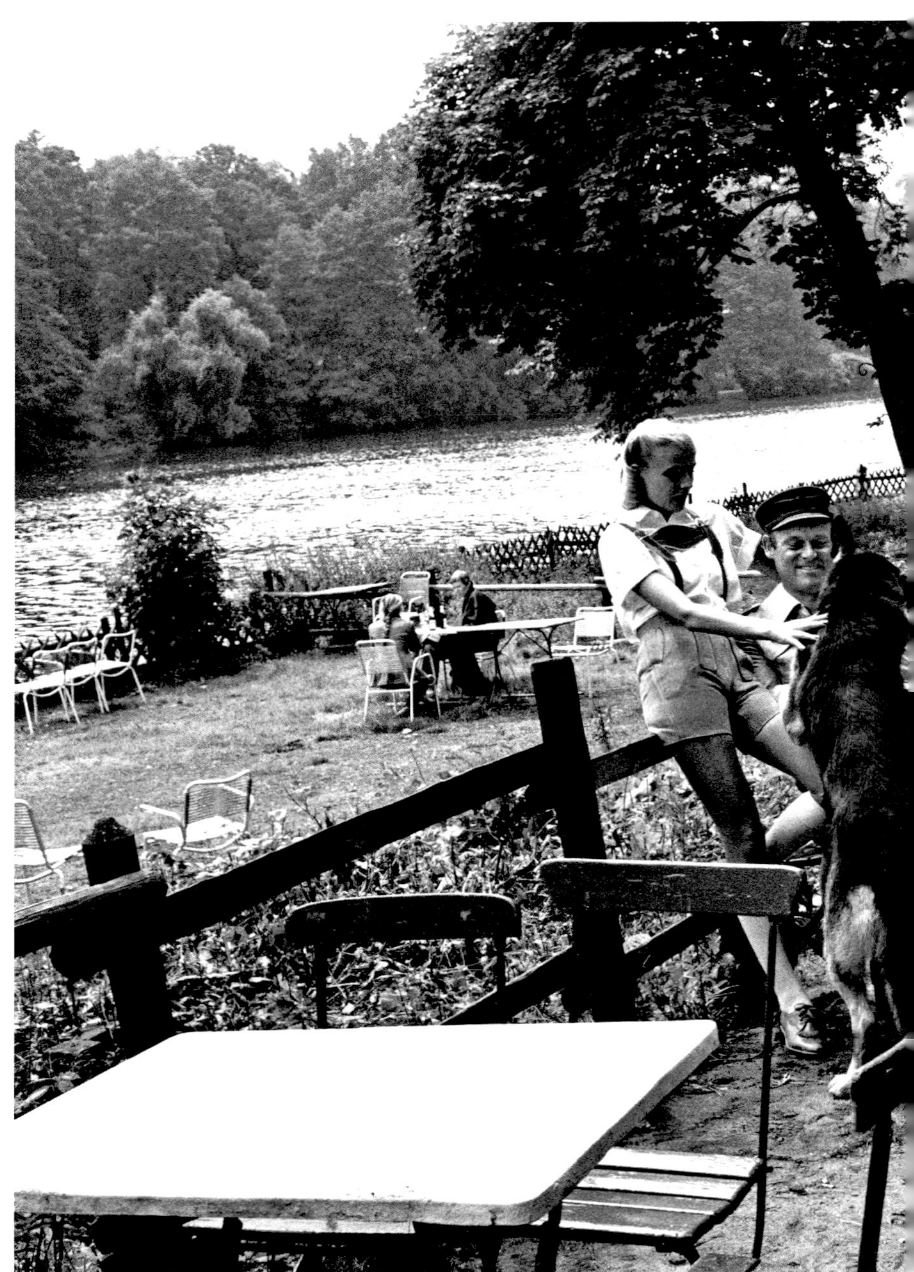

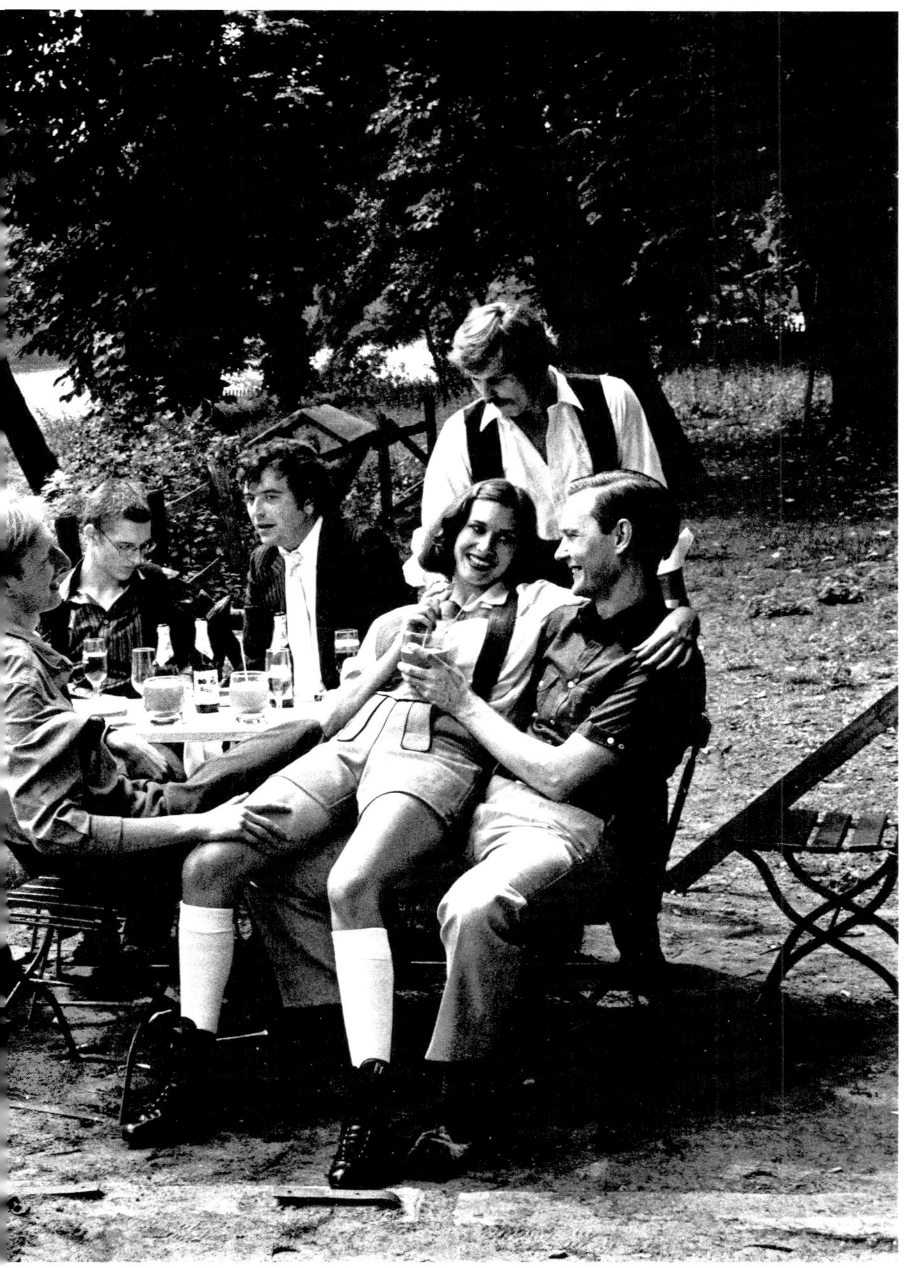

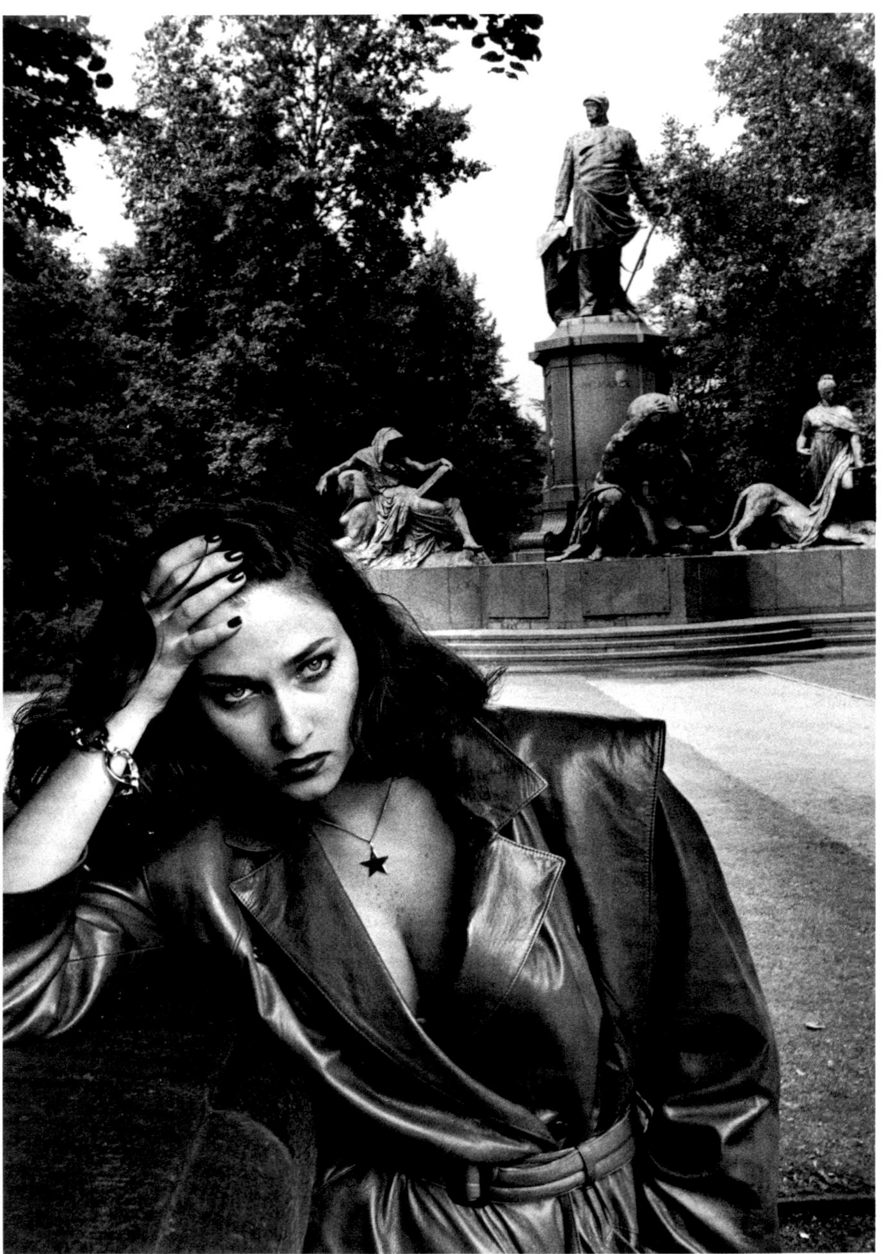

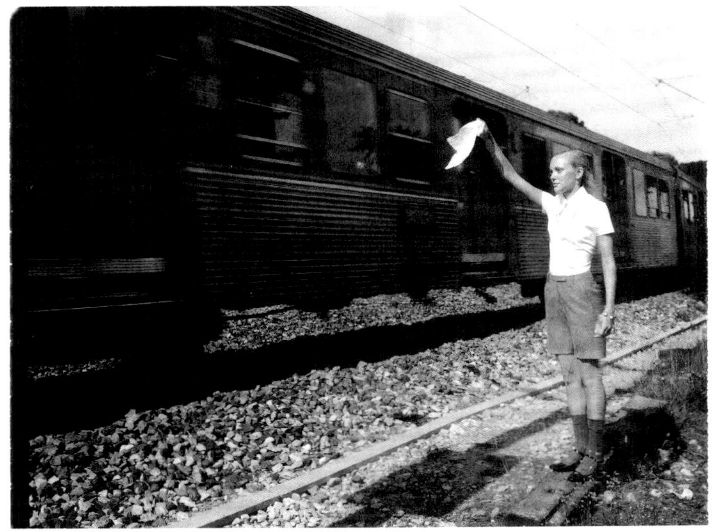

Polaroid, *Vogue Italia*, Monte Carlo, 1996

The symbolism of an adolescent waving goodbye
to a train is an unavoidably poignant evocation
of Newton's own experience as a Jewish teenager
in Berlin. In December 1938, his mother saved
him from Nazi persecution when she bought him
a ticket to board a train from Berlin Zoo station,
the first stage of a journey which took him to
Singapore. At the age of eighteen, it was the last
time he saw his parents, who later escaped to
South America.

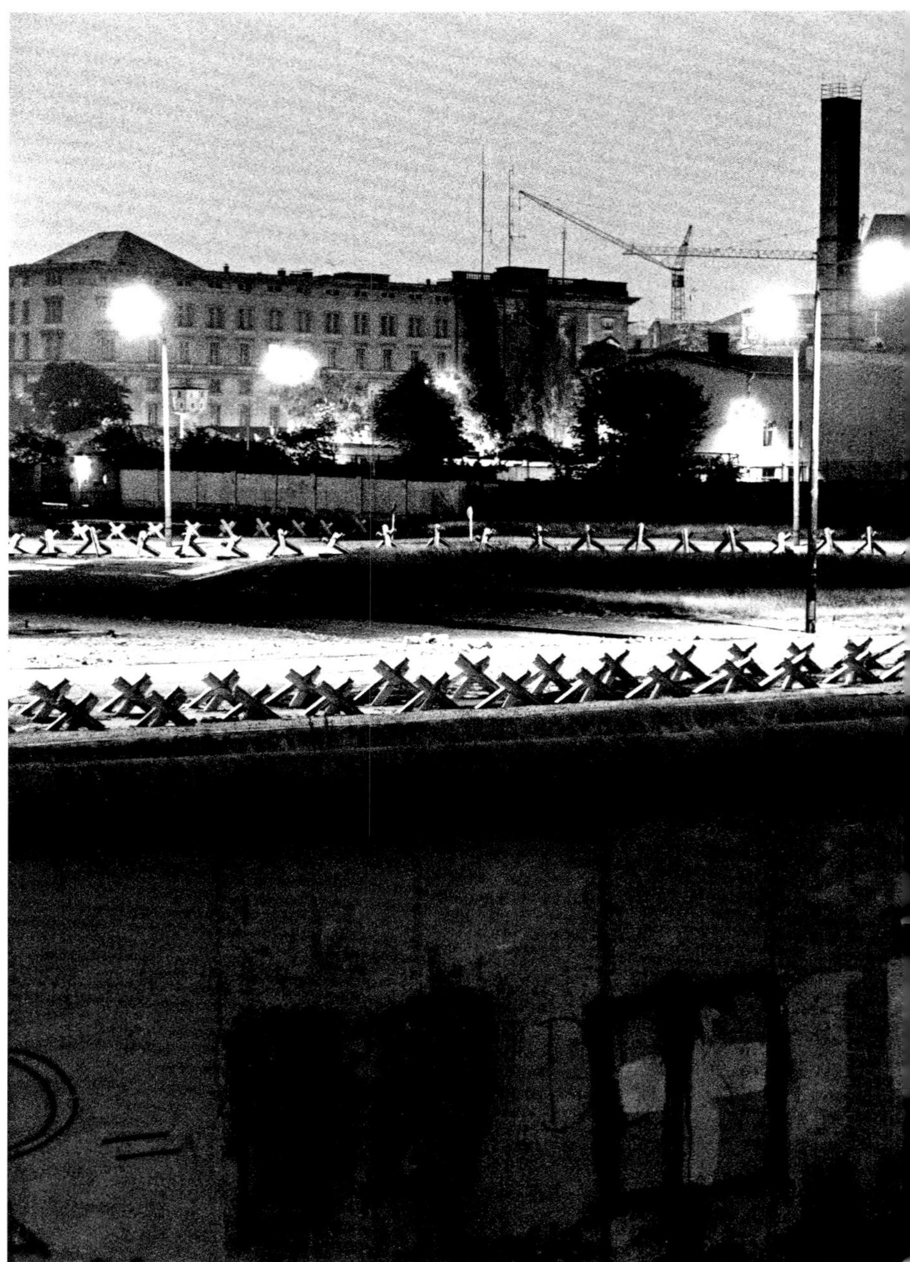

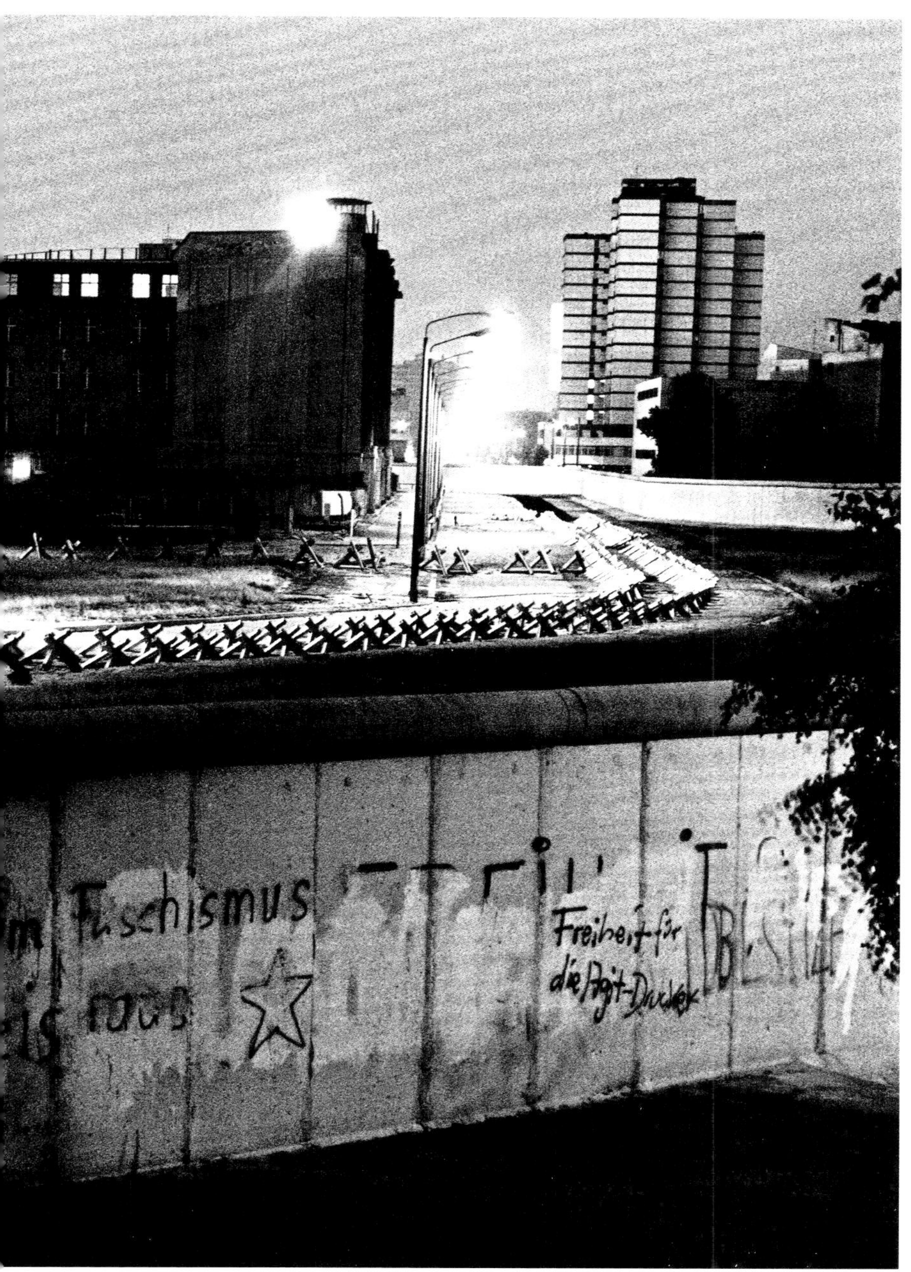
Faschismus
is raus
Freiheit für
die Agit-Drucker

***Vogue Paris*, Ted Lapidus, Paris, 1978**
Newton described in his autobiography how his controversially original phase of using shop mannequins began while working for *Vogue Paris*. "I am standing on the Pont Alexandre III. It's 5 p.m., pitch black, freezing cold, driving rain. Couture collection time. It's been like this for me now for the last twenty-four years, photographing these flimsy dresses at this impossible time of the year. I know I could always go back to the studio, but when I am faced with white paper background I seize up completely and don't know what to do. It's no fun. This time I have decided to do my *Vogue Paris* pix on store dummies. I can't possibly take real girls out in this weather. We are all huddled up in a truck waiting for a gale to subside. It's a specialist job. I have a wizard of a girl from *Au Printemps*, who will make these mannequins take on the most wonderfully lifelike positions, with the help of cardboard and rolled up newspaper. Part of the fun for me is to make them look as real as possible."

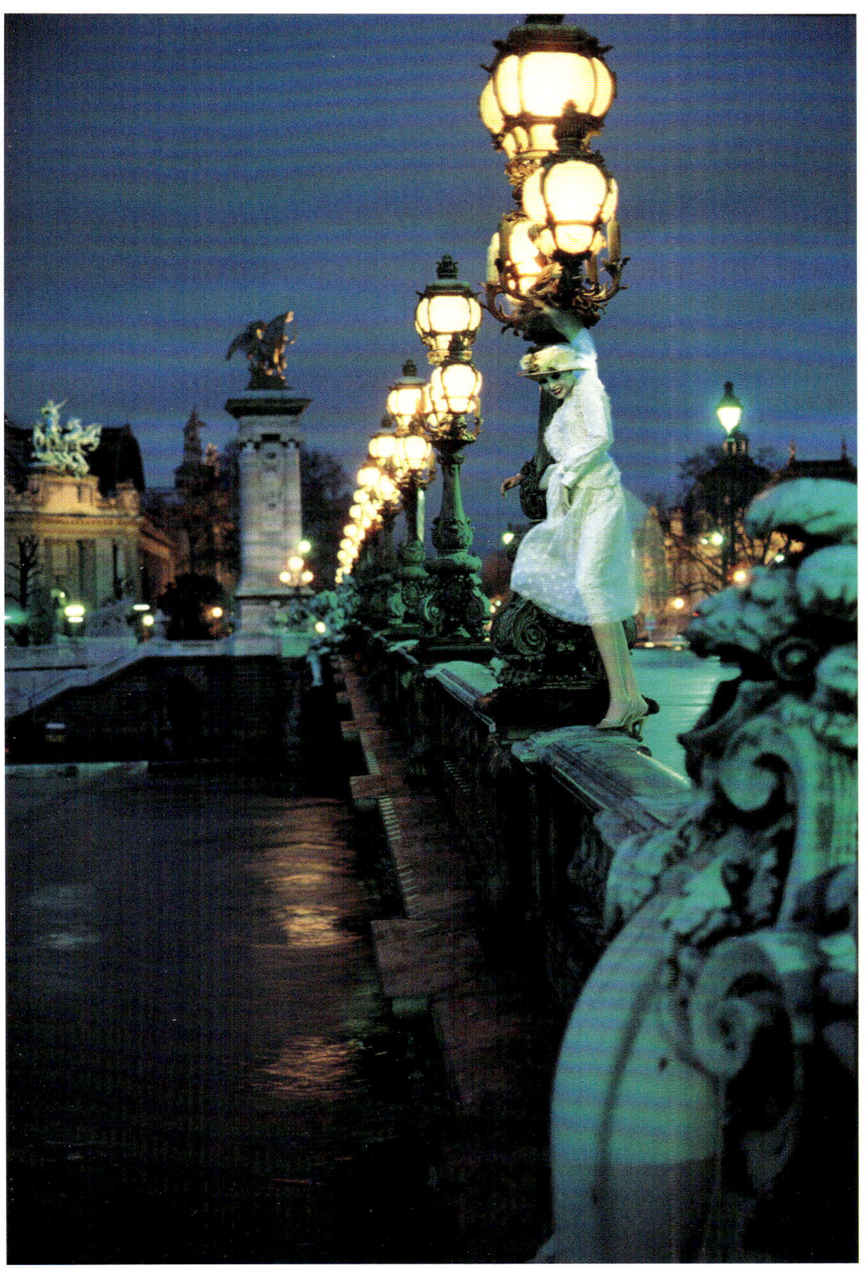

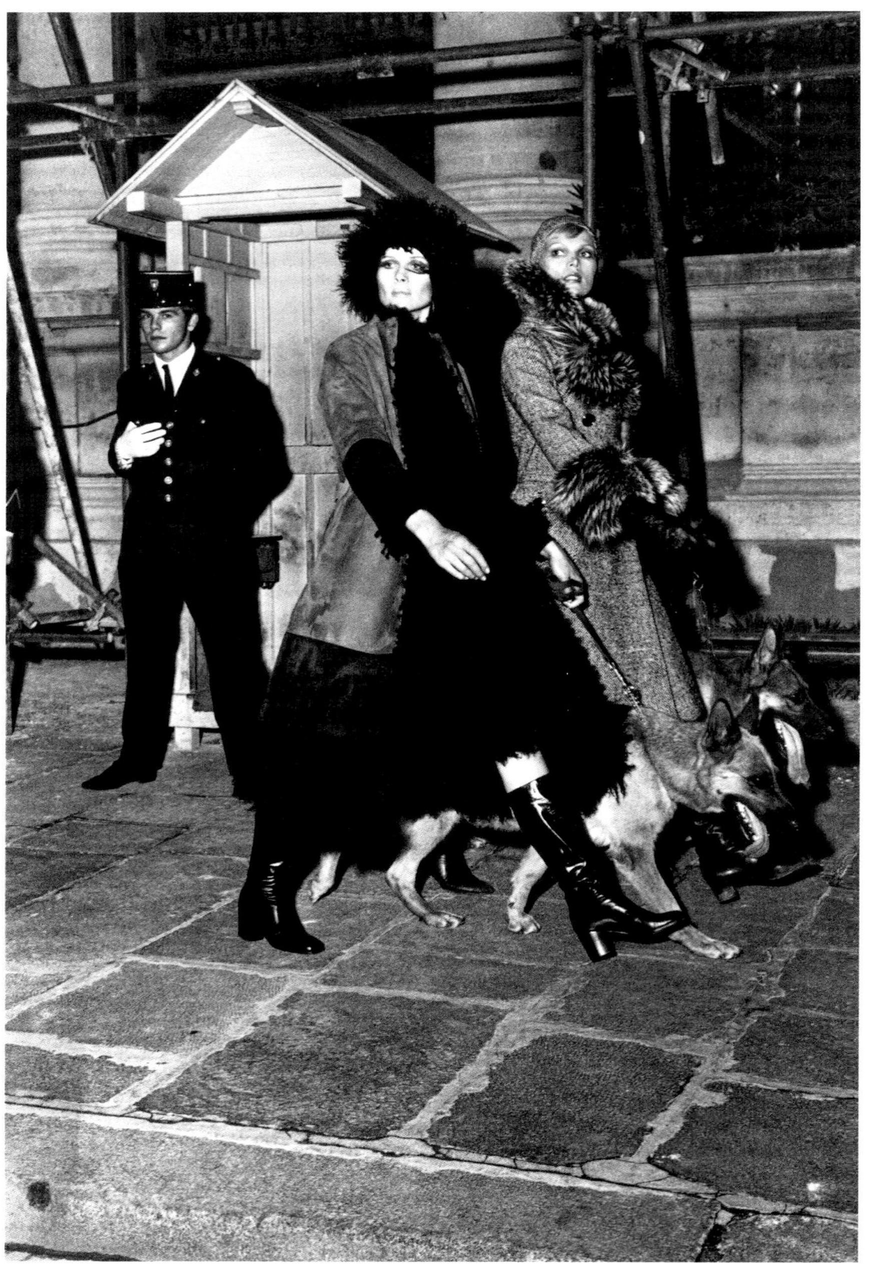

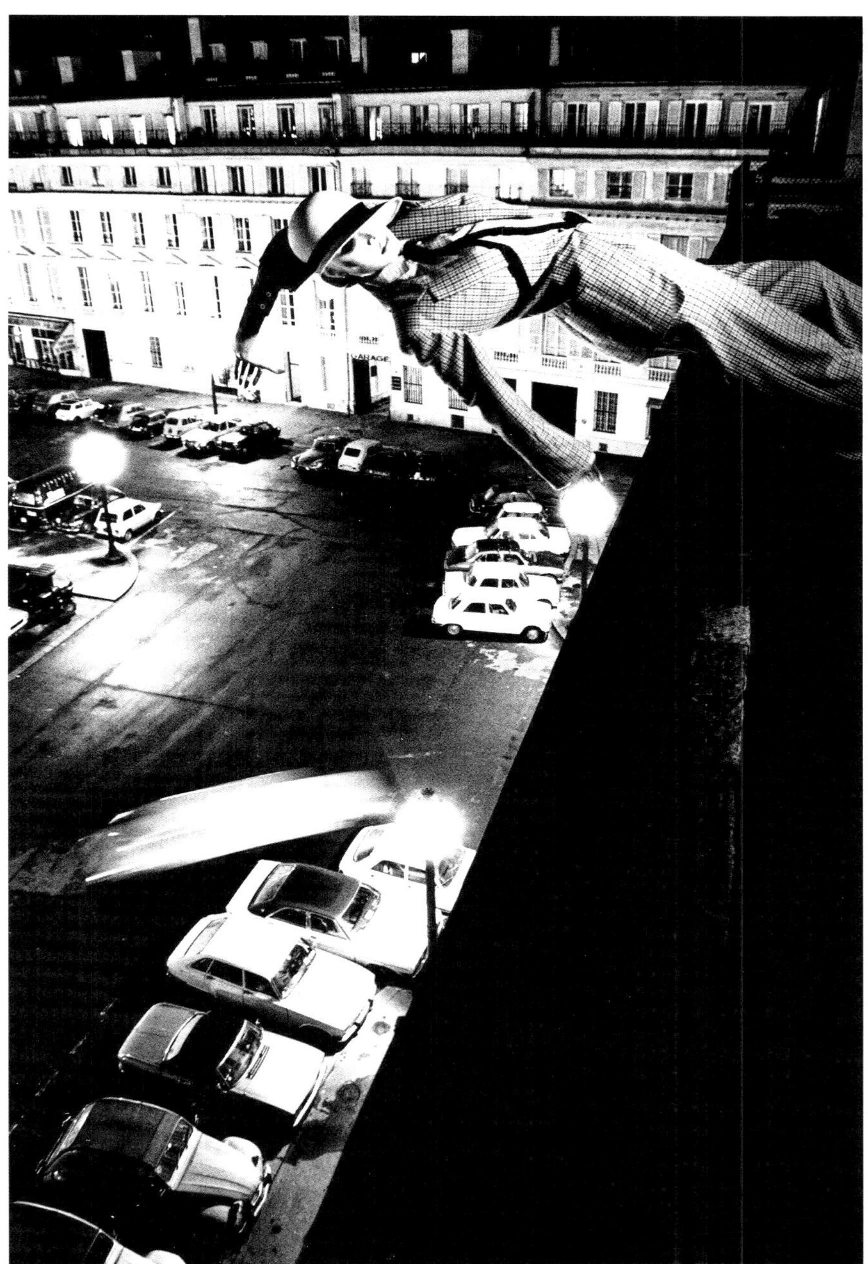

Big Nude III, Paris, 1980
Model: Henriette Allais
In 1980, Newton began to turn away from fashion
photography. Having been inspired by seeing
oversized police identity photographs of German
Baader-Meinhof terrorists, he began his *Big Nudes*.
This image is one of the first in the series, which
were shot intermittently until 1993. This particular
image has become iconic since it was the cover
of *SUMO*, the first titan in TASCHEN's epic collection, weighing in at thirty kilos. The *Big Nudes* were
Newton's only body of work taken consistently
in the studio.

Pages 118 and 119
Walking Women Dressed and Naked,
***Vogue Paris*, Paris, 1981**

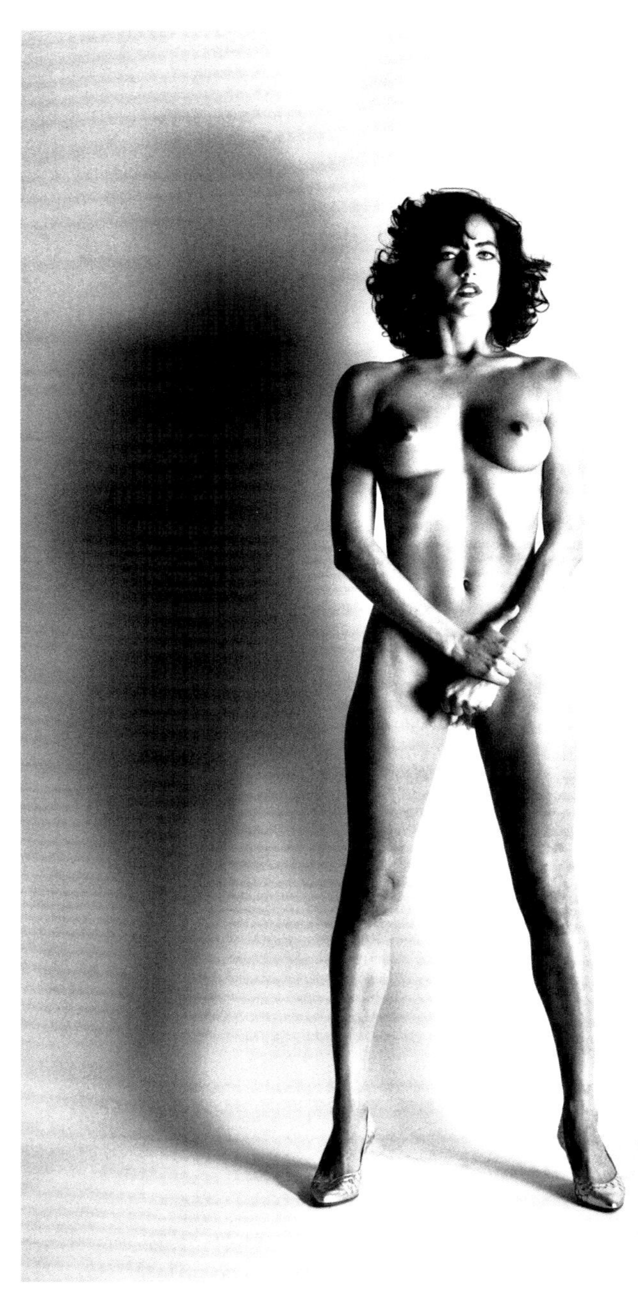

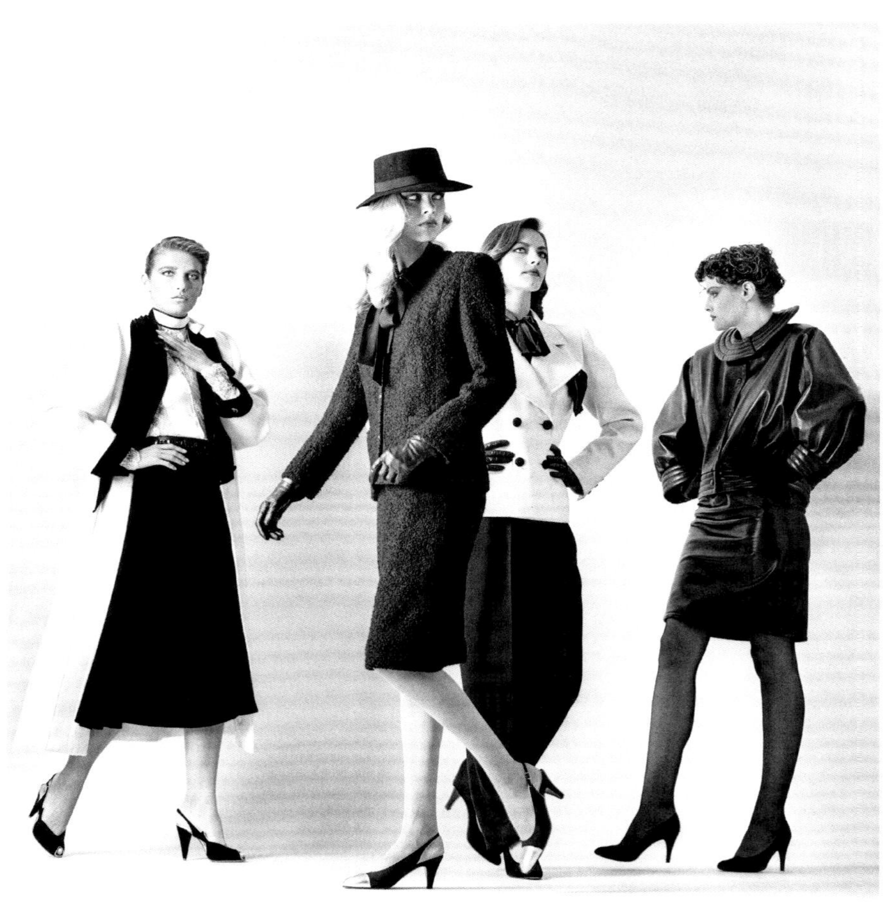

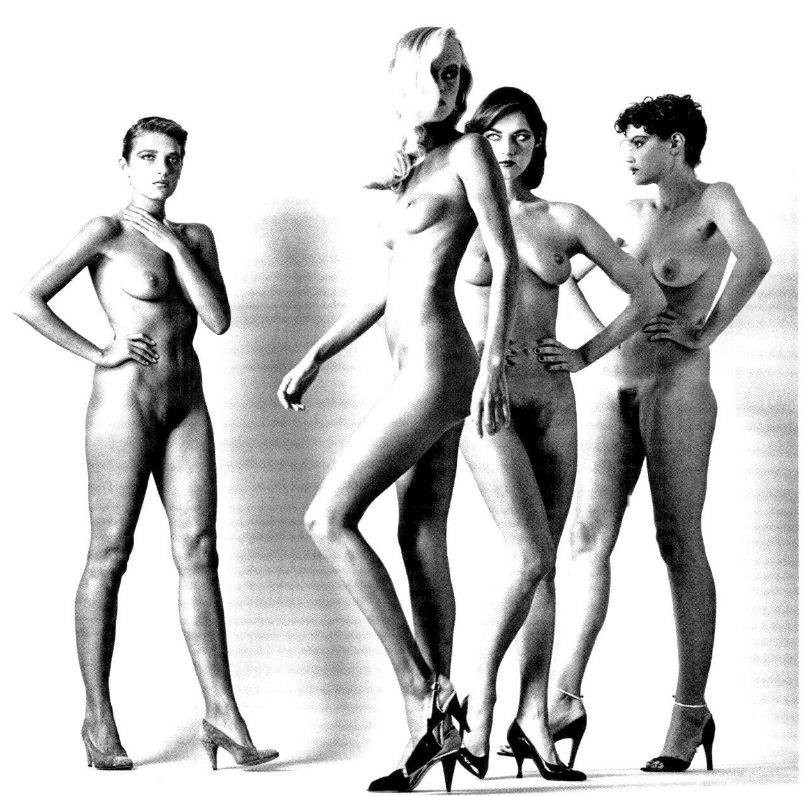

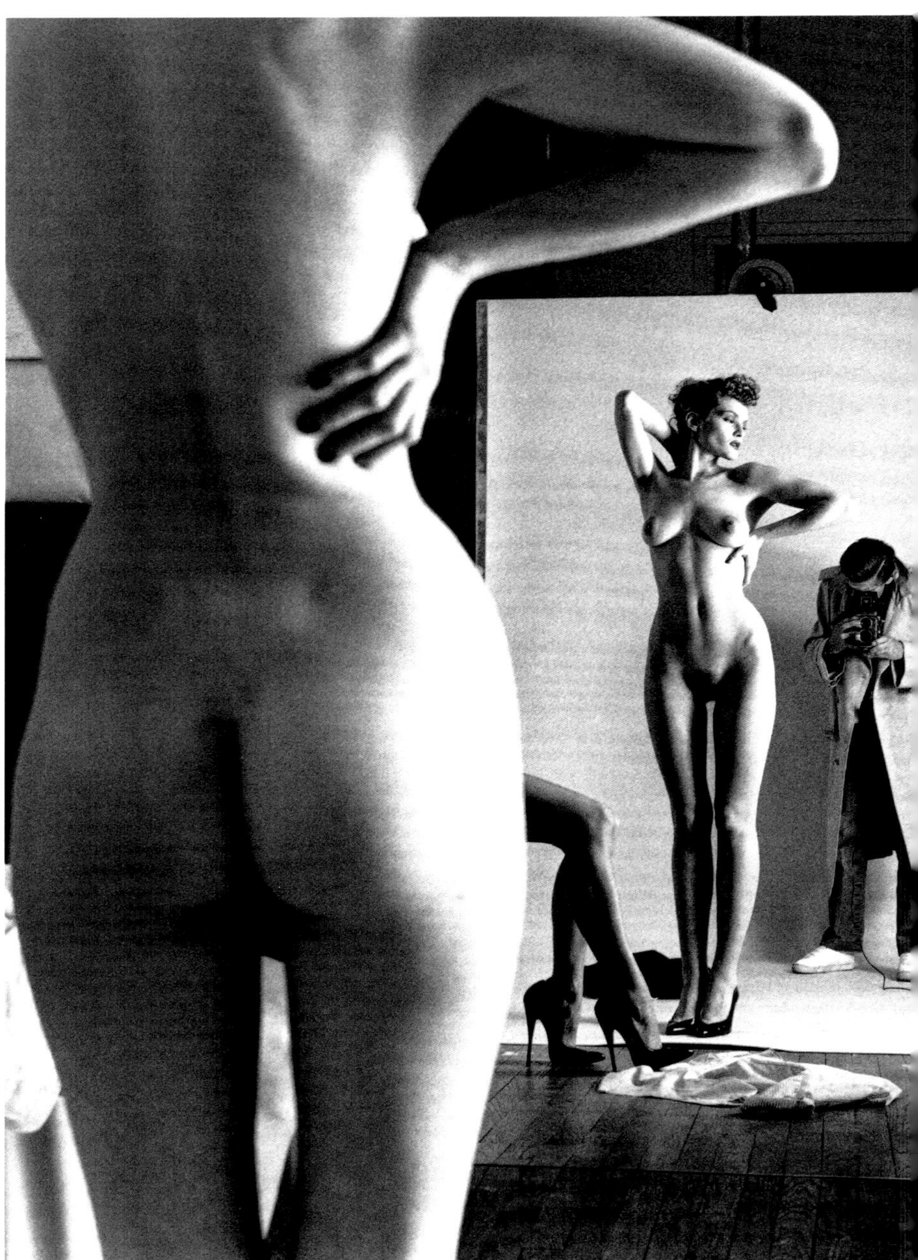

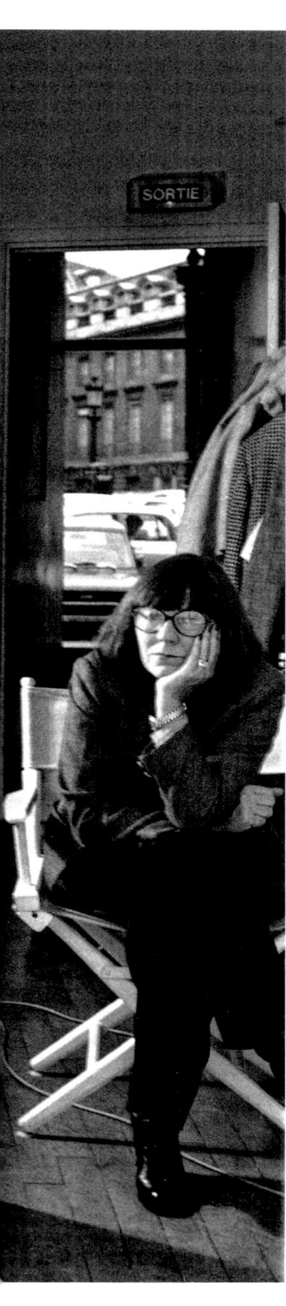

Self Portrait with Wife and Models
Vogue Hommes, Paris, 1981

With characteristic resourcefulness, and a dash of
his in-the-moment opportunism, Newton trans-
formed a potentially dull men's raincoat editorial
shoot into an image with layered messages to
send viewers reeling.

The framing and depth of the composition,
with models, mirror and the Paris street seen
through the window, coolly echo that of a Dutch
painting. It also reflects Newton playing on his
stature as a photographer of nude women – he
has wittily turned the tables of the subject of men
in trench coats onto himself, subtly skewering the
stereotype of street photographers and voyeurs
in raincoats.

Typically accomplished, formally and technically,
Self Portrait with Wife and Models also acknowledges June Newton's presence in the background
of his work, although at that moment she was
unaware he was putting her in the picture.

Raquel Welch,
Vogue Paris,
Beverly Hills, 1981

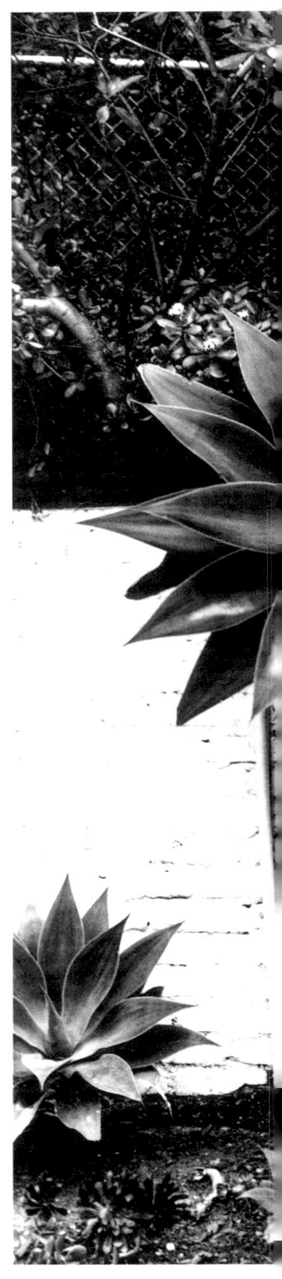

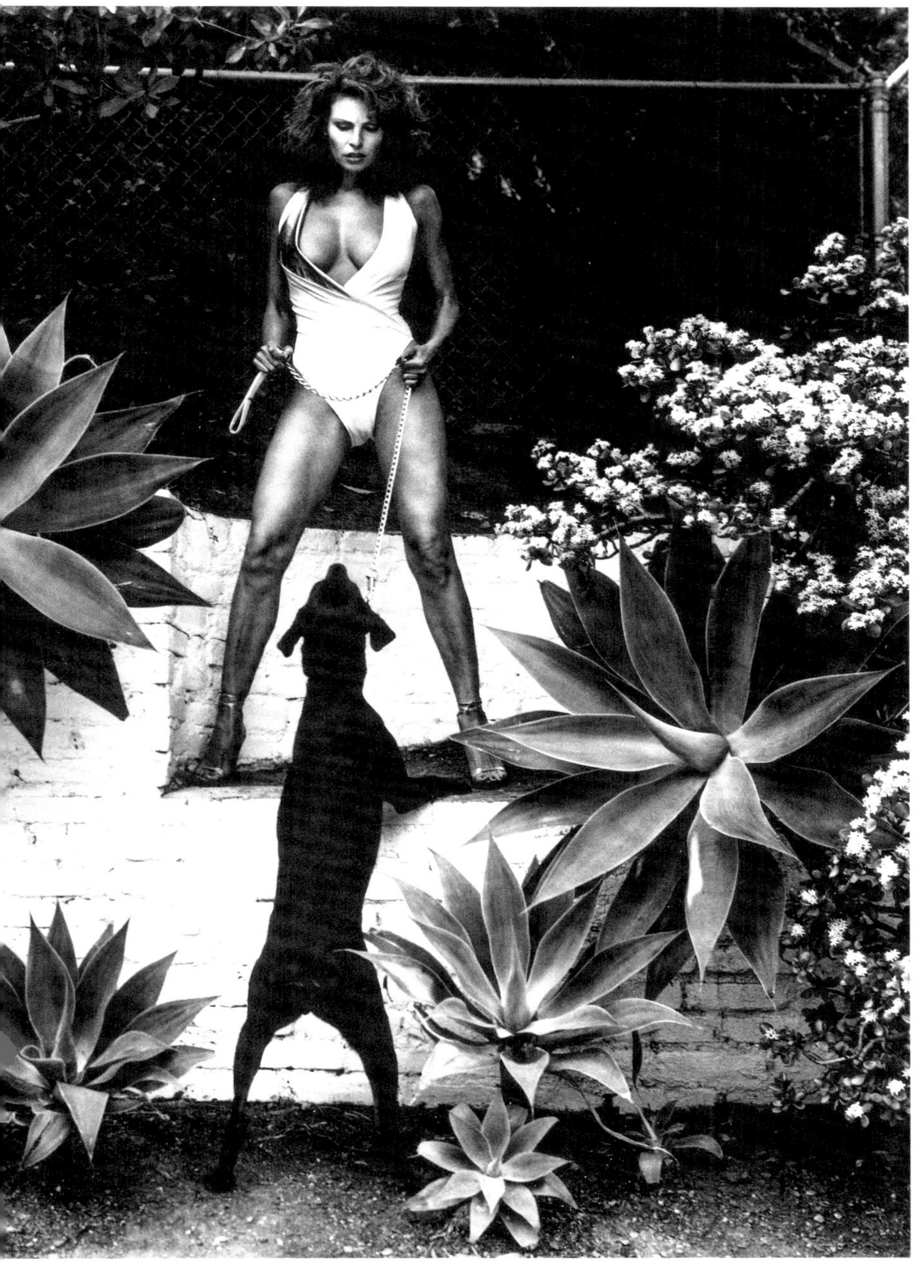

**Arielle after a Haircut,
Paris, 1982**
Model: Arielle Burgelin

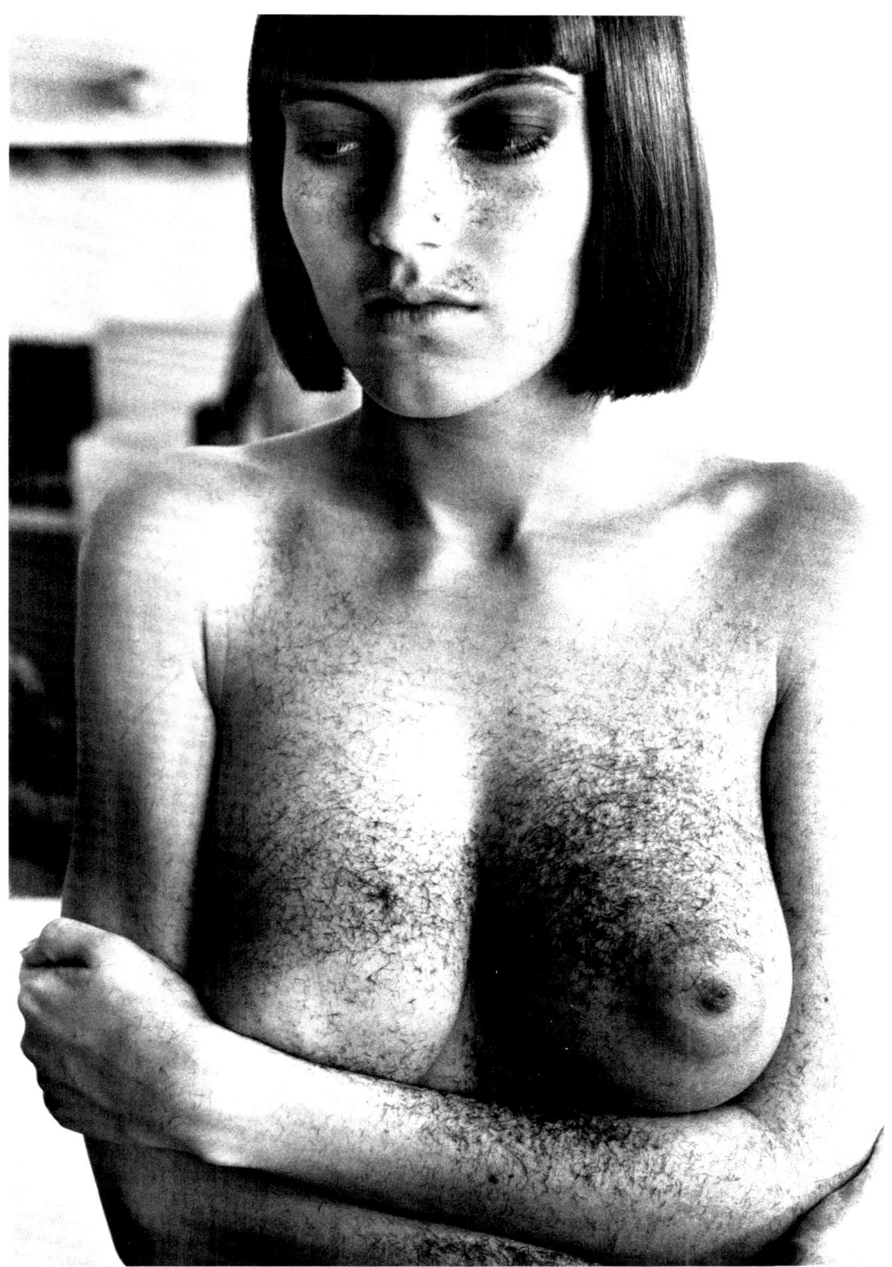

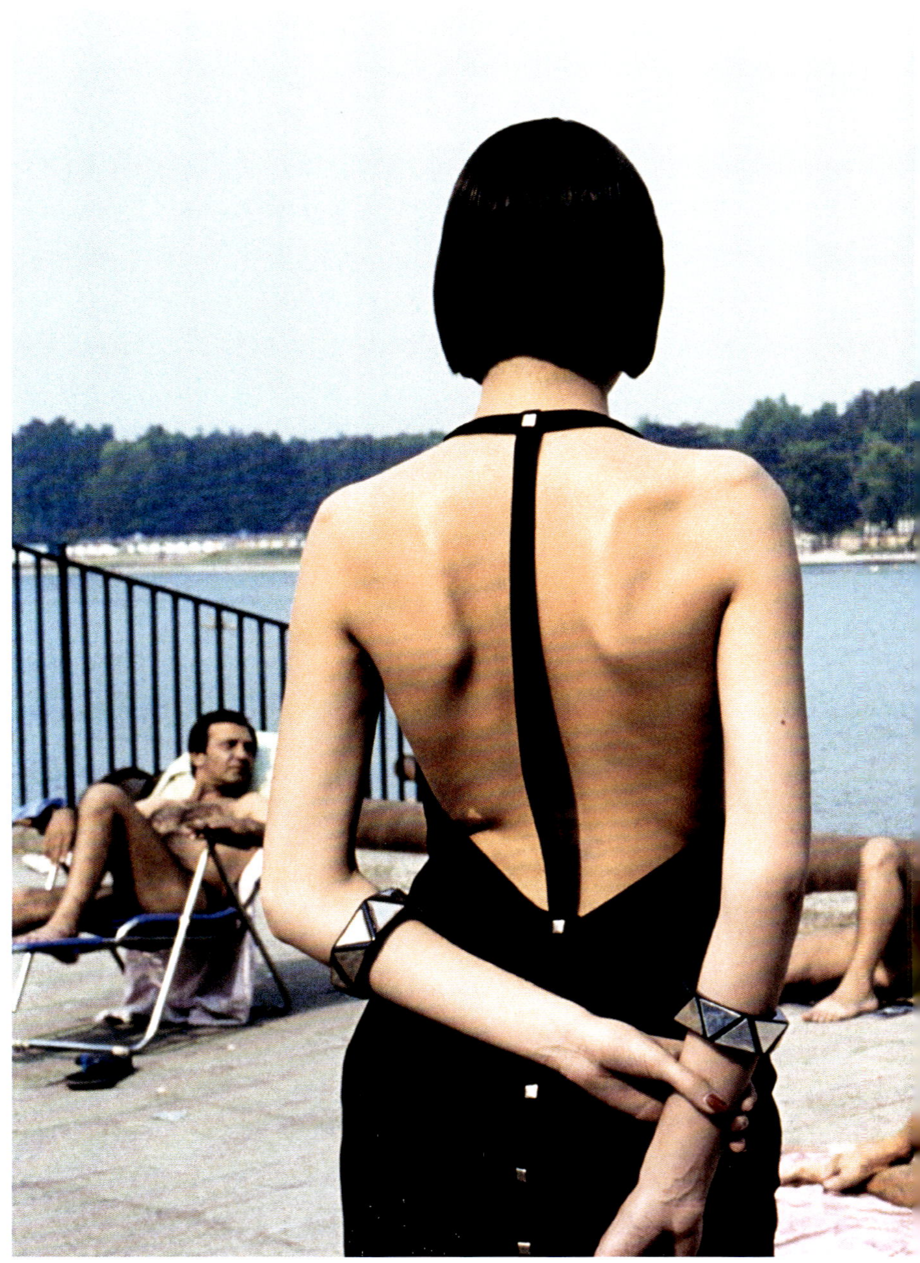

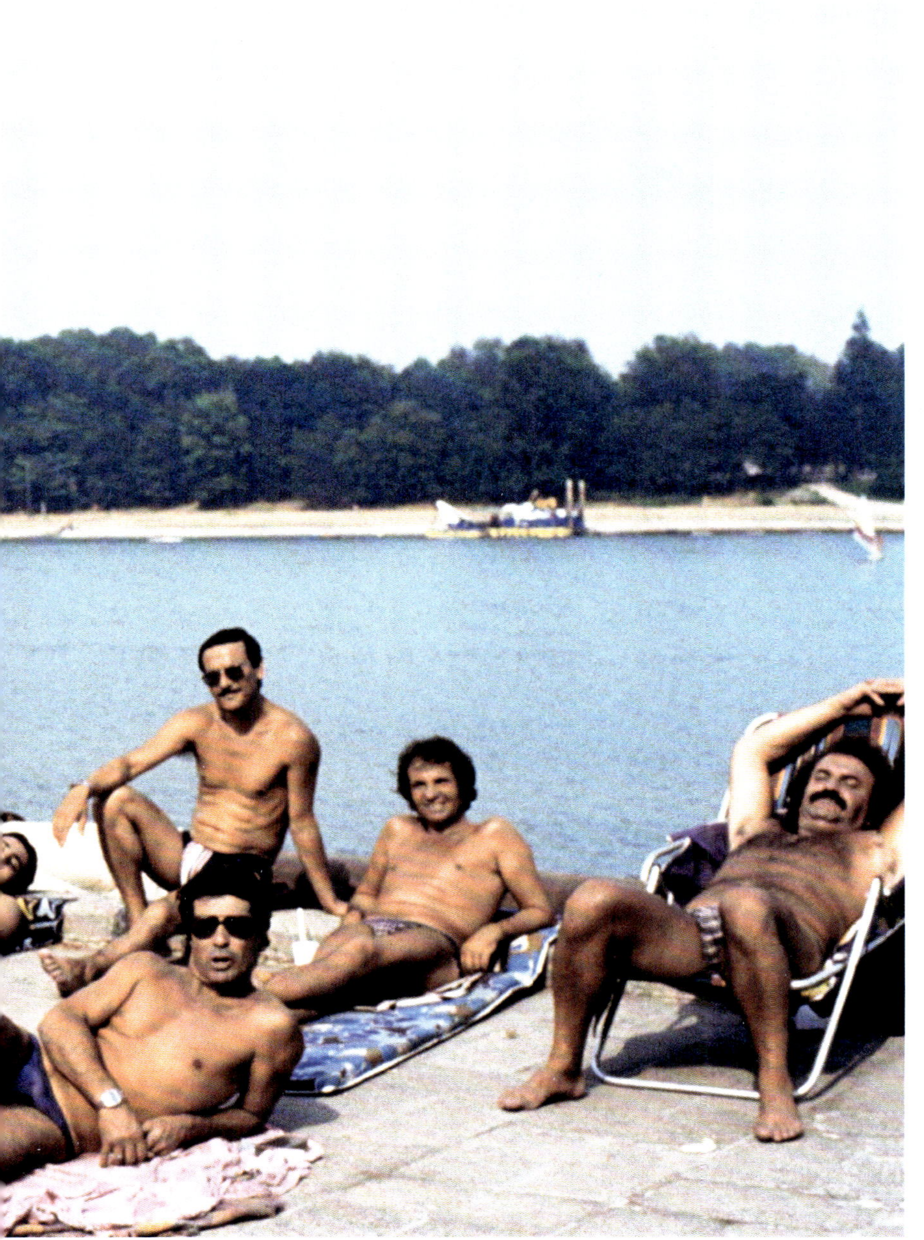

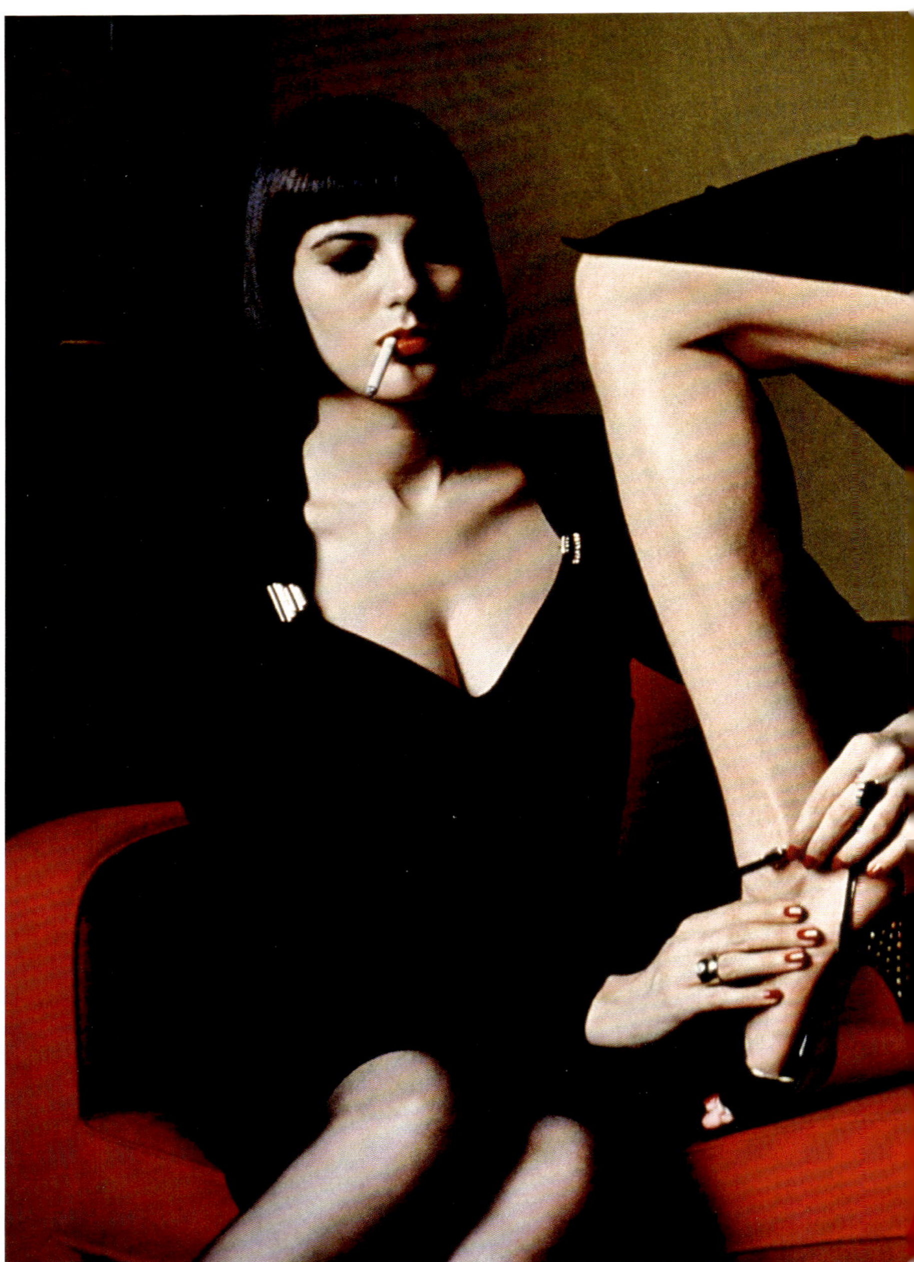

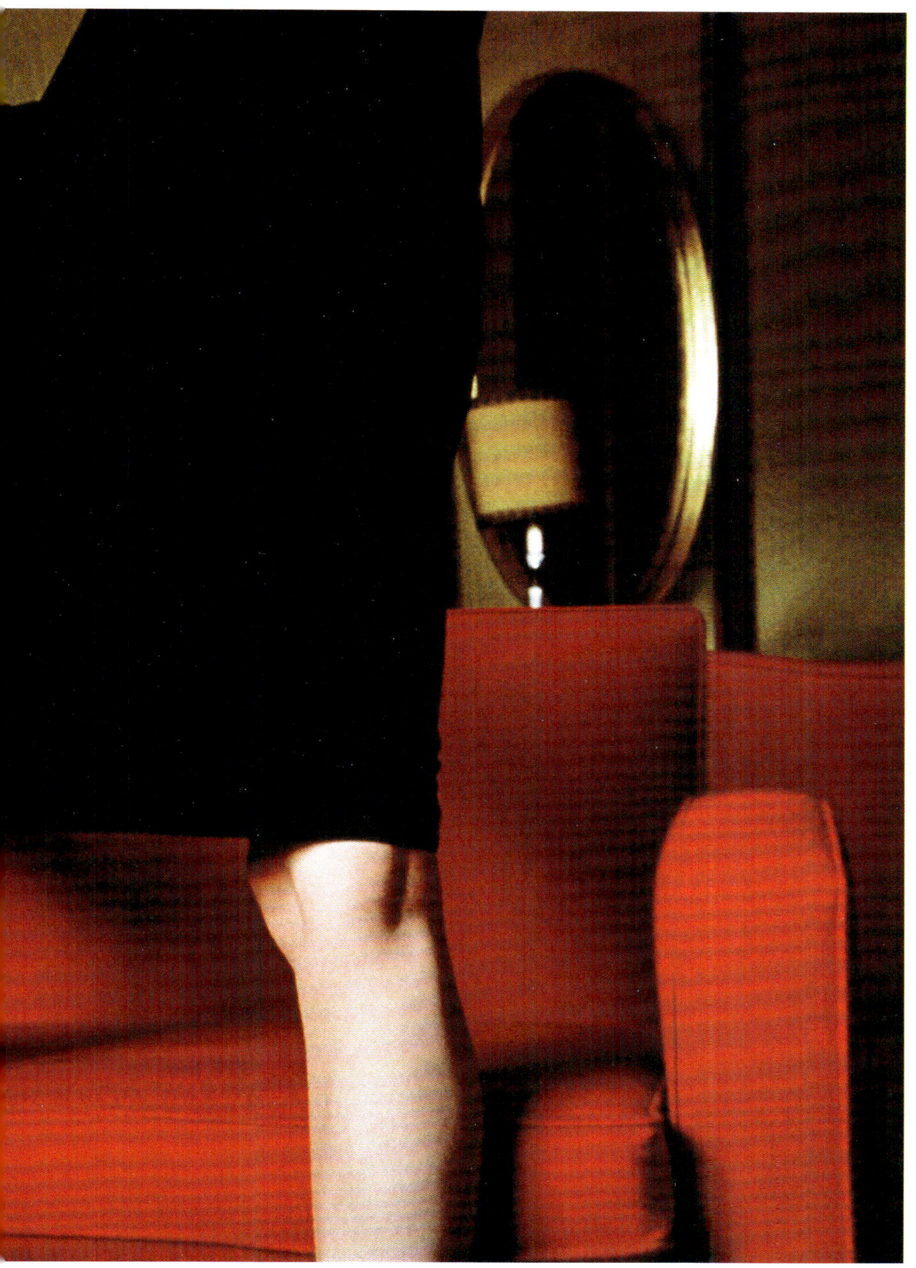

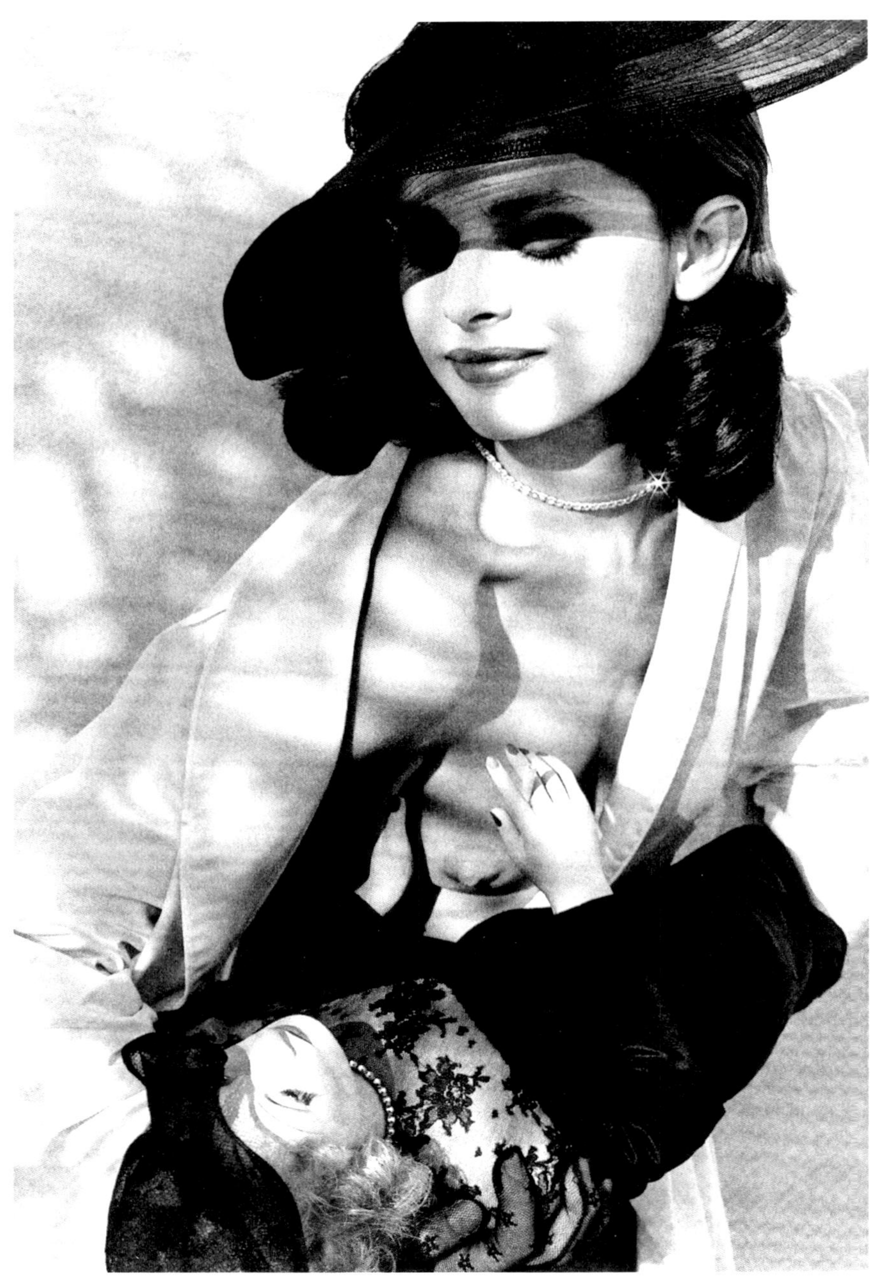

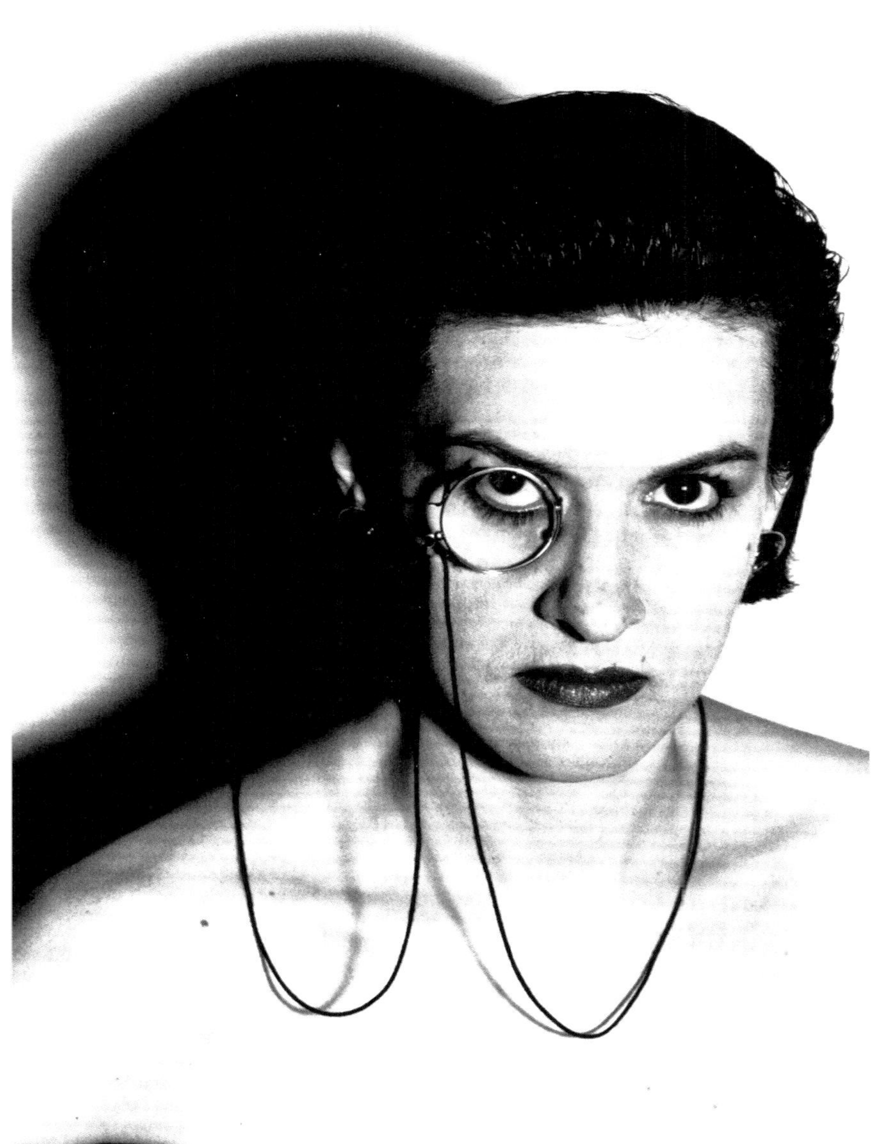

**Debra Winger,
Los Angeles, 1983**

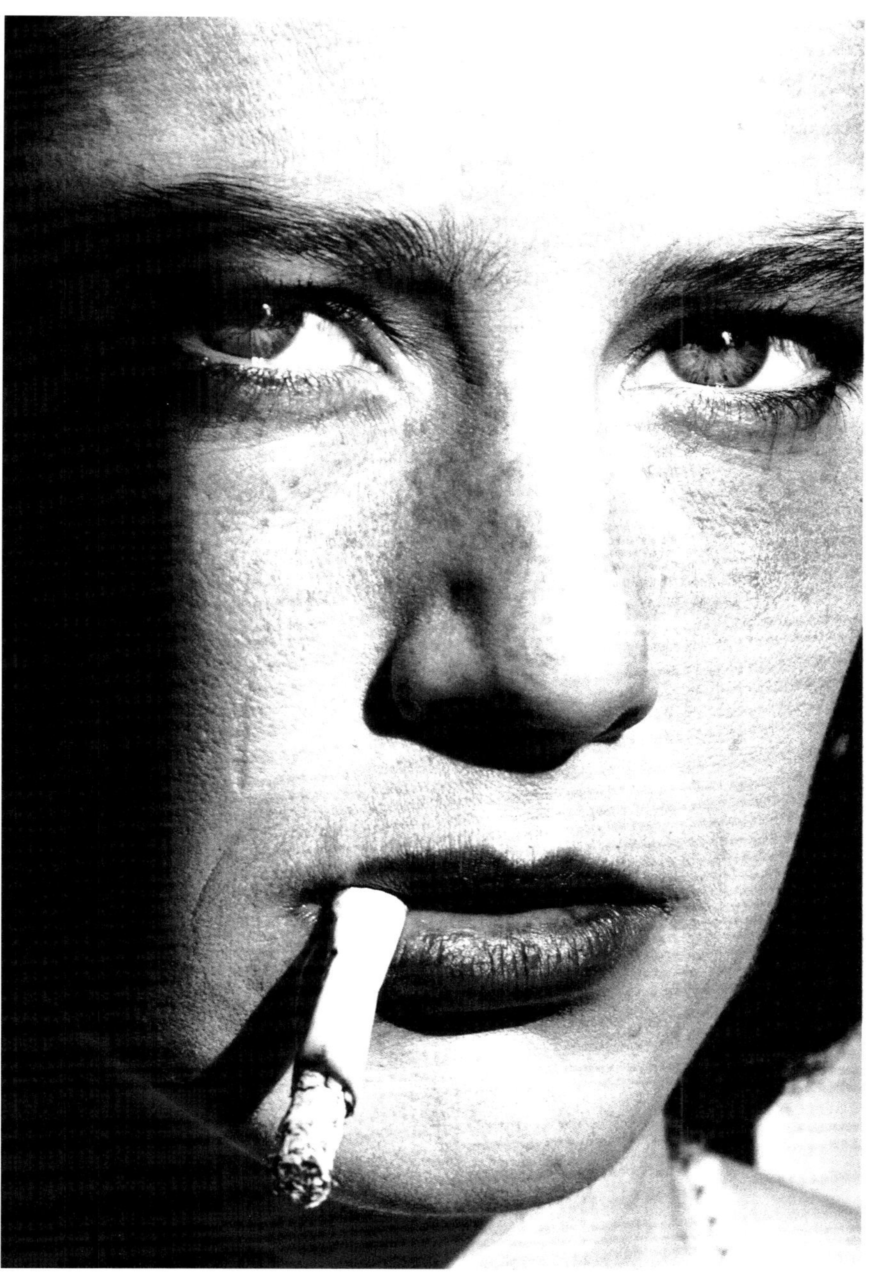

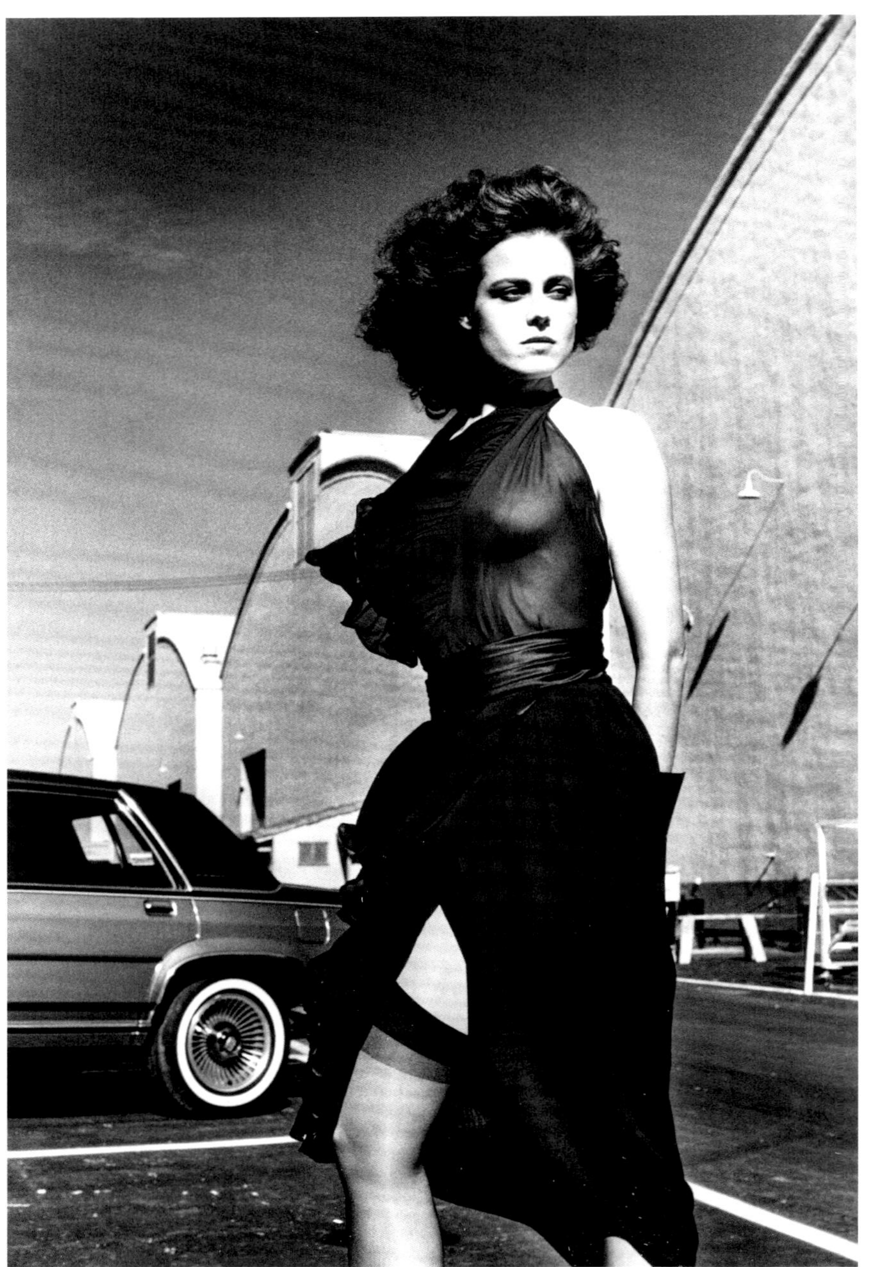

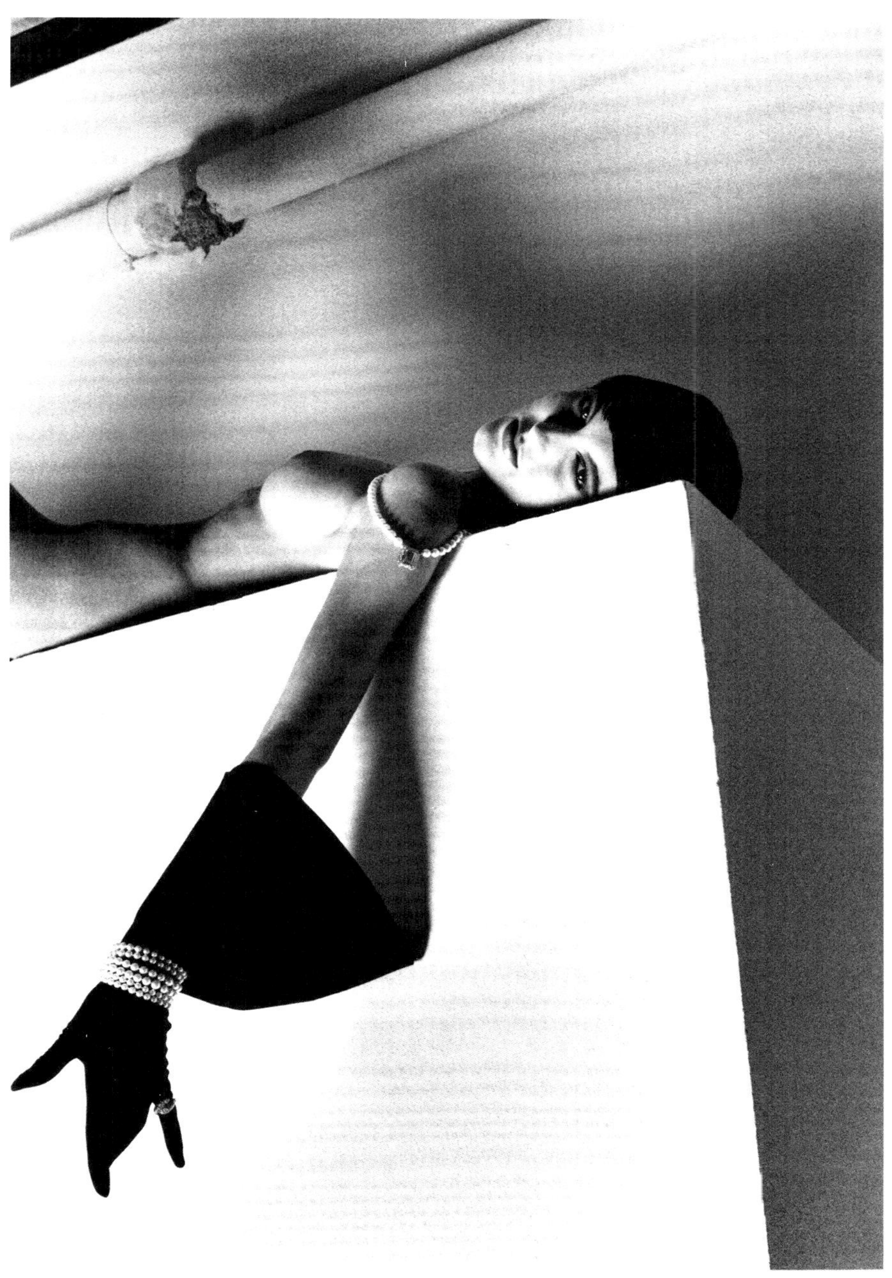

Walter Steiger Shoe,
Monte Carlo, 1983

Pages 138/139
**Pina Bausch,
Wuppertal, 1983**

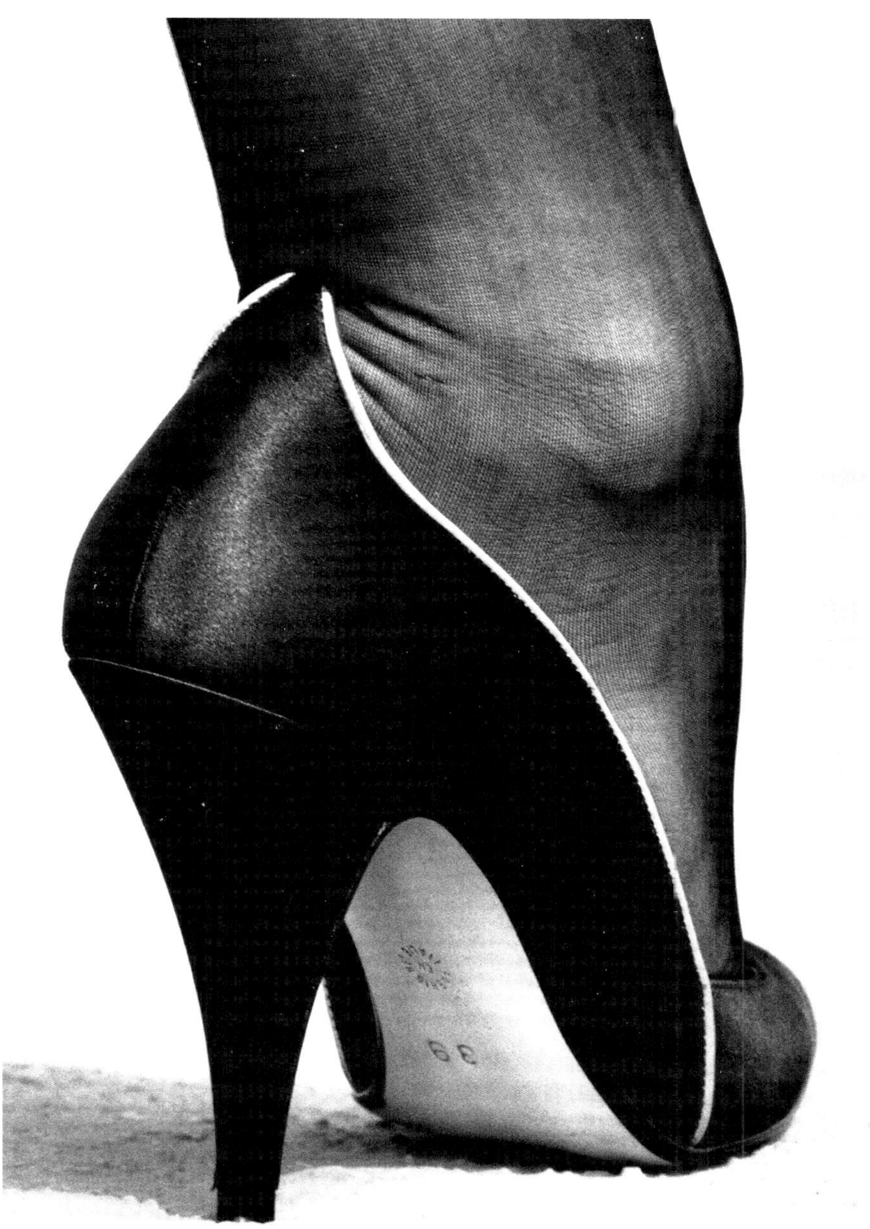

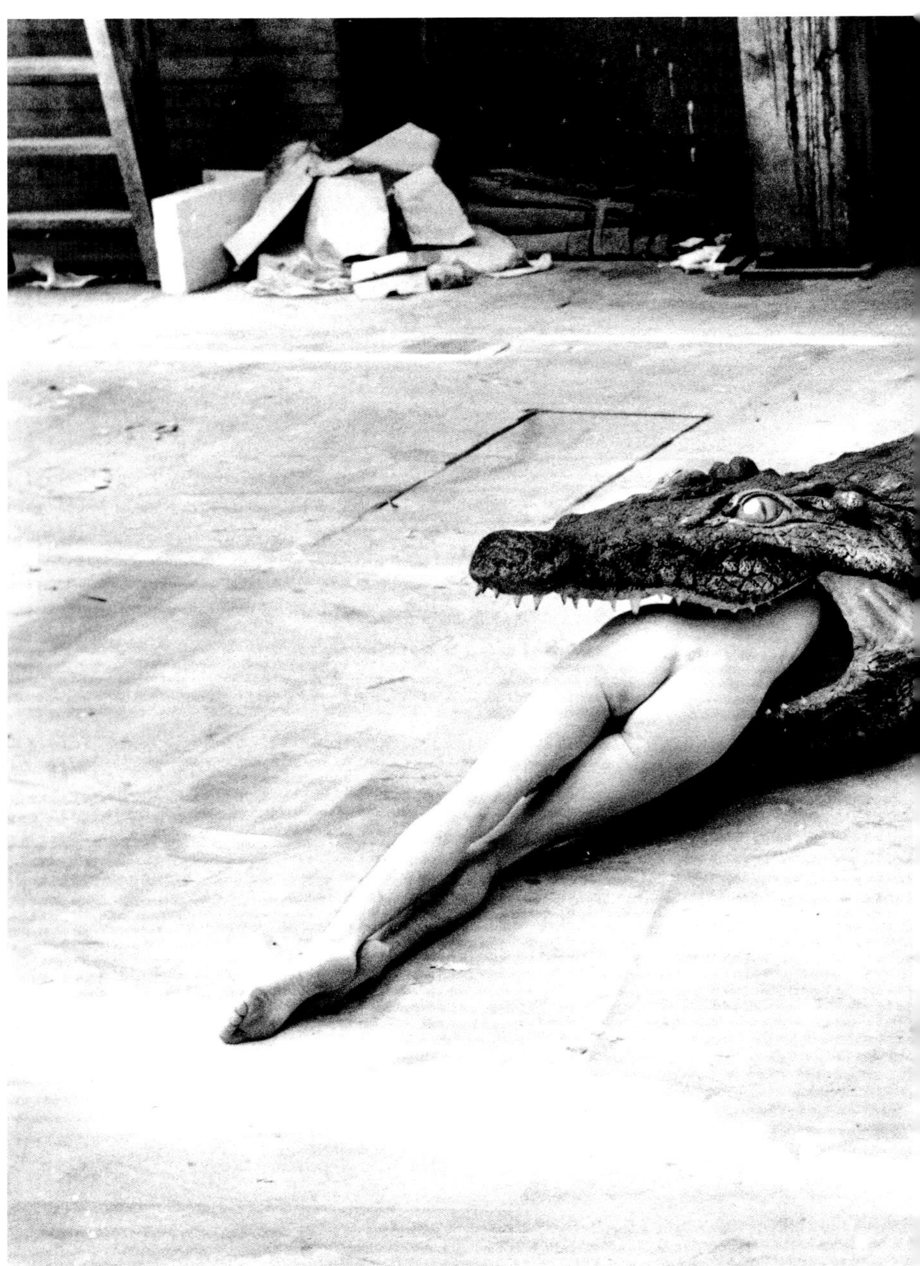

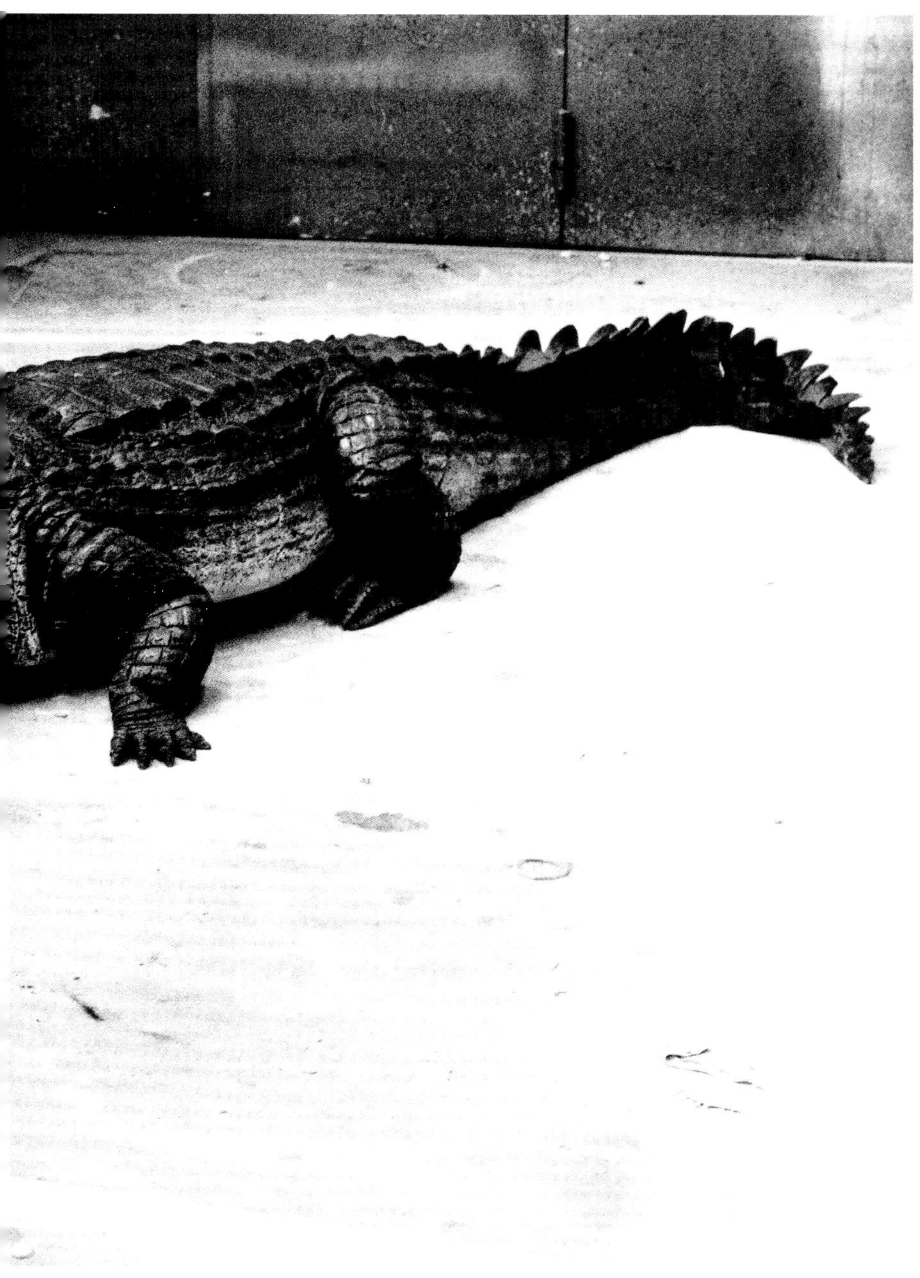

Elizabeth Taylor,
Vanity Fair,
Los Angeles, 1985

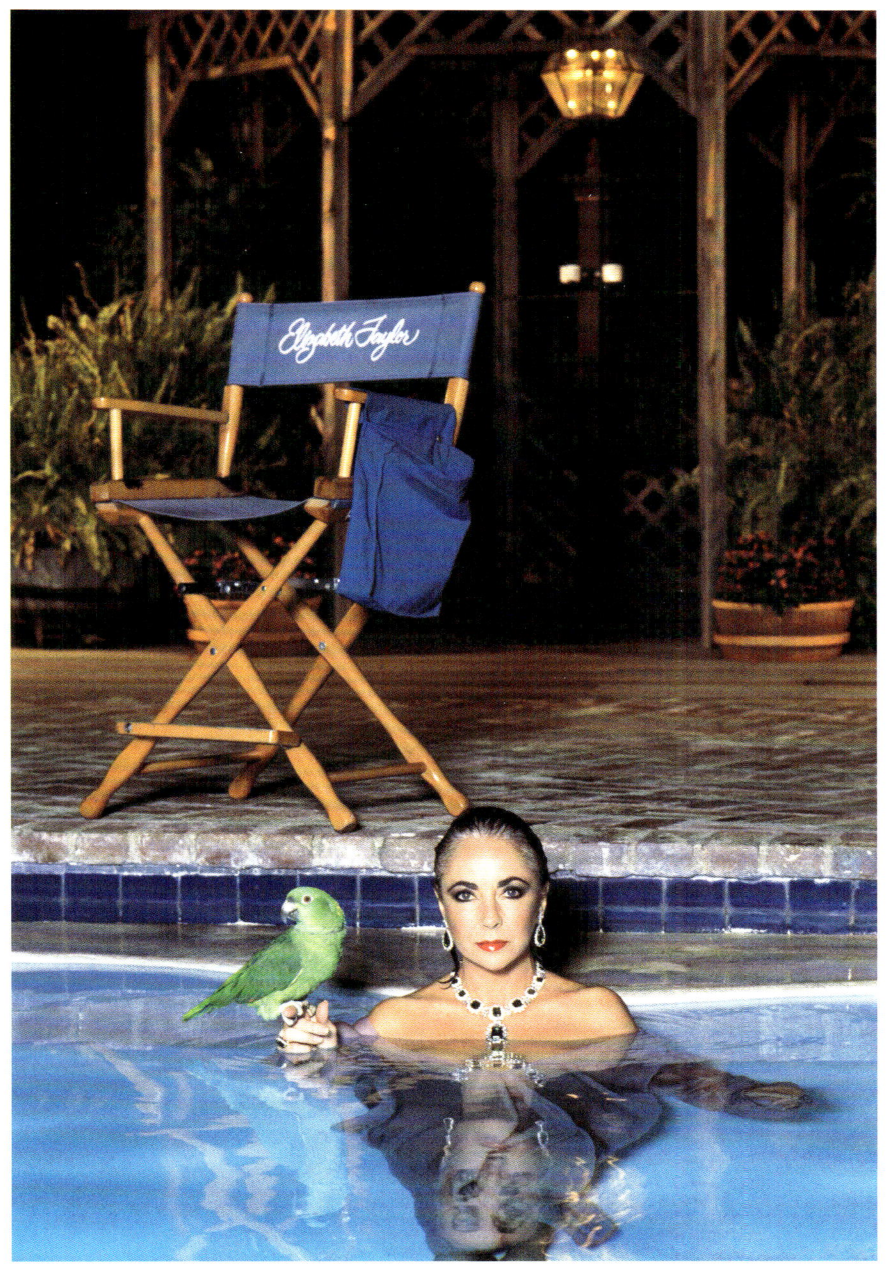
Elizabeth Taylor

Daryl Hannah,
American *Vogue*,
Los Angeles, 1984

Pages 144/145
Fat Hand and Dollars,
Monte Carlo, 1984

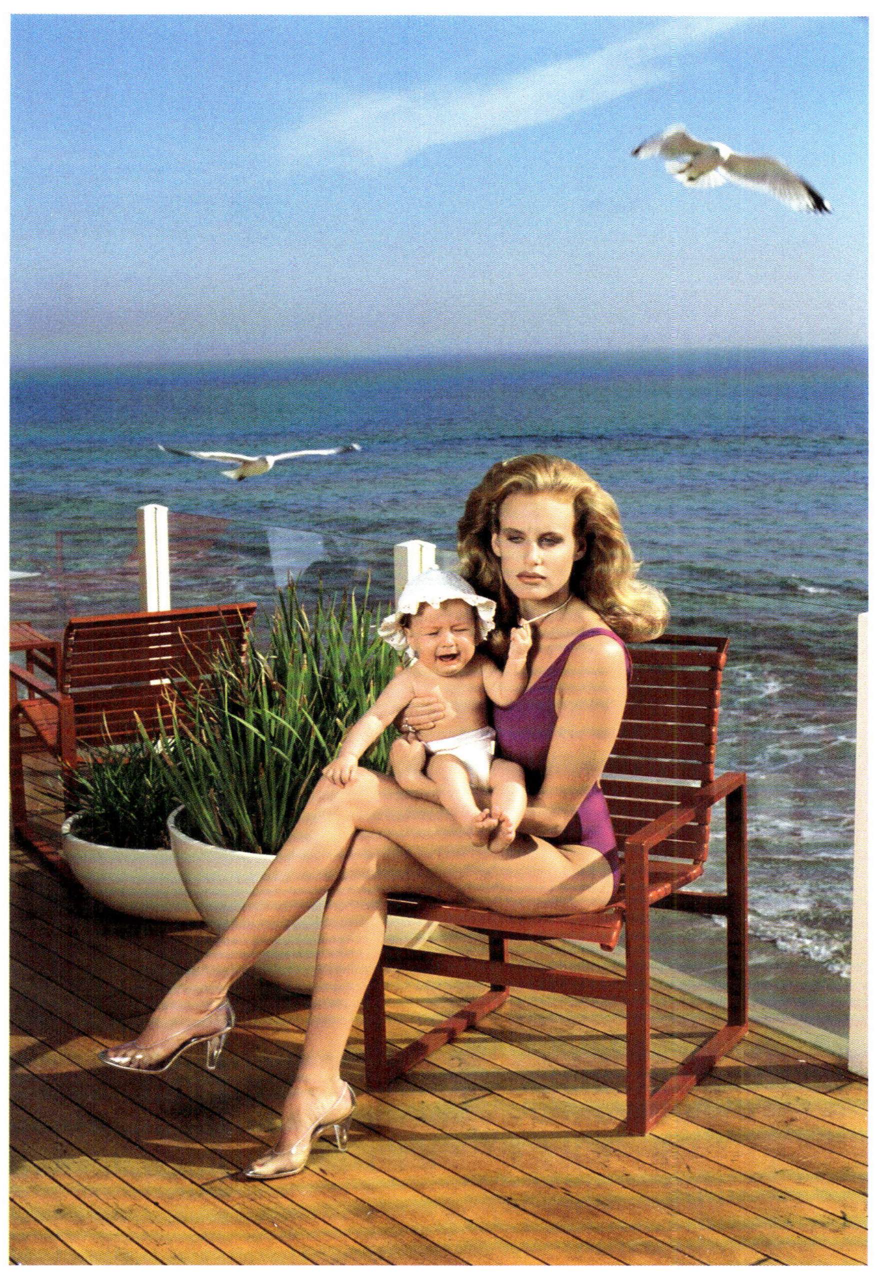

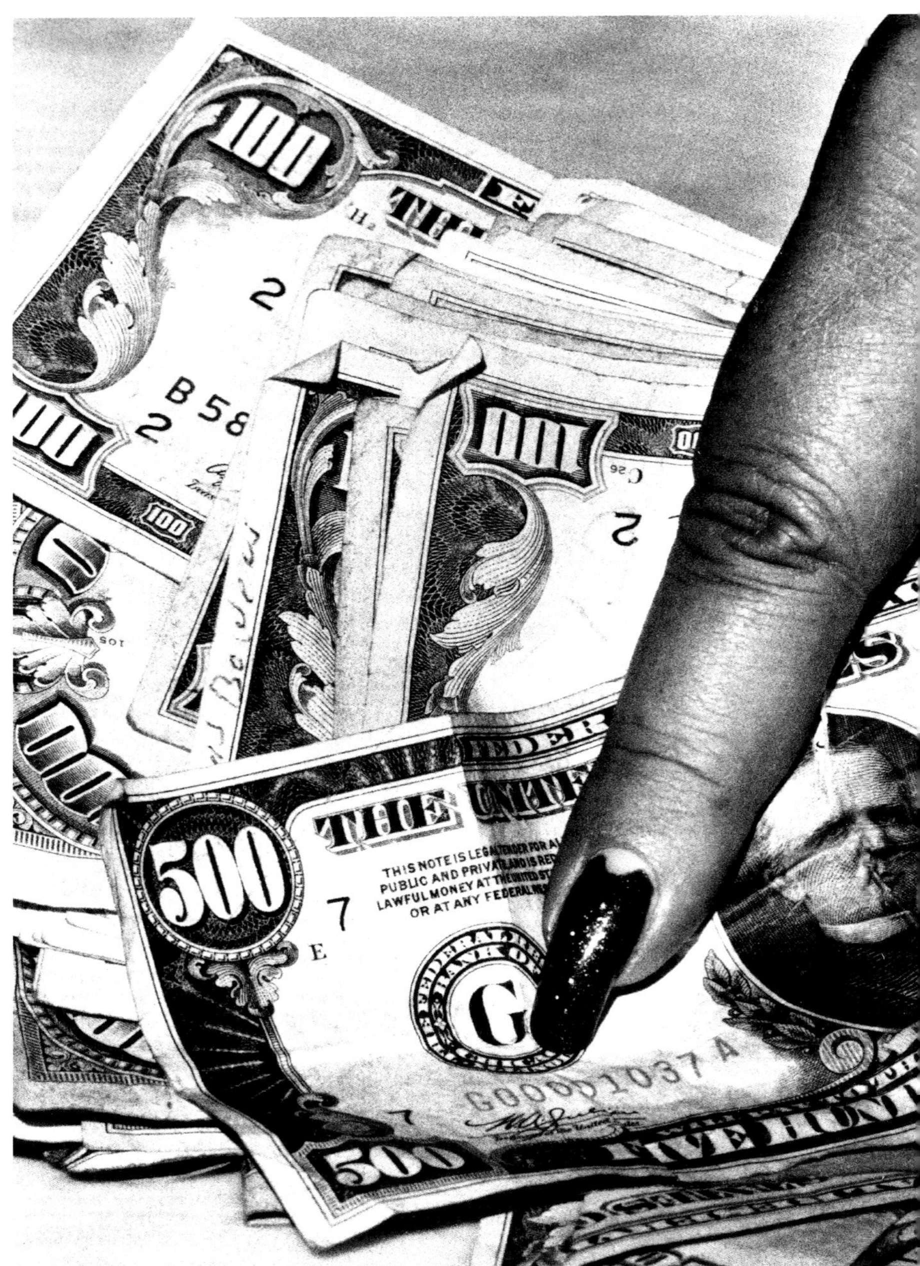

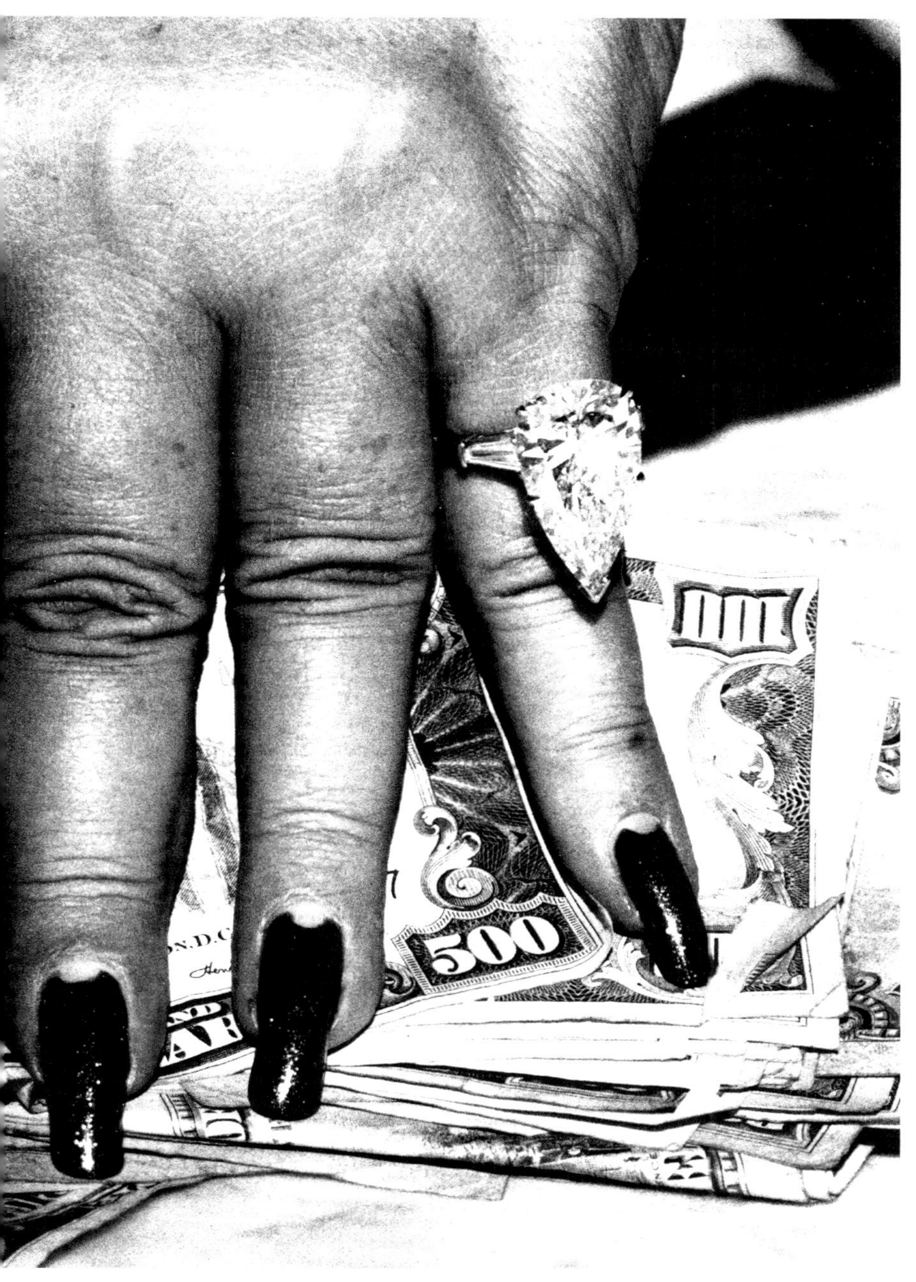

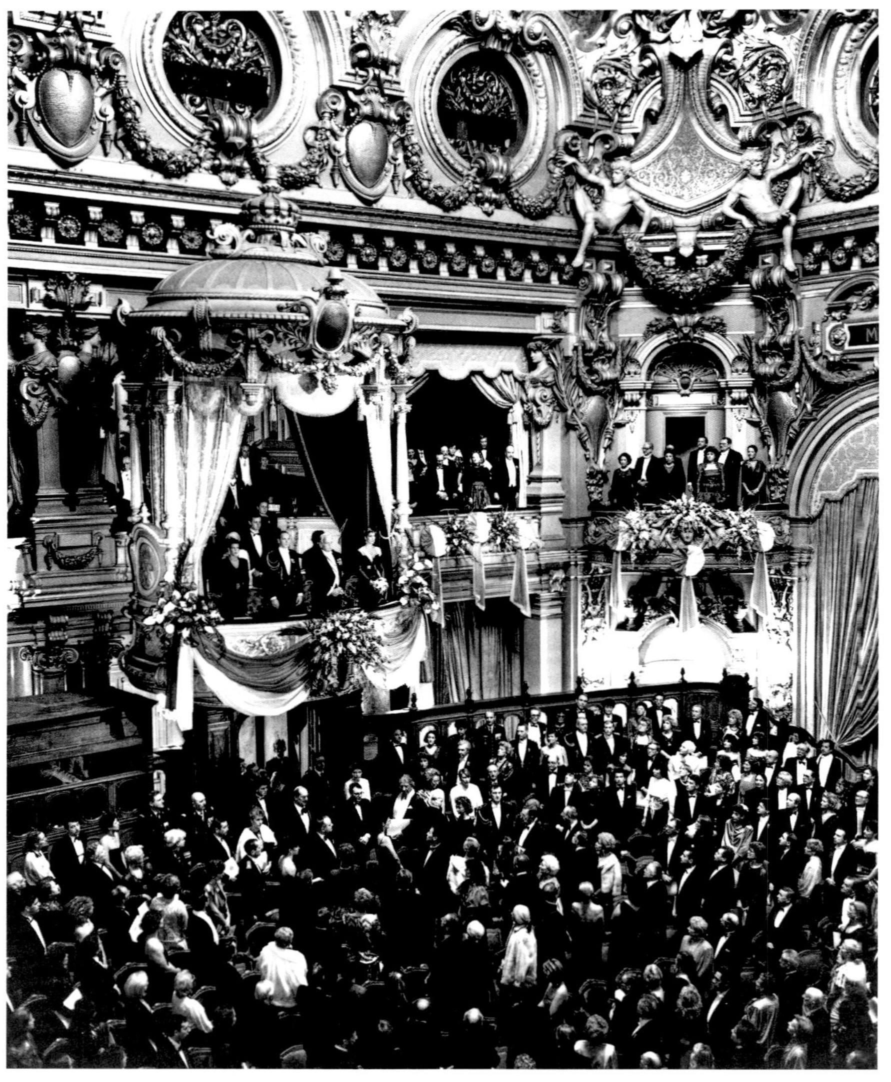

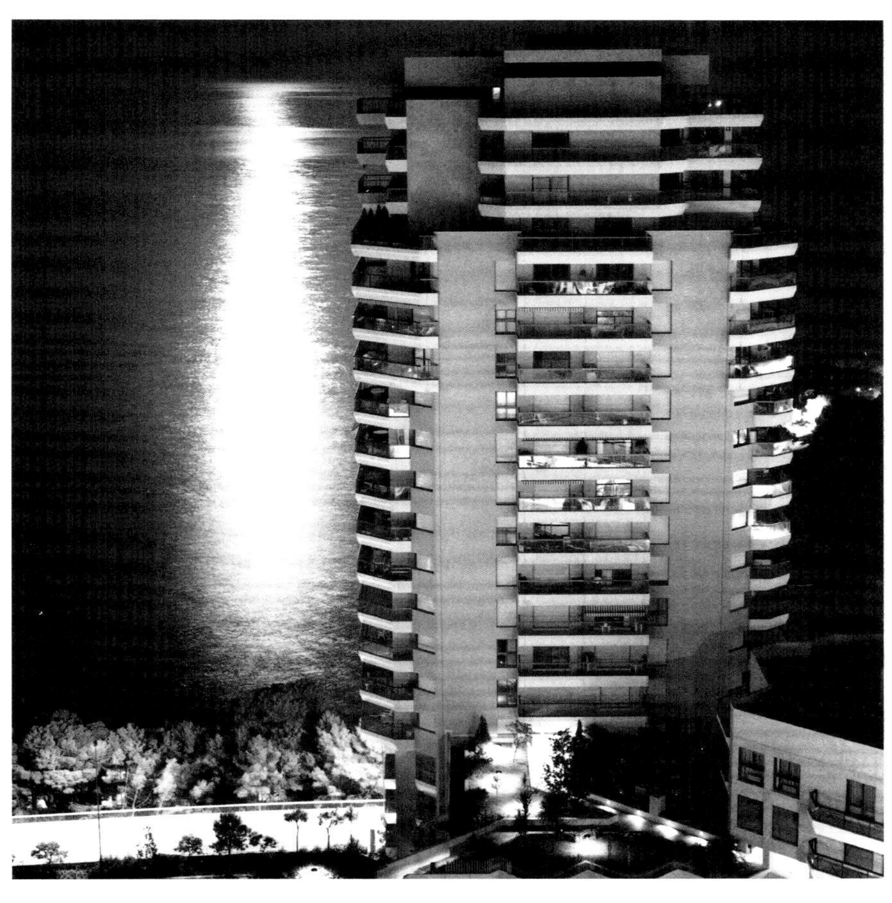

A Night at the Opera,
the Prince and Family in their Box,
Monte Carlo, 1986

Sun Tower,
Monte Carlo, 1986

**Princess Caroline of Hanover
on the Ramparts of the Palais Princier,
Monte Carlo, 1988**

Page 150
Celia, Miami, 1991
Model: Cecilia Nord

Page 151
Wolford, Monte Carlo, 1995

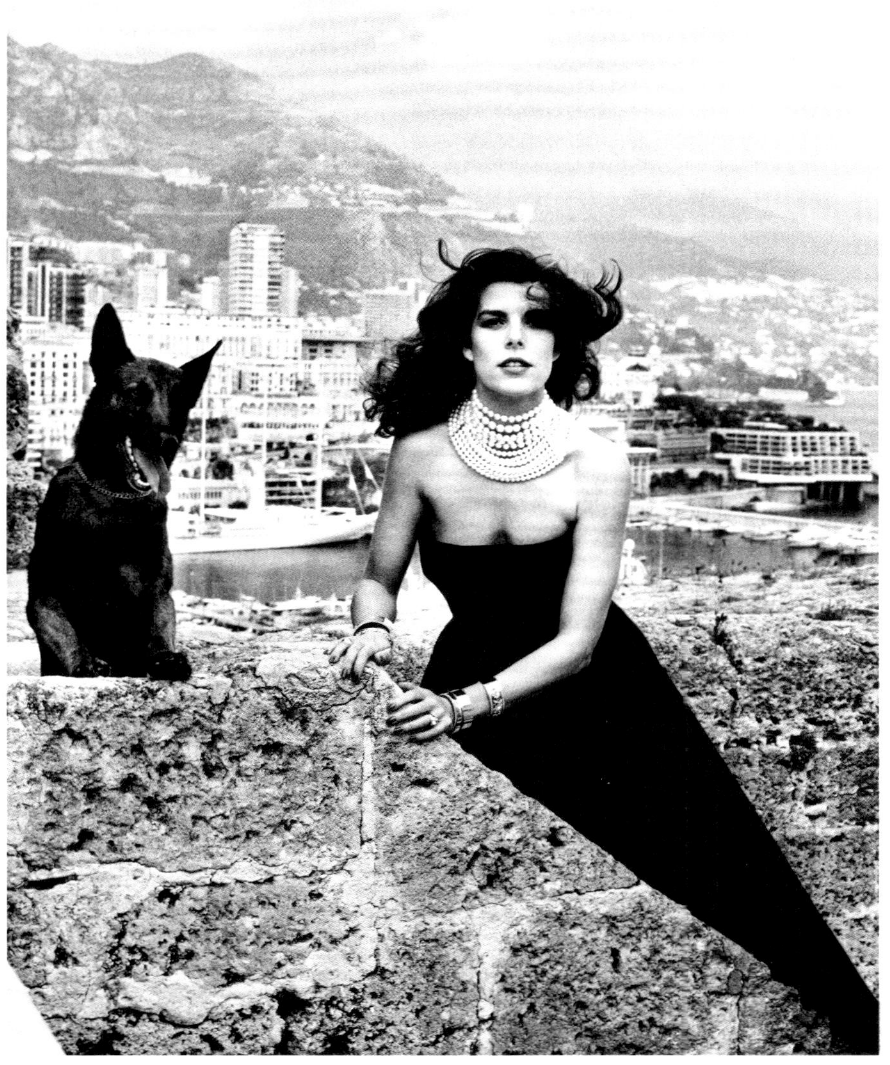

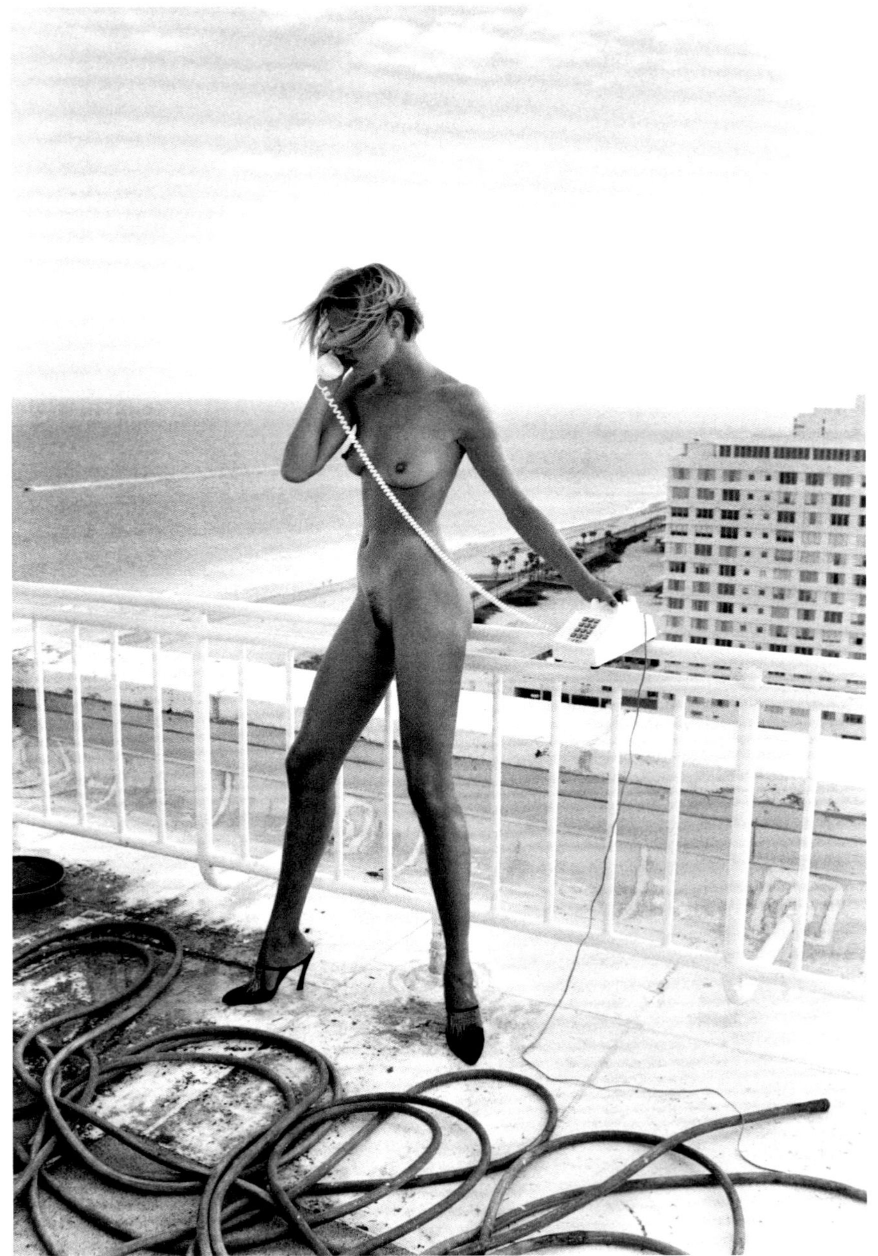

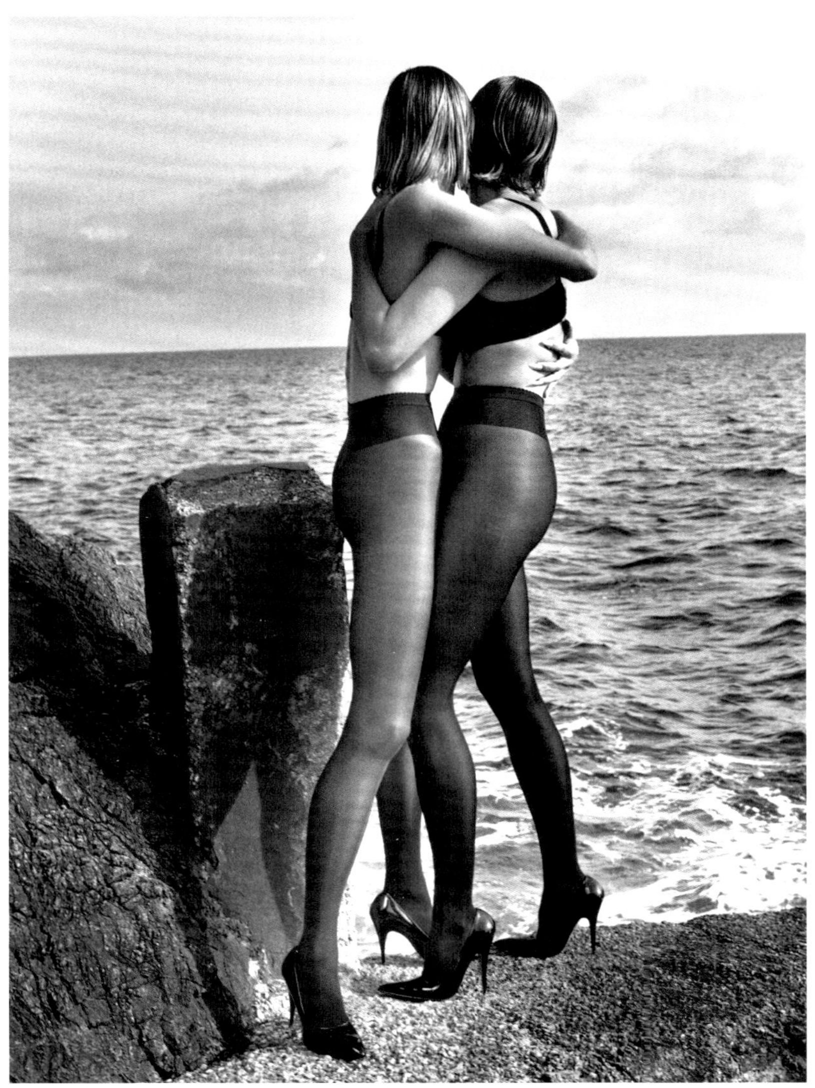

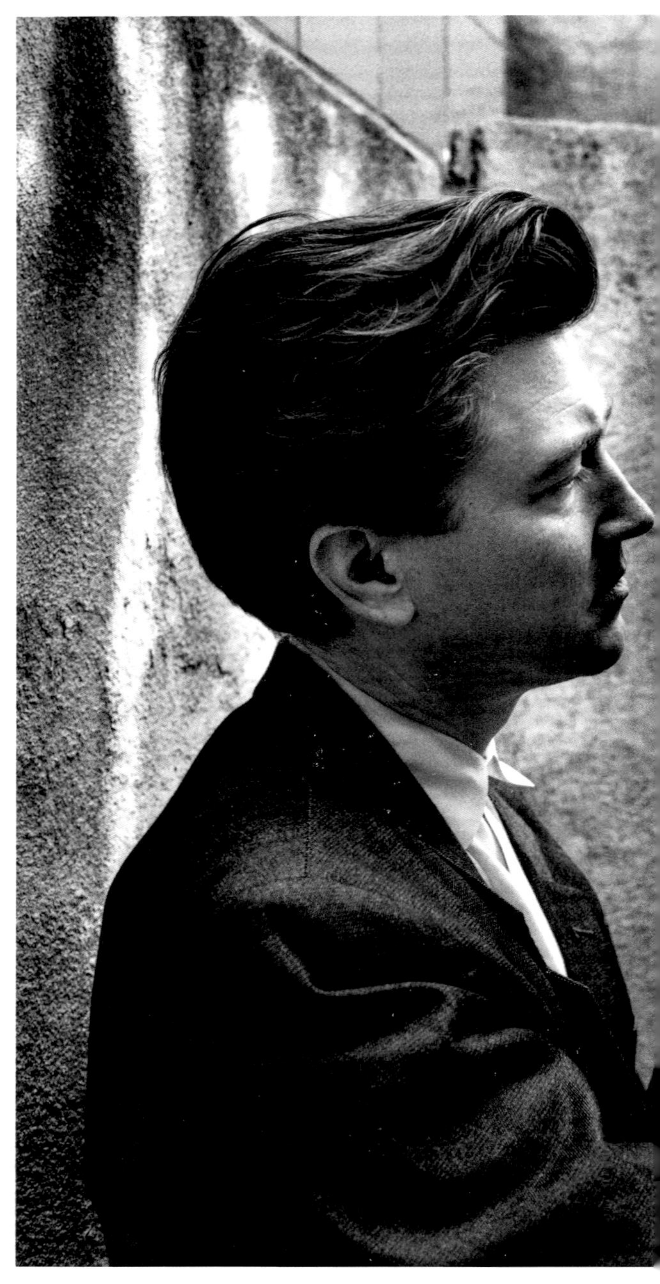

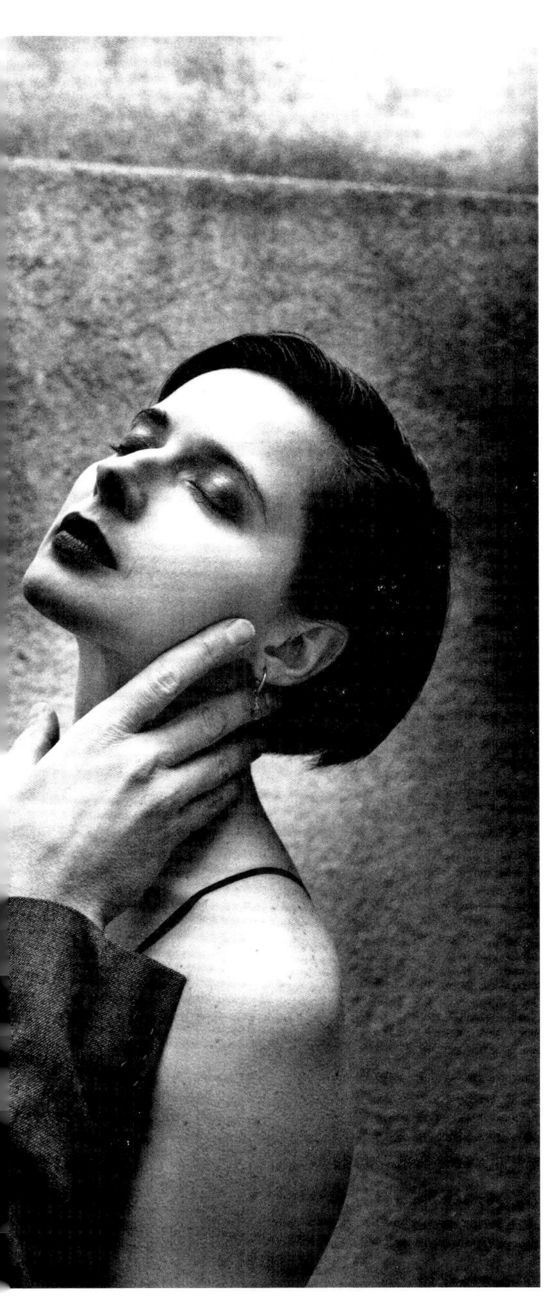

David Lynch and
Isabella Rossellini,
Vanity Fair,
Los Angeles, 1988

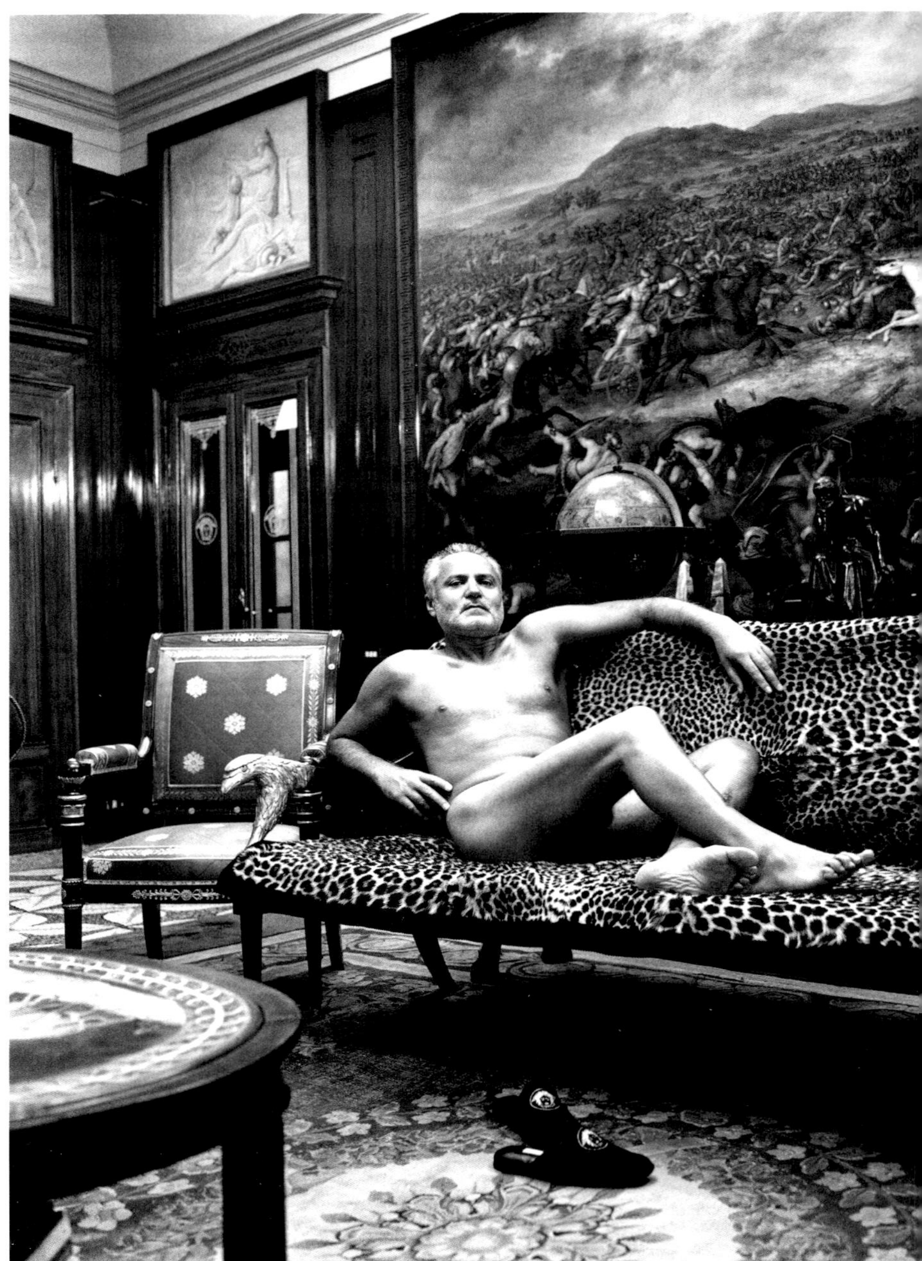

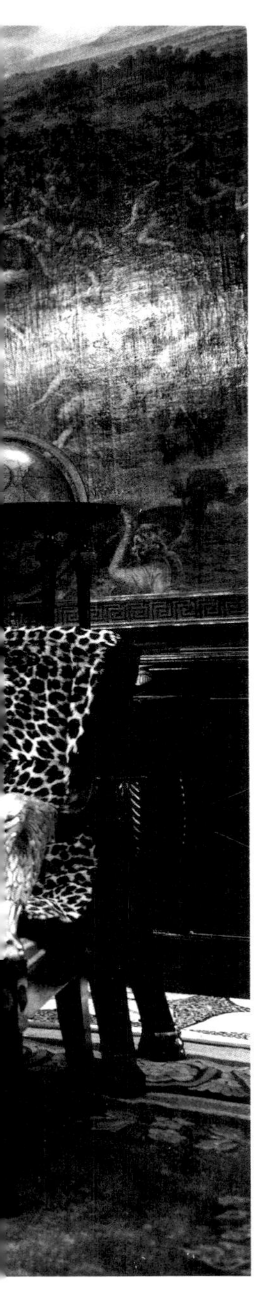

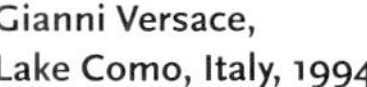

Gianni Versace,
Lake Como, Italy, 1994

Pages 156/157
Halensee, Berlin, 1990

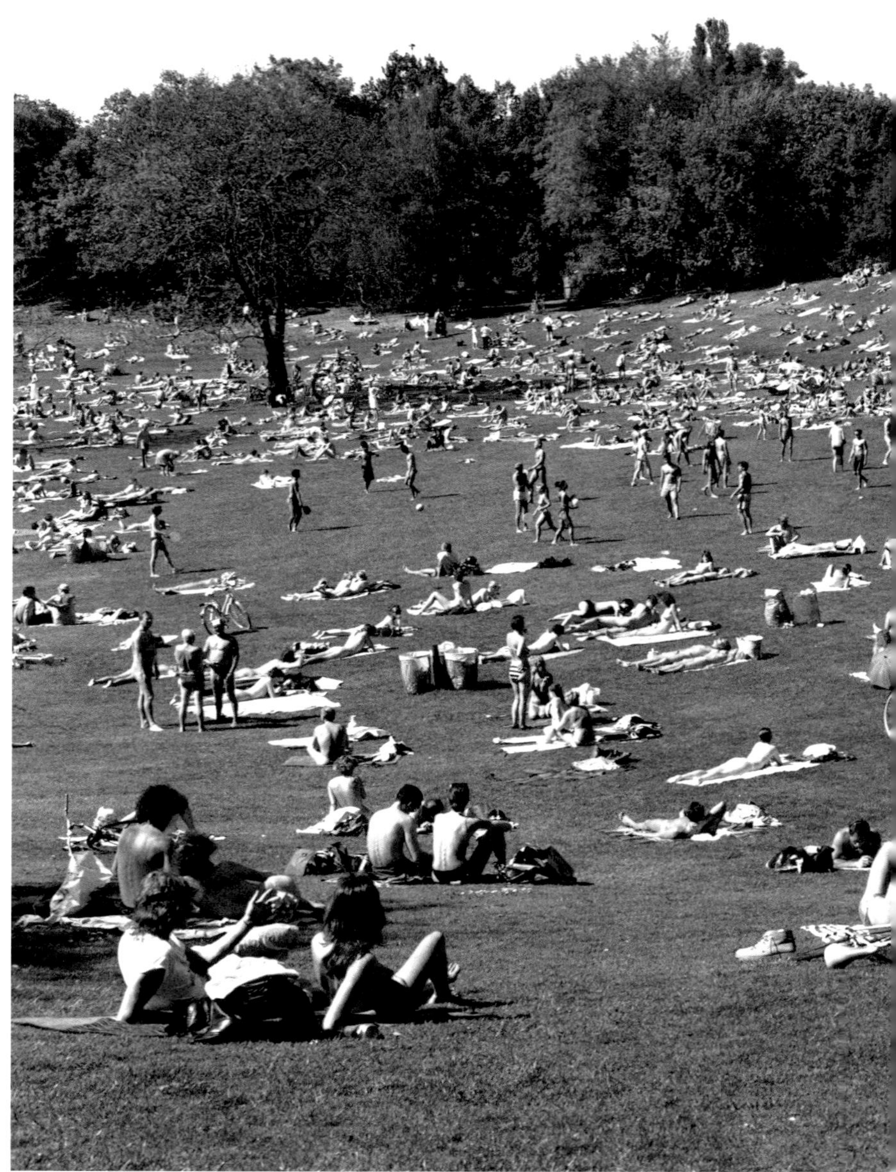

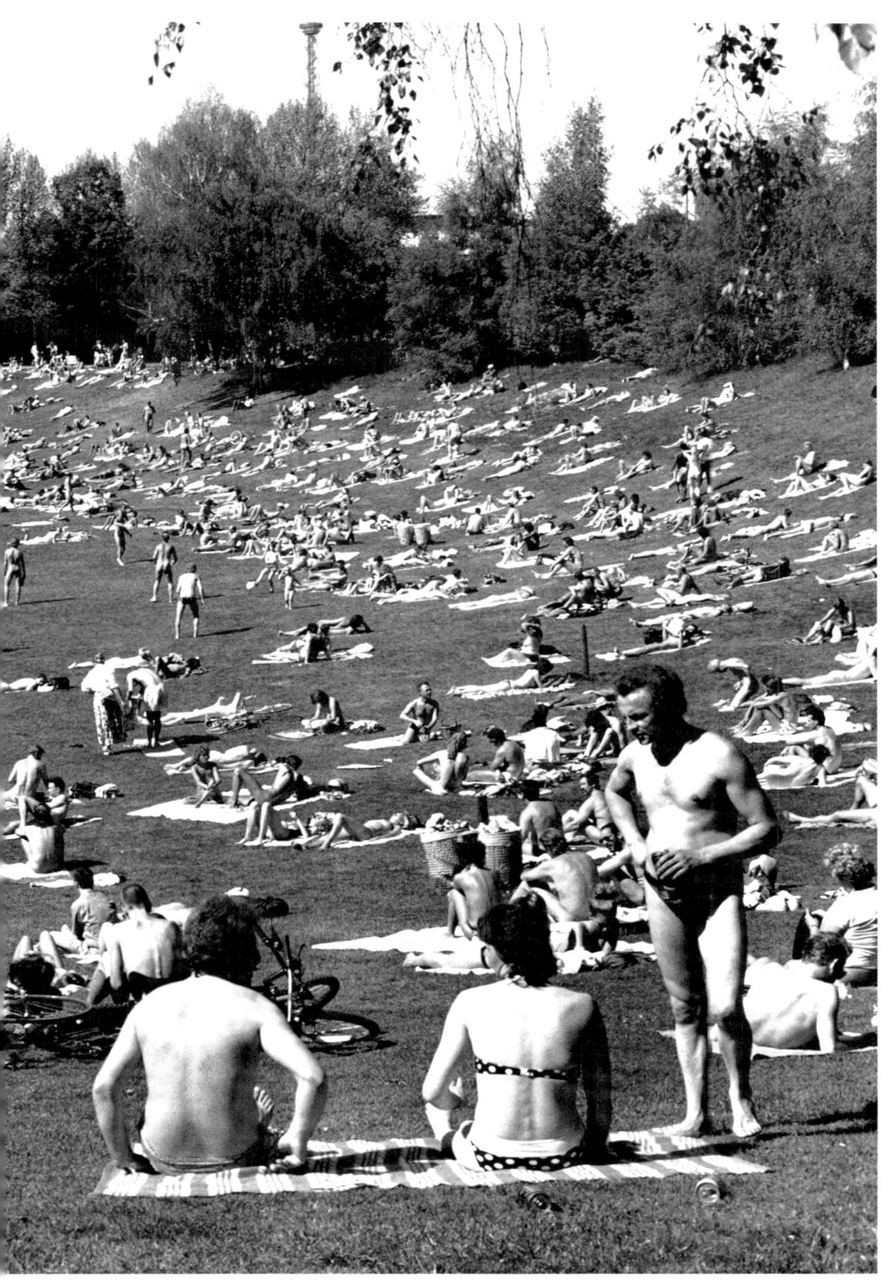

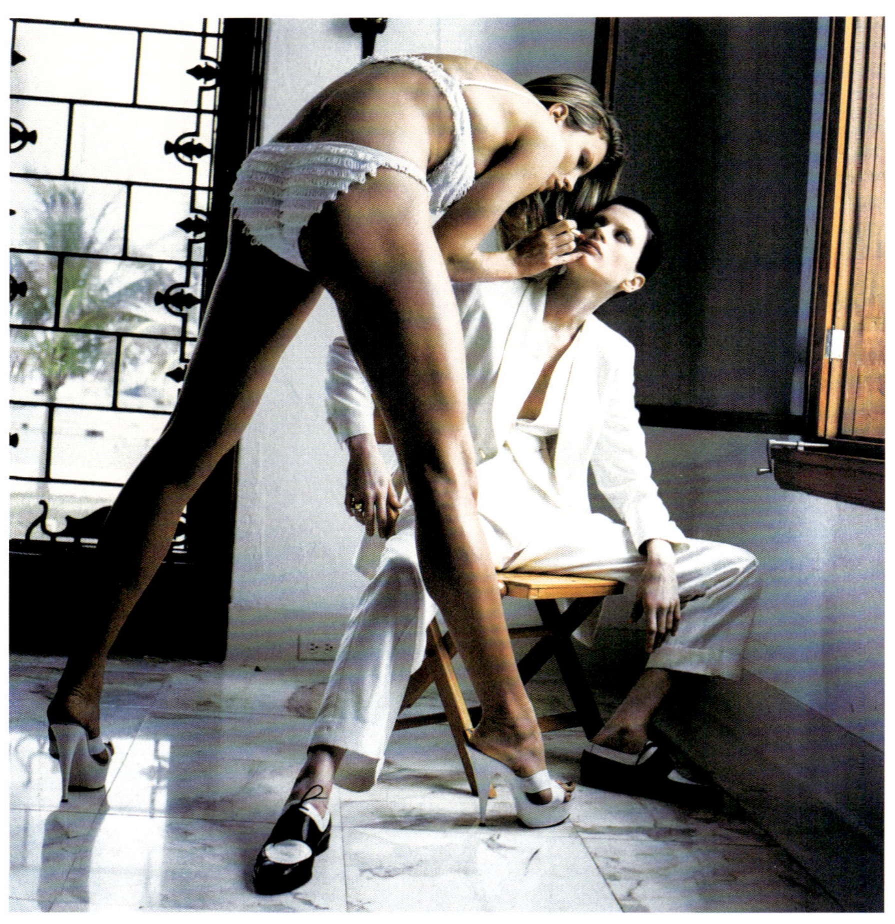

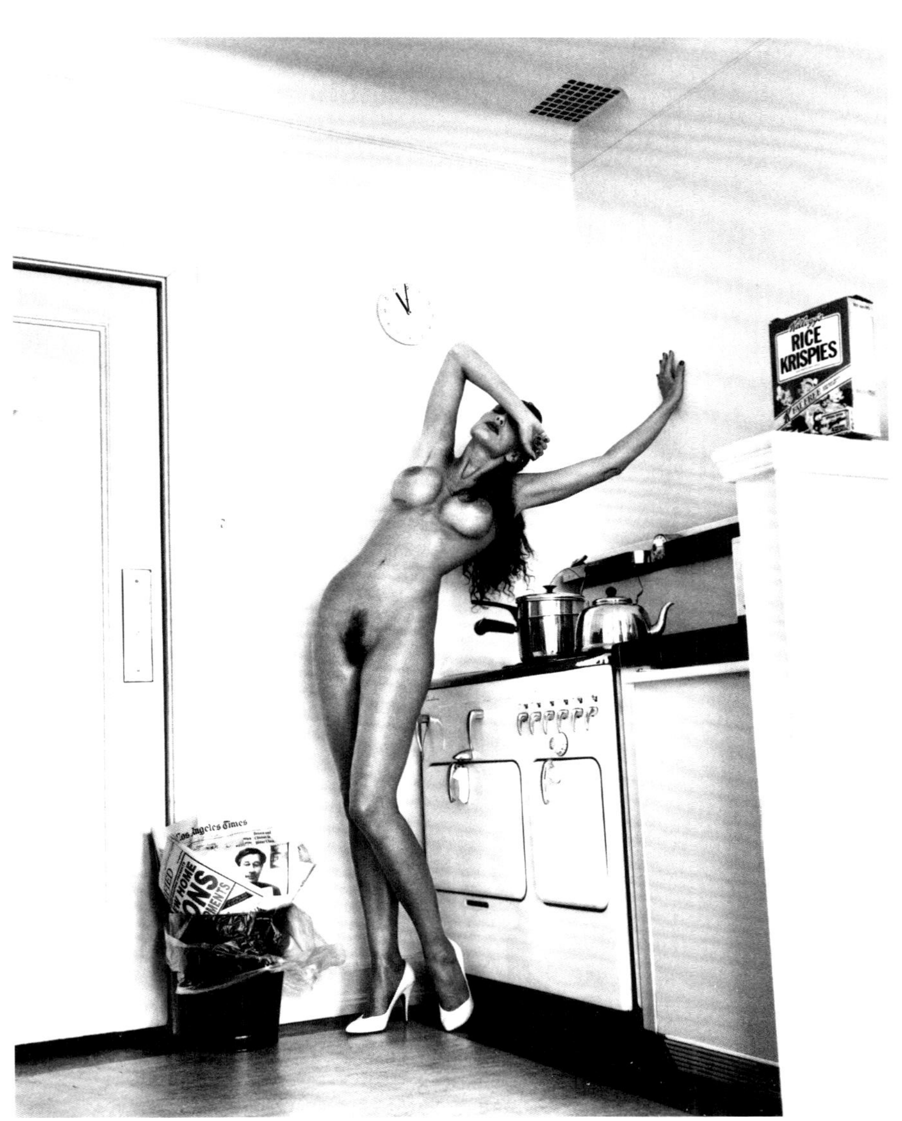
RICE KRISPIES
Los Angeles Times

**Big Nude VIII,
The Two Violetas,
Paris, 1991**
Model: Violeta Sanchez

Page 158
**White Mischief,
American *Vogue*, 1993**
Models: Rachel Williams
and Kristen McMenamy

Page 159
**Domestic Nude I,
Julie Strange in My Kitchen,
Chateau Marmont,
West Hollywood, 1992**

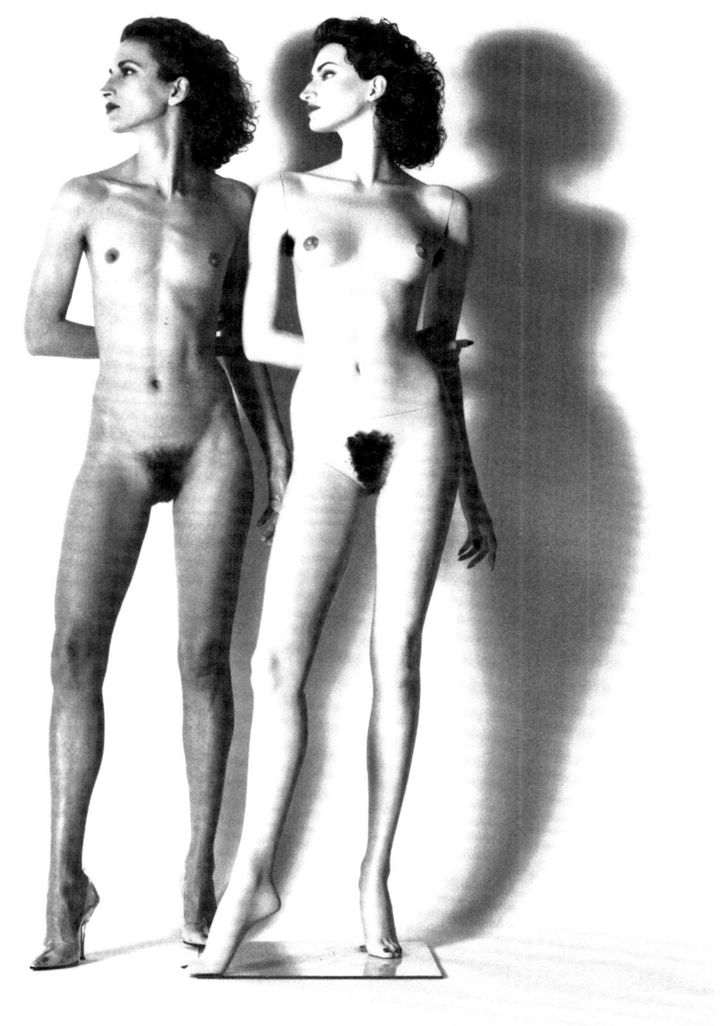

**Marchese Coccapani,
Monte Carlo, 1994**
Model: Claudia Schiffer

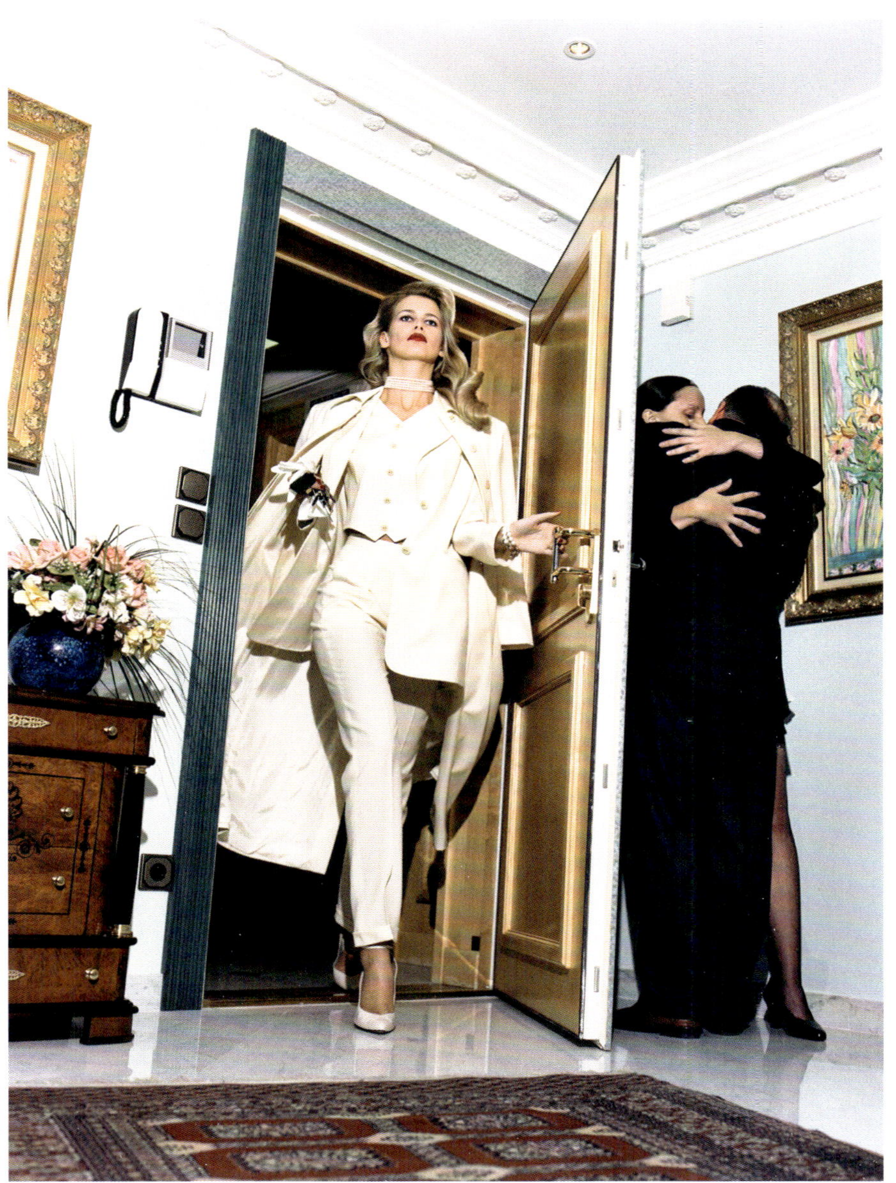

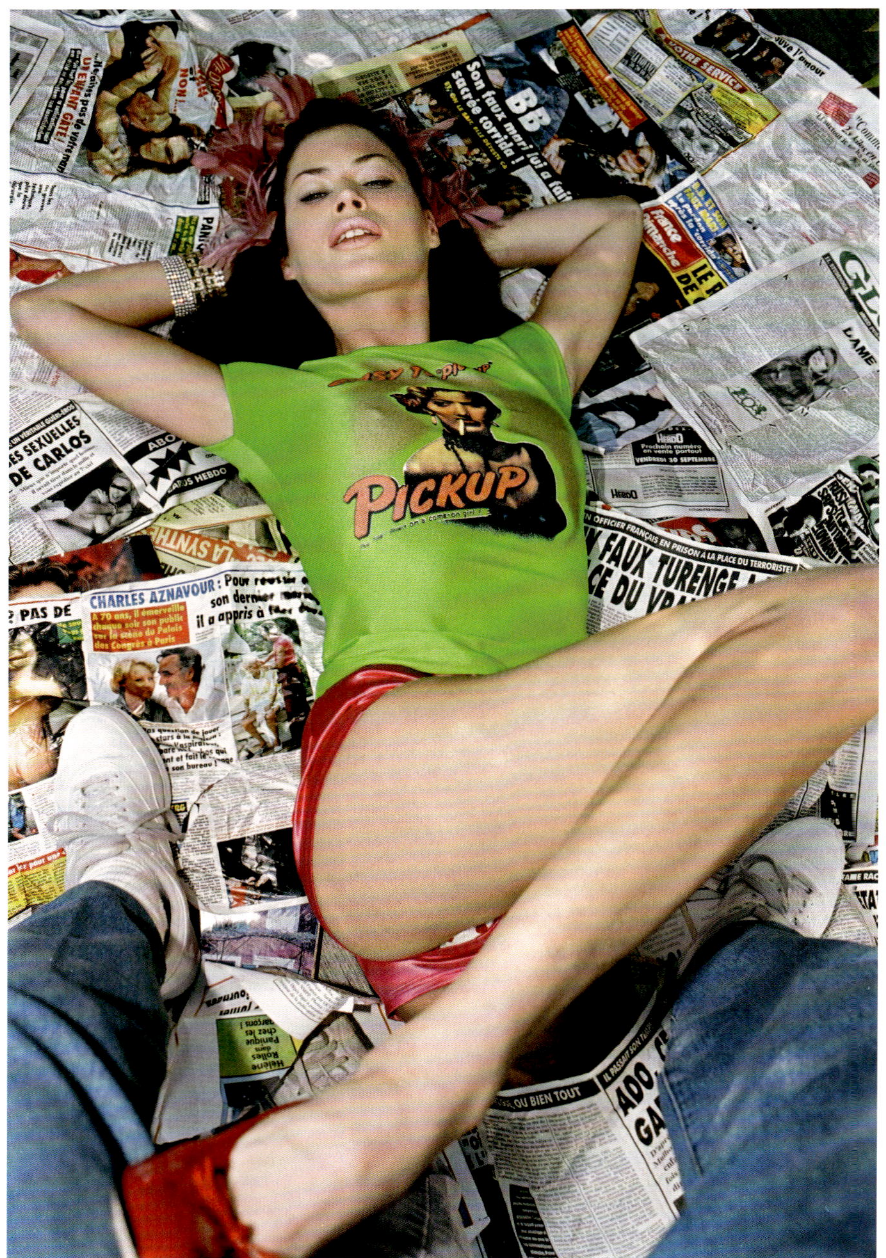
PICKUP

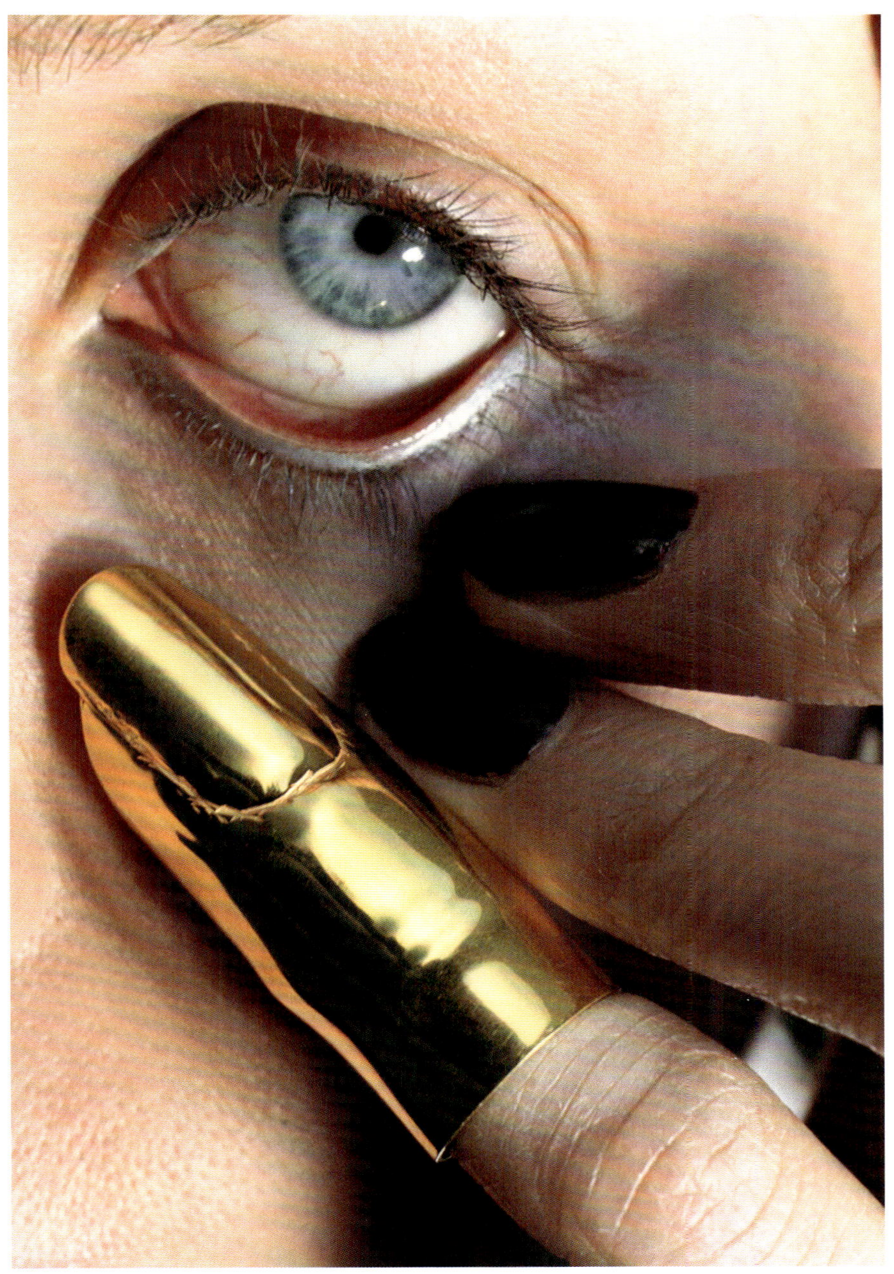

X-ray, 1995
In 1980, Newton began using X-rays in his photography. He wanted to see what was underneath
"all the flesh" and specifically a three-million-
dollar Van Cleef & Arpels diamond necklace.
In the X-ray, there was nothing to the necklace
except the metal setting. X-ray images have been
published since the nineteenth century, though
usually for medical purposes. In this X-ray, that
reveals his fascination with high heels, Newton
puts the technology to use in American *Vogue*.

Pages 168/169
Machine Age, American *Vogue*,
Thierry Mugler, 1995
Models: Kristen and Johanna
McMenamy, Claudia Lynx

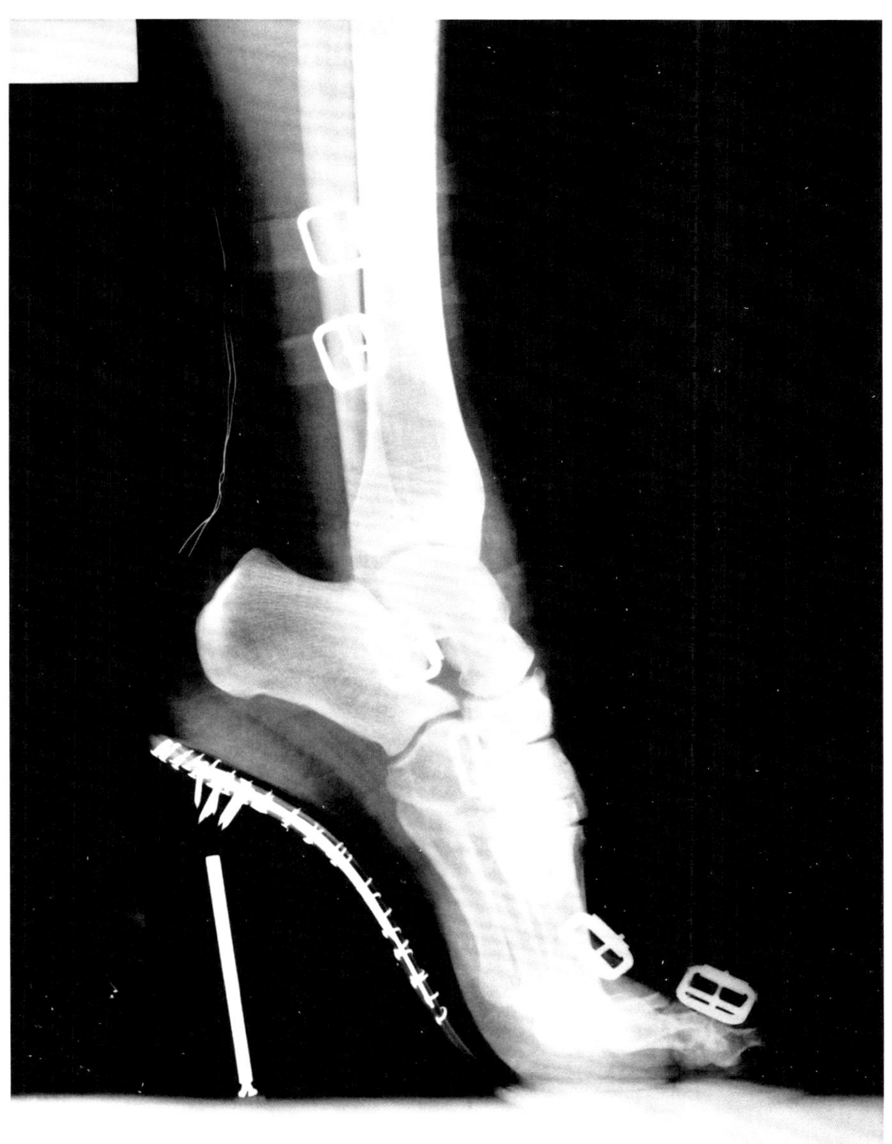

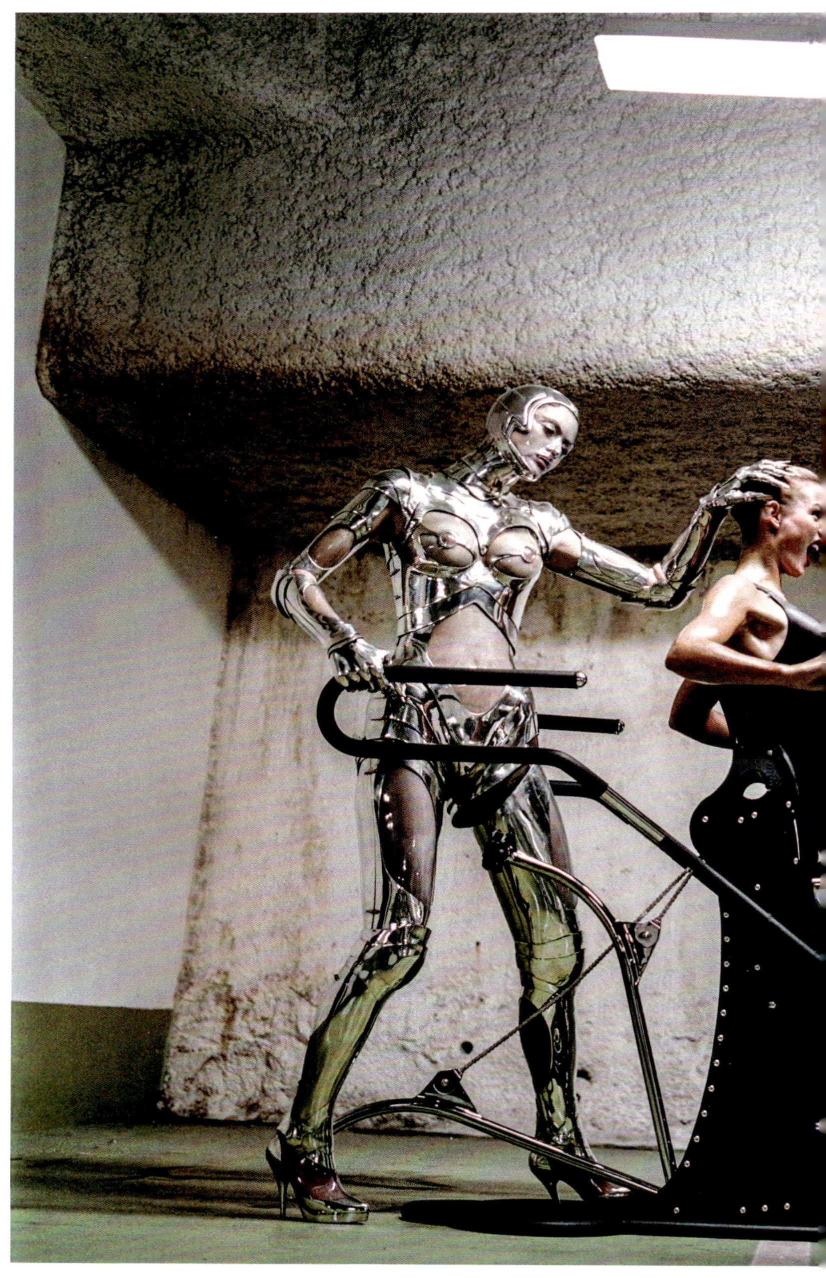

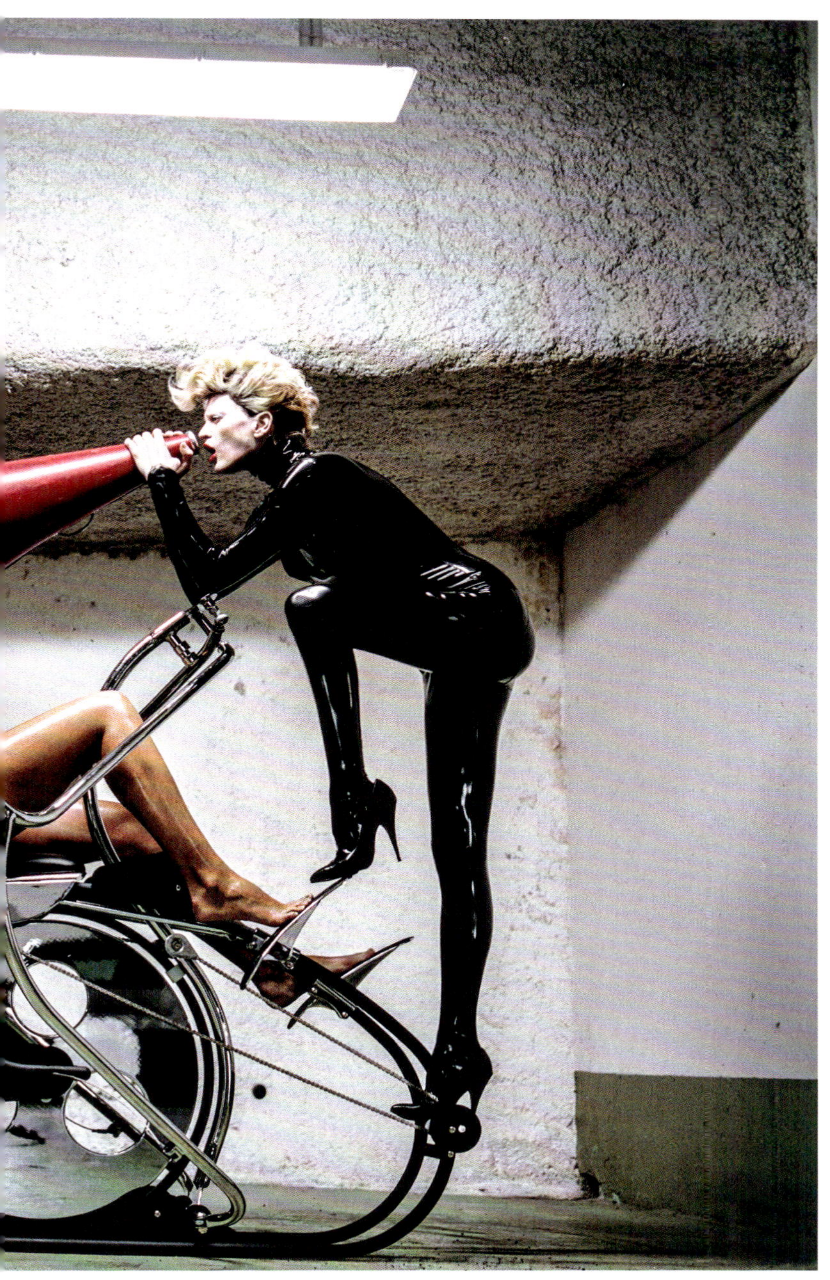

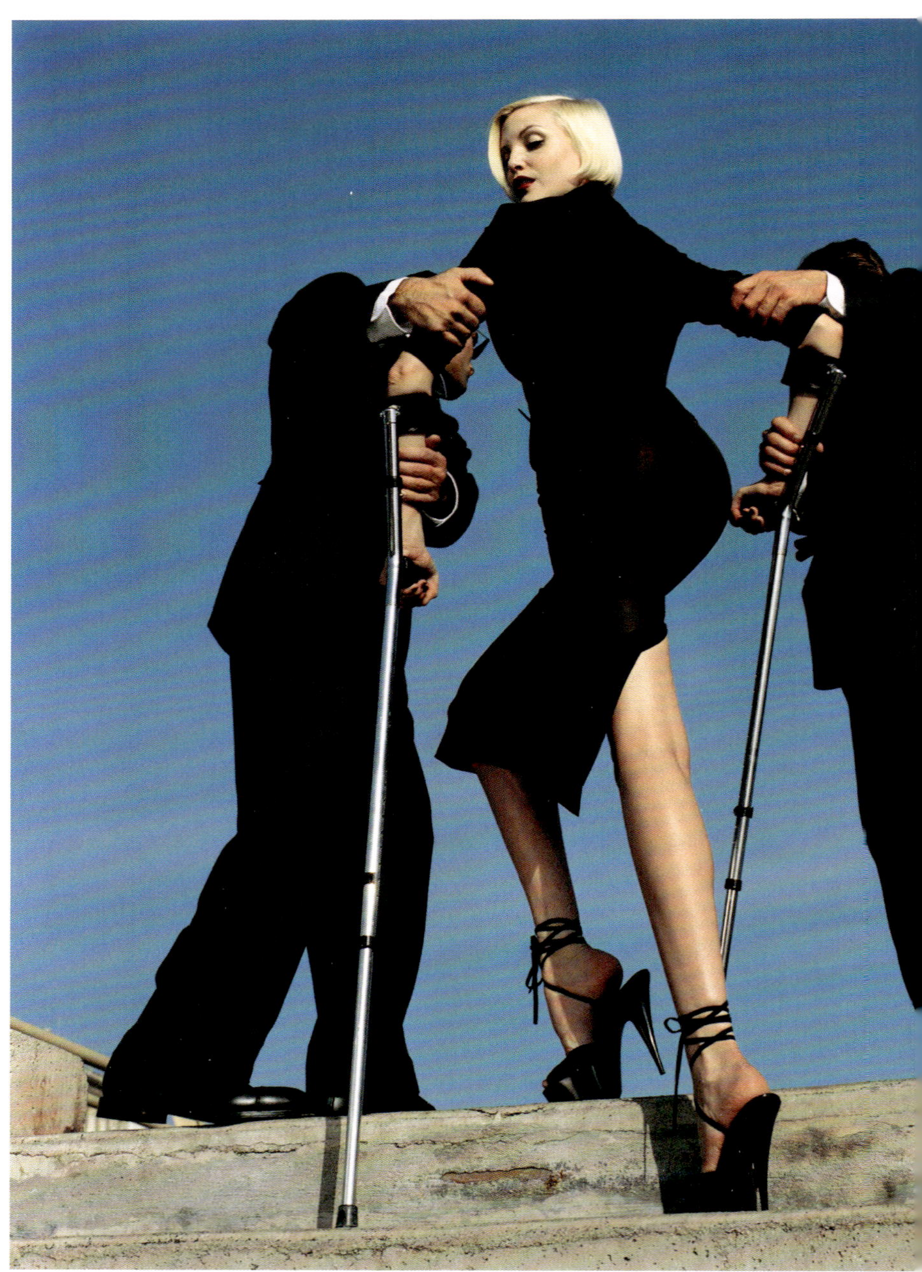

**American *Vogue*, Dolce & Gabbana,
Monte Carlo, 1995**
Model: Nadja Auermann
"When I see a woman, I always immediately look
at her shoes and hope that they are high," Newton
said, "because high heels make a woman look
sexy and dangerous." This story, titled "High and
Mighty", was the first for American *Vogue* after an
absence of shooting fashion editorial for fifteen
years, during which Newton focused on portraits,
nudes and travel, as well as his own magazine,
Helmut Newton's Illustrated. It was editor-in-chief
Anna Wintour who enticed Newton back to
American *Vogue*. Under her editorship, the magazine had become the most powerful fashion
publication at the end of the twentieth century.
Newton enjoyed a fruitful decade, photographing
fashion editorial again for American and Italian
Vogue until his death in 2004.

Jean-Marie Le Pen, *The New Yorker,* Paris, 1997
"His reputation as an extreme rightist and anti-
Semite has been well established. Just the kind of
guy I love to photograph." Newton turned his lens
on Jean-Marie Le Pen for *The New Yorker,* using
all of his charm and his sharp eye for capturing an
iconographic psychological insight. As he narrated
in his autobiography, he saw the politician's
Dobermans in the garden of his house in Neuilly-
sur-Seine, Paris, and persuaded him to pose with
them on the spur of the moment. The image was
instantly compared in the press to a well-known
photograph of Hitler posing with his dogs.

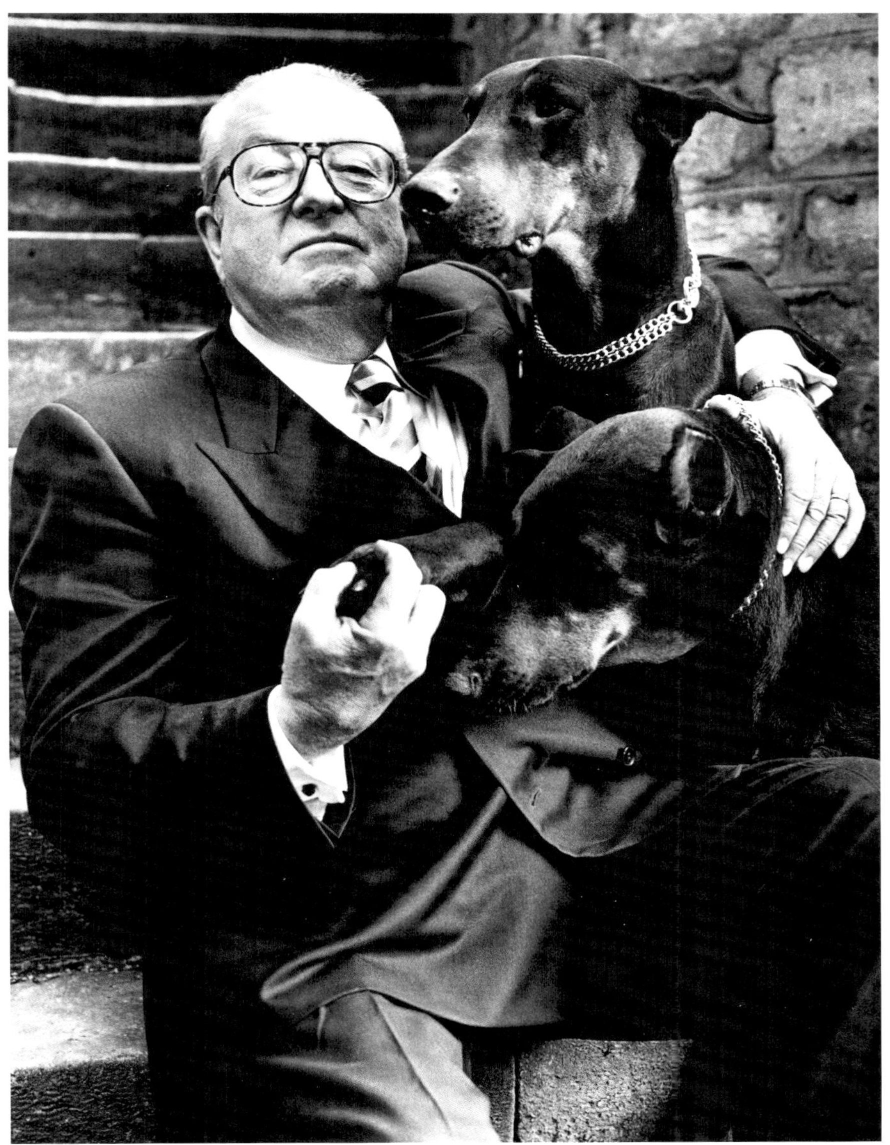

Paris Match,
Monte Carlo, 1997
Model: Eva Herzigová

Page 176
Brian, the Gambler,
Details, **Château de Gairaut, Nice, 1997**

Page 177
Naked Lunch,
American *Vogue*, Monte Carlo, 1996
Model: Kylie Bax
This was the first assertively bared breast published
in American *Vogue*, commissioned for a feature
on the current fashion for body exposure on the
runway. In the list of illustrations, Newton noted
next to this photo: "Anna [Wintour] let me get
away with this one."

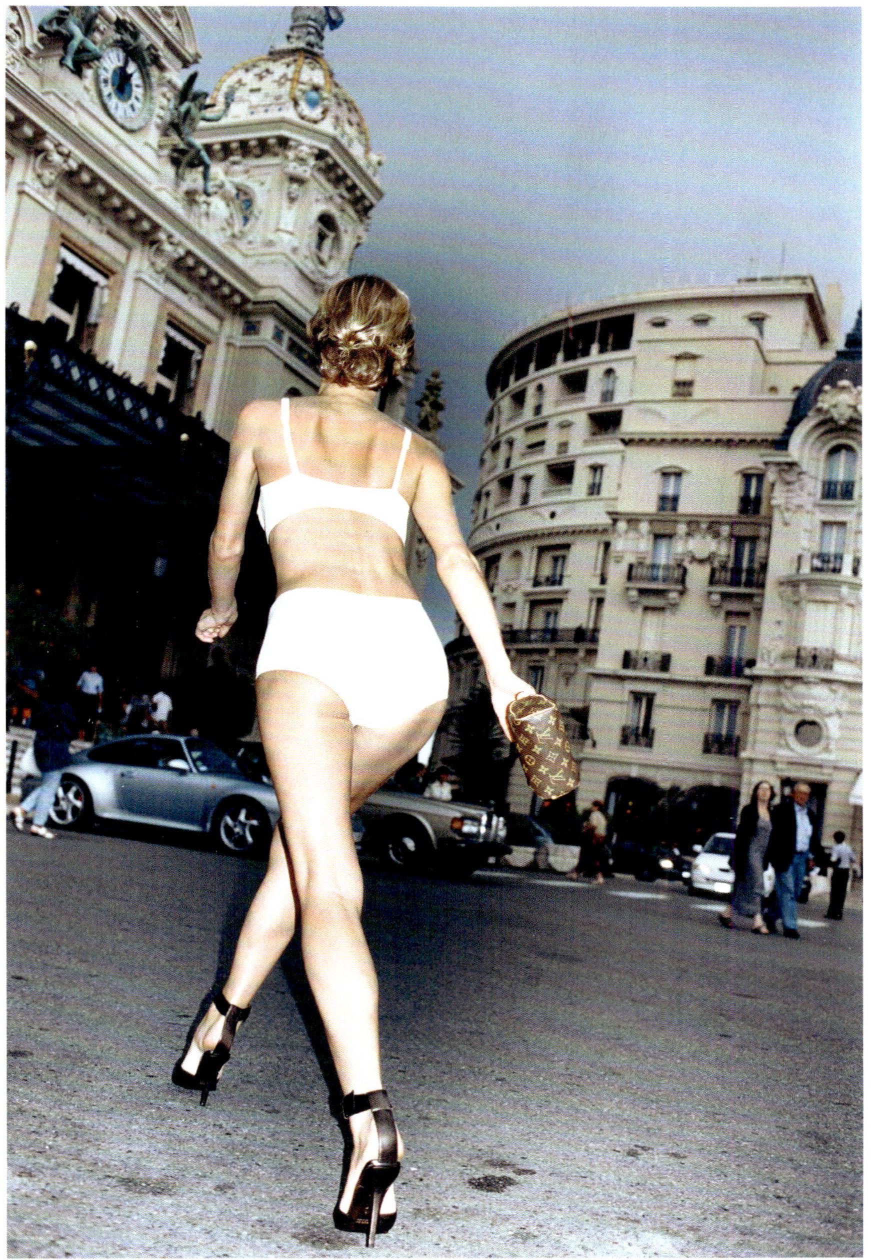

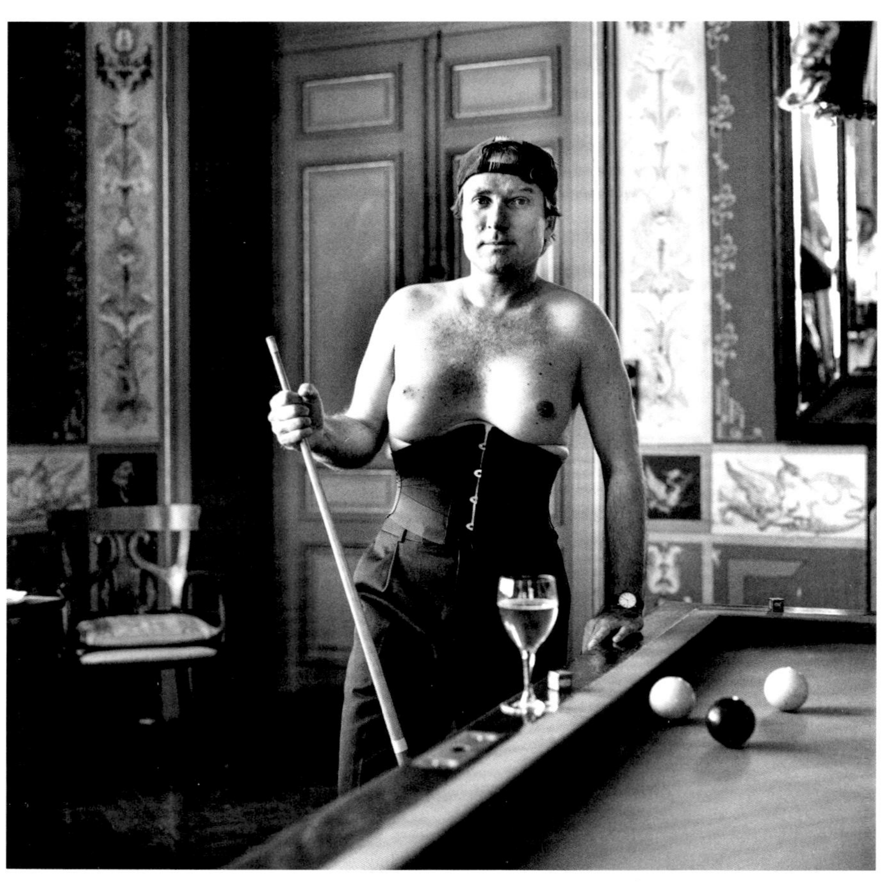

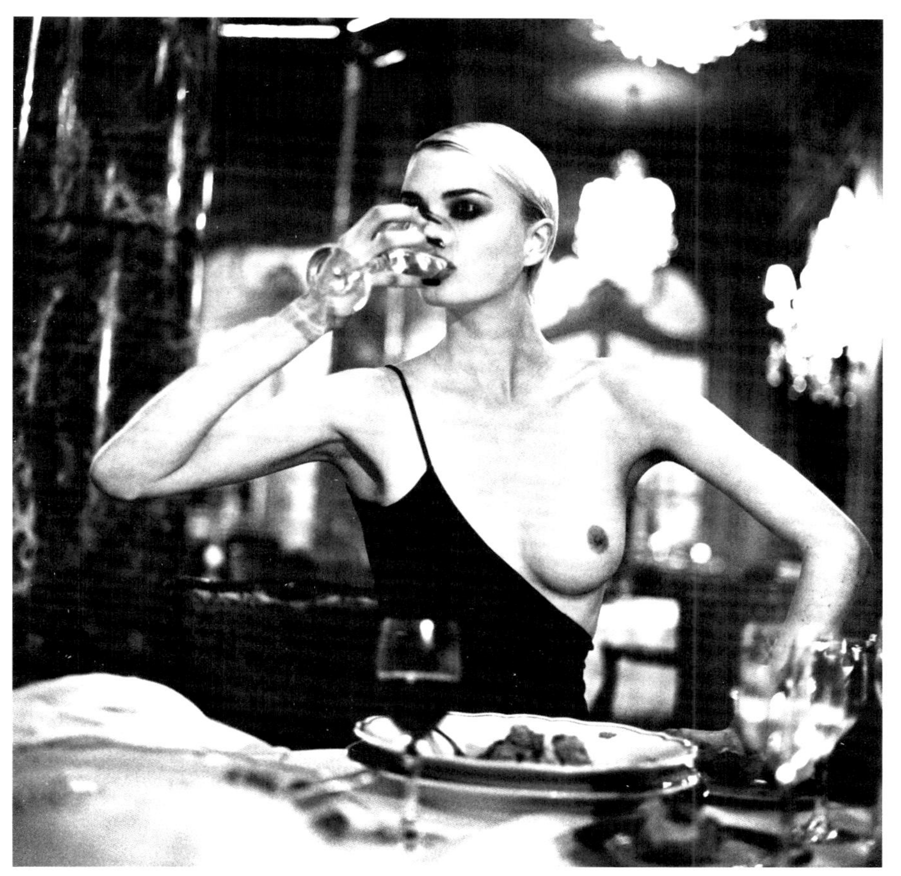

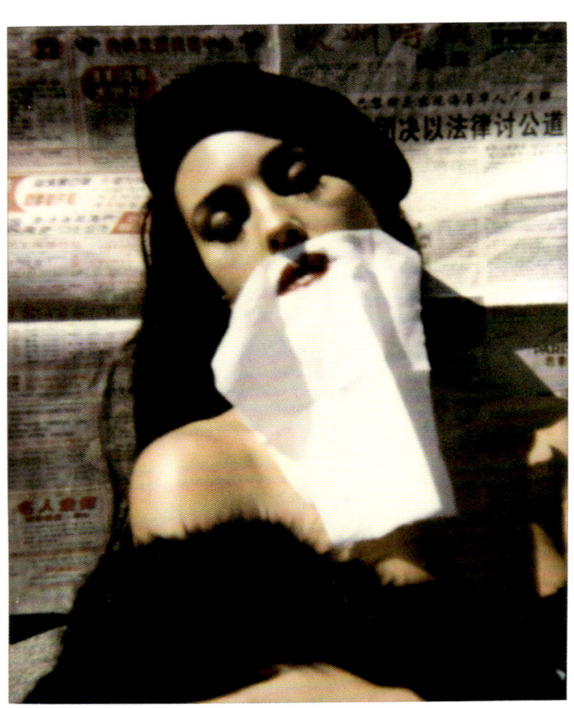

Polaroid, Monica Bellucci,
Monte Carlo, 2001

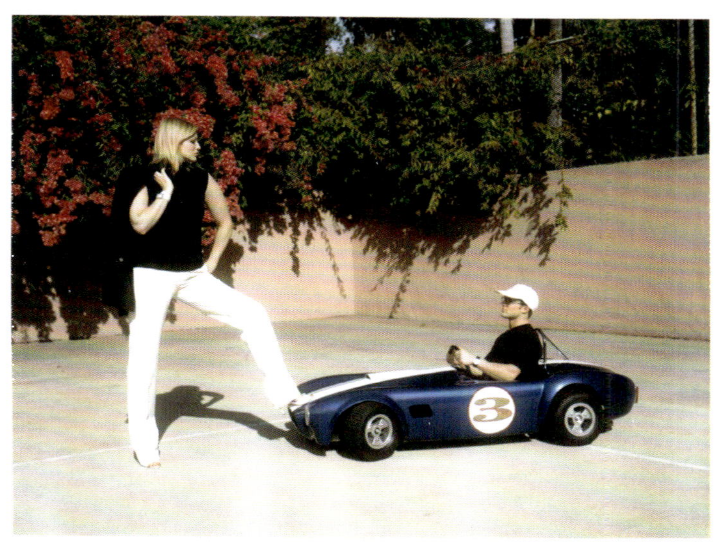

Polaroid, American *Vogue*, Los Angeles, 2002
Scale was something that Newton liked to play
with; a motif he started to use in the late 1960s.
Often, it was tall strong women with a much
smaller, scaled-down man. His liking for real
women with "flesh on their bones" is captured
in this Polaroid from an American *Vogue* shoot
in 2002.

Praise the Lard,
American *Vogue*, Monte Carlo, 2003
One of Newton's jokes about the male ability to
see sex in anything appeared in this still life for a
cookery feature on fried chicken in American *Vogue*
in 2003. "Chickens! They're so sexy. I saw it when
I was passing the kitchen once, and it was sitting
there with its legs open waiting to be cooked," he
remarked in an interview with *The New York Times*.
Planning this version of a favourite theme, he
asked the magazine's Phyllis Posnick to procure a
tiny pair of shoes. After sourcing them from the
Doll Museum in Paris, she and an assistant of
Newton's took them to the butcher just up the
hill from his Monte Carlo apartment to cast a
chicken – as she recounted – "with the best legs".
However, the story does not end there. Newton
was constantly delighted by angry readers' letters,
and this photograph gave rise to the final one,
dated the day that he died in Los Angeles. It was
short, badly typed and went along the lines of
"How could you have a chicken killed just for a
fashion shoot?"

Pages 182/183
Daria on a Bed of Nails,
American *Vogue*, Monte Carlo, 2004
Model: Daria Werbowy
Phyllis Posnick, the executive fashion editor
for American *Vogue* who is best known for editor-
ials on beauty, health and portrait sittings, worked
with Newton frequently in the last decade he
worked for the magazine. She said, "Helmut
could do strong photos anywhere – day or night,
in noon sun, under a street lamp, in a phone
booth, using a car's headlights, or in the underground garage of his building." This is exactly
what he did for this image illustrating a story on
cosmetic injections. Shot on the Corniche, a road
cut into the cliff in Monte Carlo with heavy traffic
and fast cars going past, the bed of nails was
delivered from Nice and had tiny pads covering
the sharp ends so the model Daria Werbowy
could lie down. The day's shooting over, the small
fashion team packed and prepared to leave;
Newton had second thoughts and decided to re-
shoot at night. The bed of nails was redelivered
from Nice, where it had been returned only hours
earlier. This is the shot he was satisfied with, and
the one that was later published in the March
2004 issue, two months after his death.

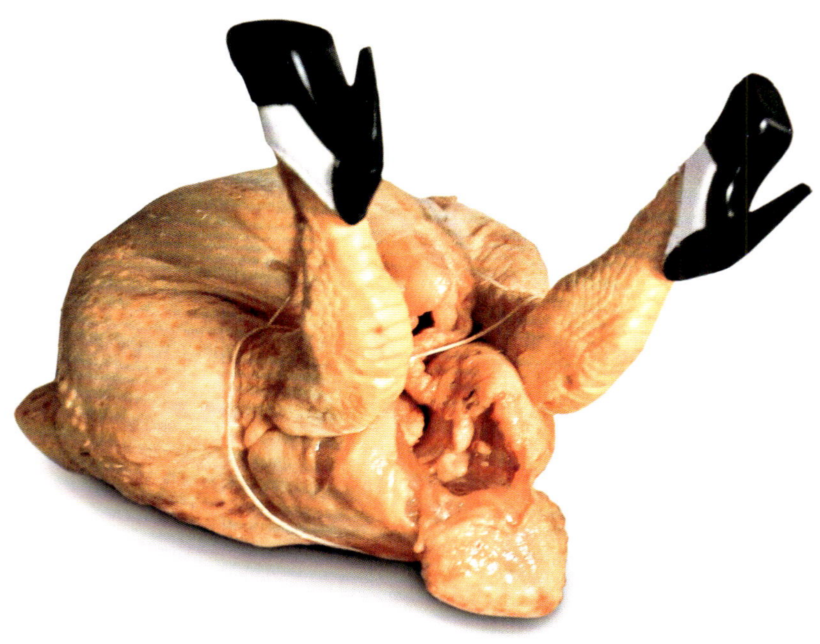

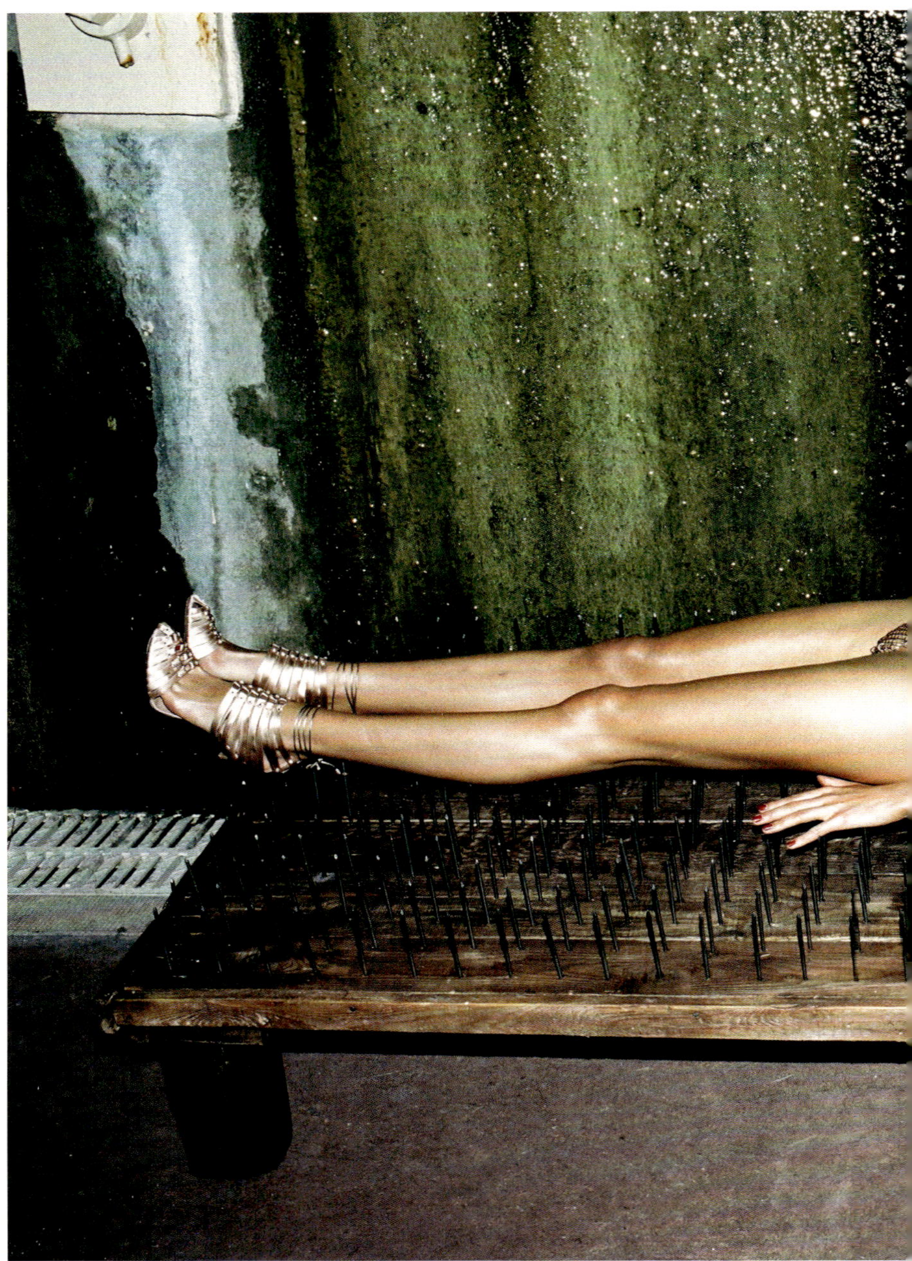

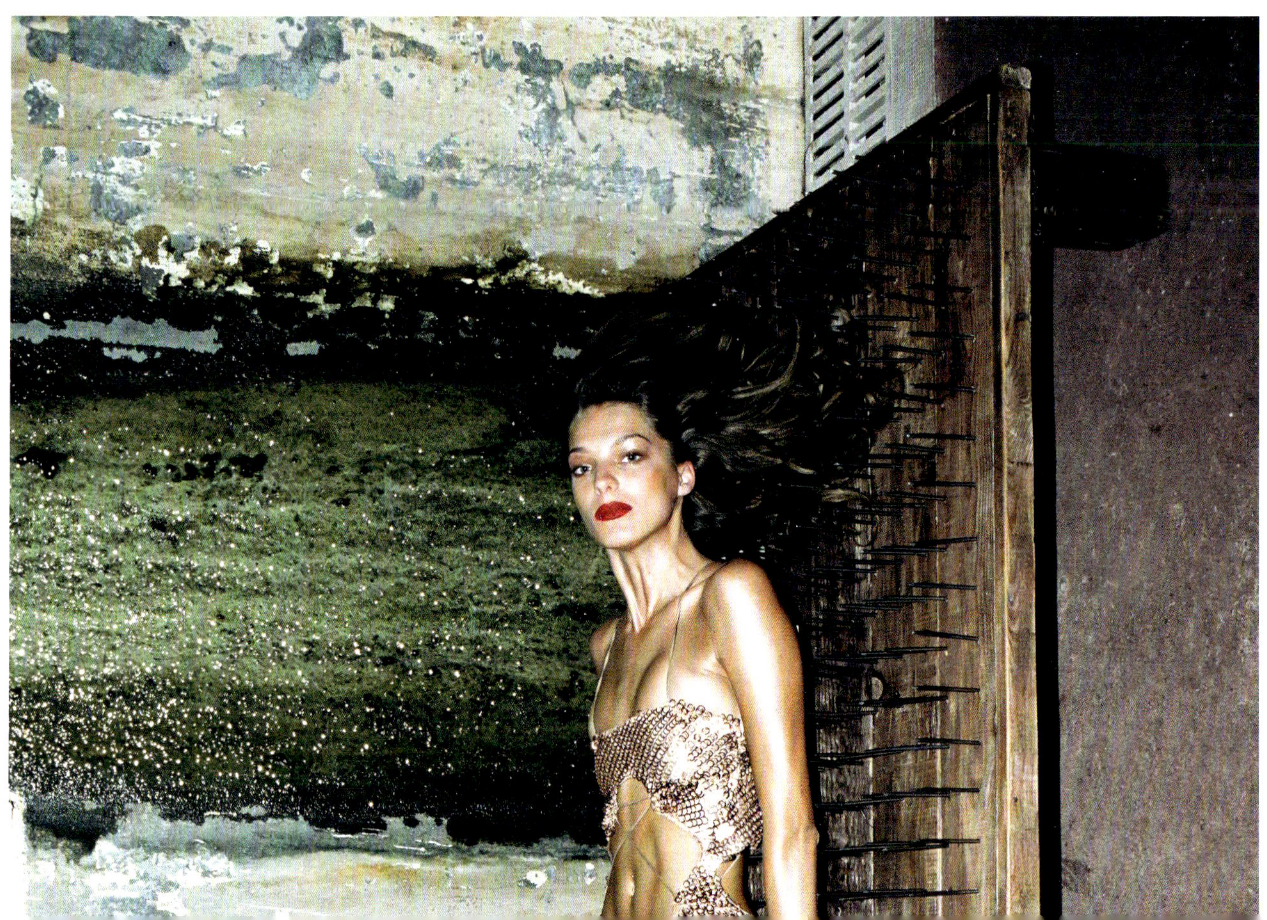

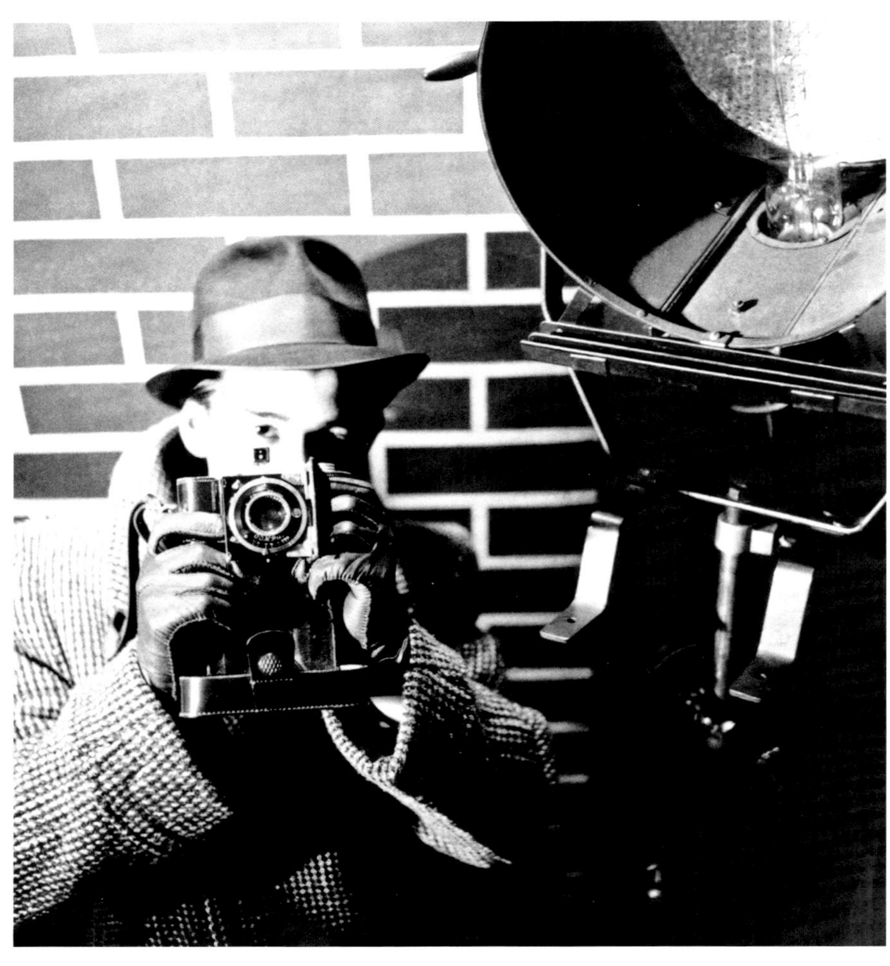

Self Portrait in Yva's Studio,
Berlin, 1936

Life & Work
1920–2004
By Philippe Garner

1920

Helmut Neustädter is born on October 31 in Berlin into a well-to-do Jewish family living in the Schöneberg district. His father Max runs the largest button manufactory in Germany, inherited by his wife Claire (also known as Klara) on the death of her first husband. From this earlier marriage, Newton has a half-brother a decade older than him, Hans Egon Hollander.

Newton enjoys a privileged bourgeois childhood punctuated by well-appointed travels with his family around Germany and Europe, staying in grand hotels that fuel his lifelong fascination with the symbols of a certain way of life and the trappings of prosperity.

1935

Following the passing of the Nuremberg Race Laws imposing the segregation of Jewish pupils from Aryans, Newton's father enrols him in the American School, where he studies in English.

Newton shows little interest in academic studies. His principal interests are girls, swimming and photography, the latter encouraged by his first success with his first camera, aged 12, as he recounts in his autobiography.

1936

Newton's father, against his better judgment, allows his son to pursue his ambition to become a photographer, taking up an apprenticeship in the Schlüterstrasse studio of Yva (the professional name of Else Ernestine Neuländer-Simon), a prominent photographer specialising in portraits, fashion and nudes. Under her tutelage, he learns the practical elements of his craft.

As persecution of Germany's Jews intensifies remorselessly, the family business is sequestered, exposing the Neustädters to increasing peril.

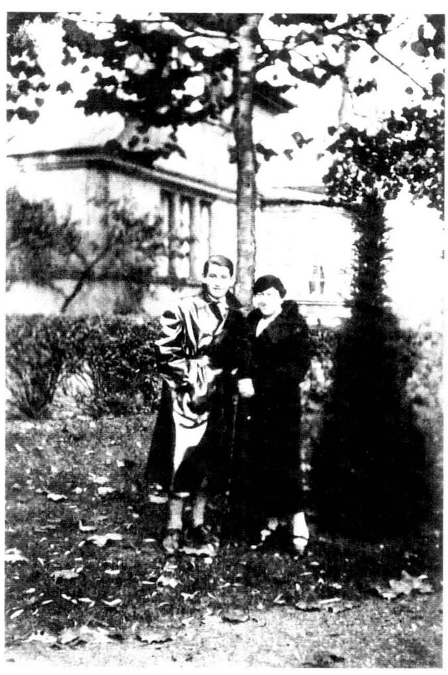

Newton with his mother in the garden on Friedrichsruher Strasse, 1935

1938

Following the trauma of the Krista lnacht pogrom on November 9–10, he goes into hiding, while his mother, using cash saved from the sale of a car, organises his escape from the country.

He flees Berlin on December 5, taking a train to Trieste from the Zoologischer Carten station, opposite which stands the handsome building,

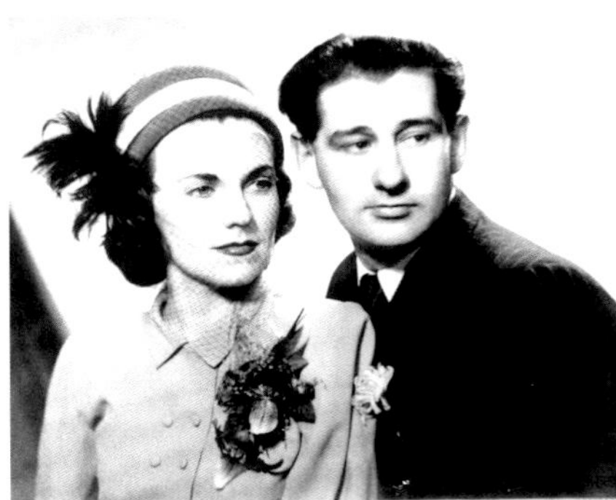

Helmut and June Newton's wedding photograph, Melbourne, 13 May 1948

formerly a Prussian officers' club, that today houses the Helmut Newton Foundation.

In Trieste, he boards a ship, the *Conte Rosso*, to Singapore, where he secures a job as a reportage photographer on *The Straits Times*.

His tenure is brief, and he acknowledges he is not suited to this genre of photography.

He becomes a gigolo, supported by an older woman, Josette Fabien, with whom he lives for a while in the Raffles Hotel.

1939
His parents escape from Germany to Argentina, where they join Hans, now established as a farmer.

1940
Helmut is detained as an "enemy alien" and deported by the British from Singapore to Australia, where he is interned in the Tatura One camp near Melbourne until the summer of 1942.

1942
He takes up an opportunity to join the Australian army and spends four years mostly kicking his heels, working as required.

1946
After the end of hostilities and his discharge from the army, Australia grants him citizenship and a passport. He changes his family name to Newton and is at last free to focus on his career as a photographer.

He sets up a small professional studio in Flinders Lane, Melbourne, seeking work as a portrait photographer, also taking on fashion and advertising work, and weddings.

1947
He meets actress June Brunell (her professional name; she was born June Browne) and makes promotional portraits of her. They become lovers.

1948
He and June marry on May 13.

His work soon starts to reveal his individuality and inventiveness in making a striking picture. his preference for strong-looking models and his flair in posing them.

1953
He has his first recorded exhibition, *New Visions in Photography*, with fellow Berlin-born émigré photographer Wolfgang Sievers, at the Federa Coffee Palace Hotel, Melbourne, May 25–30.

1957
The work he has produced on assignments for the Australian supplement of British *Vogue* leads to an offer of a 12-month contract with the magazine.

En route to London, he and June make a trip around Europe in a newly bought white Porsche, starting in Germany, and taking in France and Italy.

He does not take to the London of the late 1950s and cuts short the contract; they move for a while to Paris, a city that captivates them.

He finds Paris hugely inspiring and works hard, notably for *Jardin des Modes*, travelling also to West Berlin to shoot fashion for *Constanze*.

1959
He returns to Melbourne with a contract for Australian *Vogue*.

He sets up a new, larger studio in Bourke Street in partnership with his friend Henry Talbot.

1961
Helmut and June move definitively to Paris

In May, he signs a contract with *Vogue Paris*.

The couple soon find, buy and settle in the rue Aubriot apartment that will be their home for 14 years.

1964

They find and buy a small, dilapidated building amid vineyards at La Croix-Valmer, near Ramatuelle on the Saint-Tropez peninsula. They restore and extend the house, which becomes a regular second home for as long as they are based in Paris.

He works intensively in the fields of fashion and related advertising, steadily earning respect and building his reputation.

An impactful shoot presenting the revolutionary designs of André Courrèges for *Queen* leads to the termination of his *Vogue Paris* contract for what the magazine perceives as a betrayal.

He works ever harder for a range of French and British titles, including *Elle*, *Marie Claire*, *Queen* and British *Vogue*.

1966

He renews his *Vogue Paris* contract under fashion editor and eventual editor-in-chief Francine Crescent, entering into what will prove the single most fruitful editorial relationship of his career.

Helmut and June Newton in their Paris apartment, rue Aubriot in the Marais, 1965

1971

Helmut suffers a serious heart attack and is hospitalised while in New York shooting fashion at the invitation of Alex Liberman, creative director of American *Vogue*. This trauma makes him rethink his priorities, and he determines henceforth to push the limits of his imagination in his work.

He starts to file his negatives and contact sheets systematically.

1975

He has his first solo exhibition, presented at the Galerie Nikon, Paris. It shows his most recent work, including images destined for his first book.

1976

His first London show follows, held at the Photographers' Gallery.

His first book, *White Women*, is published in numerous international editions. It wins the Kodak Photobook Award and plays a key role in establishing his reputation with a new and far wider audience.

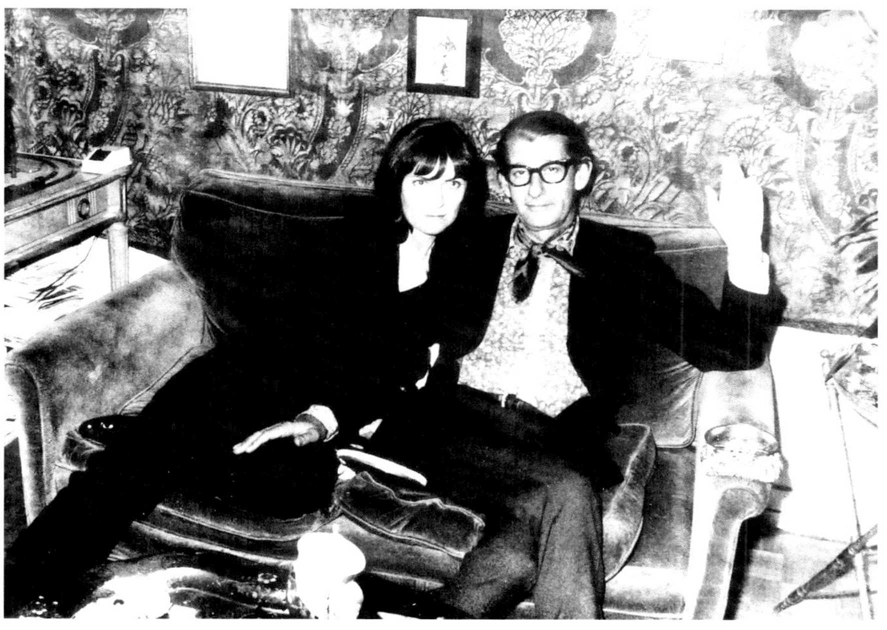

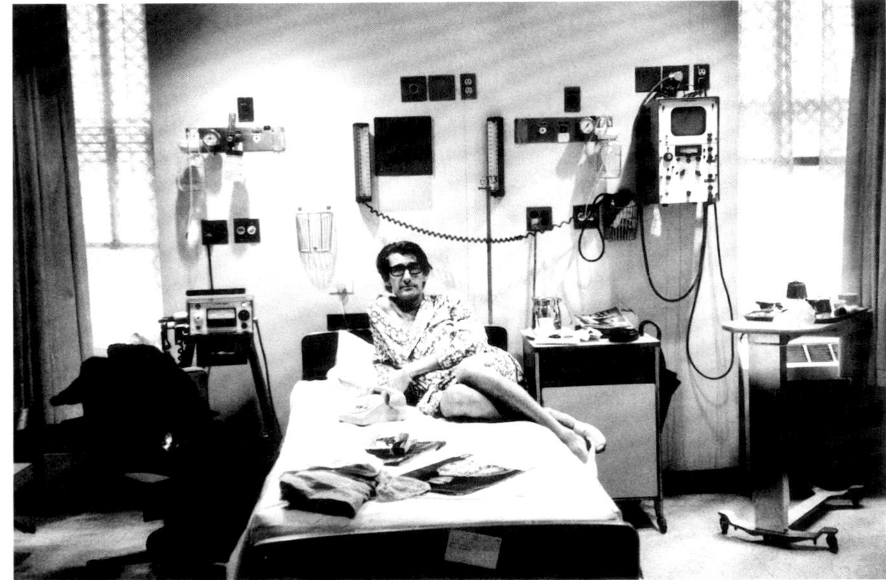

1977

He and June leave the rue Aubriot for an apartment in the rue de l'Abbé-de-l'Épée, near the Jardin du Luxembourg.

He starts what is to become an intermittent but fruitful working relationship with the newly launched *Égoïste*, issued periodically by Nicole Wisniak.

1978

His second book, *Sleepless Nights*, is published.

1979

He presents an innovative projection-based exhibition at the American Center, Paris.

The first documentary on him, produced and directed by Michael Whyte, is screened by Thames Television, London.

He publishes a large-format selection of black-and-white work of the 1970s, *Helmut Newton. Special Collection, 24 Photo Lithos.*

1981

He holds an important exhibition, *Photographies 1980–81*, at the Galerie Daniel Templon, Paris. This presents large-format prints, notably his first

In Lenox Hill Hospital, New York, after his heart attack, 1971 Photo: Alice Springs

series of *Big Nudes*, one of which, *Big Nude III*, the poster image for the exhibition, was destined to become one of his most celebrated and emblematic works.

The exhibition is commemorated with the publication of *Helmut Newton*, soon revised, and republished with an introductory text by Karl Lagerfeld as *Helmut Newton – 47 Nudes*.

He and June leave Paris at the end of the year to take up residence in Monte Carlo as Monégasque citizens.

They establish what becomes a pattern of making an extended winter stay in Los Angeles in the Chateau Marmont.

1982

Newton is destabilised when June undergoes major surgery; for a while, he loses his creative direction.

Passing through the low-key Italian seaside town of Bordighera, just beyond the border with France, his imagination is rekindled, and he

returns there to shoot with fresh ideas, most
notably with his series *Bordighera Details*, published in *Vogue Italia* and in issue 7 of *Égoïste*.

1984

Newton's exhibition *Portraits* at the Musée d'Art
Moderne de la Ville de Paris, curated by Françoise
Marquet, is his first major museum show, an
achievement in which he takes considerable pride.
It is accompanied by a catalogue.

He publishes *World Without Men*, a retrospective anthology of his fashion photography.

1986

He publishes a new anthology, *Portraits*, in several
international editions. Portraiture becomes an
ever more important aspect of his work with
numerous commissions, notably, since 1983,
from *Vanity Fair*.

He meanwhile develops his interest in photographing places that intrigue him, including
commissions for *Condé Nast Traveler*.

1987

He publishes *Helmut Newton's Illustrated No 1.
Sex and Power*, the first in what will become a
series of four issues of a tabloid-format journal
inspired by his recollections of the illustrated
press of his youth in Germany, specifically the
Berliner Illustrirte Zeitung.

1988

He has an exhibition, *Portraits*, at the National
Portrait Gallery, London.

1989

He is appointed Chevalier de l'Ordre des Arts et
des Lettres by Jacques Lang, the French Minister
of Culture.

He is awarded the Grand Prix de la Ville de
Paris by Jacques Chirac, the city's mayor.

1990

He is awarded the Grand Prix National de la
Photographie by Jacques Lang.

1992

He publishes *Pola Woman*, introducing his audience to his Polaroids.

His exhibition *Archives de Nuit*, sponsored
and hosted in Paris by the bank Crédit Foncier de
France, introduces important new work, including
his *Domestic Nudes* and *Panoramic Nudes*, and
a range of more personal images. It is accompanied by a catalogue of the same name.

He is awarded the Großes Verdienstkreuz der
Bundesrepublik Deutschland (Grand Cross of
Merit of the Federal Republic of Germany) for his
contribution to culture.

He is appointed Chevalier de l'Ordre du
Mérite Culturel by Her Serene Highness Princess
Caroline of Monaco.

1995

He is the subject of an intimate documentary,
Helmut by June, shot by his wife.

1996

He is elevated to Commandeur de l'Ordre des
Arts et des Lettres by Philippe Douste-Blazy, the
French Minister of Culture.

**Helmut Newton with one of the first copies
of *SUMO* in the courtyard of TASCHEN's
headquarters, Cologne, 1999** Photo: Alice Springs

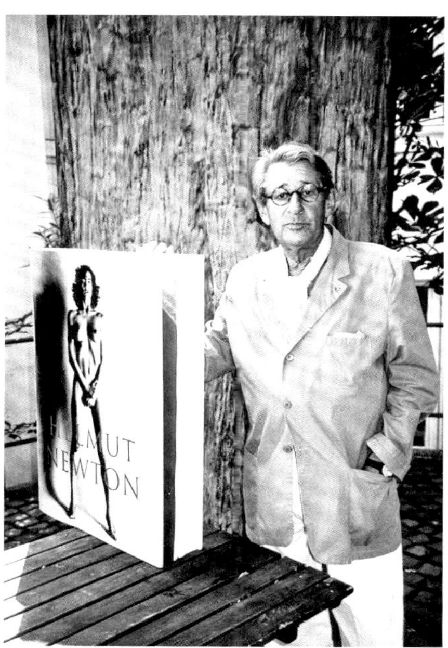

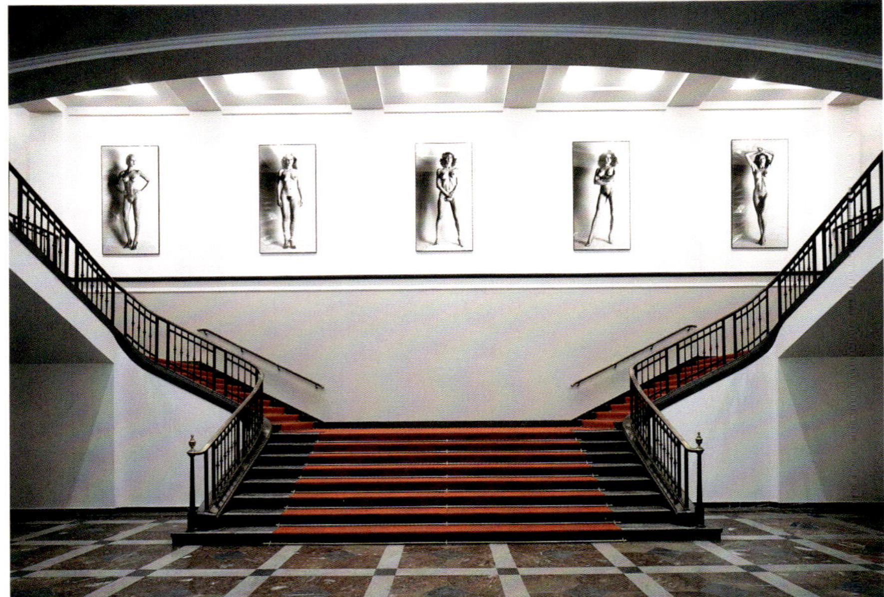

1998

He publishes *Pages from the Glossies: Facsimiles 1956–1998*, a compendium of magazine pages and covers covering his career as a fashion photographer.

1999

He publishes two significant books. *Helmut Newton, Alice Springs: Us and Them* is an intimate and insightful volume that presents together the work of the couple, notably their portraits of one another and their distinct respective portraits of the same subjects (June Newton assumed the professional name Alice Springs after she started to take on photographic commissions in 1970); and *SUMO*, conceived in close collaboration with publisher Benedikt Taschen as a monumental-format tribute to Helmut's long career.

2000

He celebrates his 80th birthday with a major retrospective exhibition at the Neue Nationalgalerie, Berlin and with the accompanying publication *Work*. The exhibition travels to cities around the world, including London, New York, Moscow and Prague.

The foyer of the Helmut Newton Foundation with five two-metre *Big Nudes* facing the entrance, circa 2004 Photo: Stefan Müller

Prince Rainier of Monaco promotes him to Officier de l'Ordre du Mérite Culturel.

2001

His exhibition *Sex and Landscapes* at the de Pury & Luxembourg Gallery in Zurich marks a significant step up in the market for his prints.

2002

His *Autobiographie* appears first in its German-language edition, followed by the English-language *Autobiography* and other international editions.

2003

He agrees the formal arrangement with the Prussian Cultural Heritage Foundation (Stiftung Preussischer Kulturbesitz) for the use of the former officers' club opposite the Bahnhof Zoo station and establishes the Helmut Newton Foundation in Berlin.

2004

He dies in Los Angeles on January 23 after suffering a heart attack at the wheel of a Cadillac, while exiting the garage of the Chateau Marmont on his way to an advertising shoot.

His ashes are interred on June 2 in a grave of honour, conferred by the Senate of Berlin, at the Friedhof Schöneberg III cemetery, Berlin.

2012

The extensive retrospective *Helmut Newton 1920–2004*, co-curated by June, is the first photography exhibition hosted by the Grand Palais, Paris.

2020

His centenary is celebrated with an extensive outdoor exhibition in Berlin. A major retrospective, *Legacy*, delayed by the Covid pandemic, is held at the Helmut Newton Foundation and subsequently travels to Vienna, Milan, Rome and Venice, and is accompanied by a substantial new monograph.

2021

June Newton dies on April 9.

The Helmut Newton Foundation inherits the rights to Helmut and June's archives and assumes its responsibility to preserve and promote their achievements.

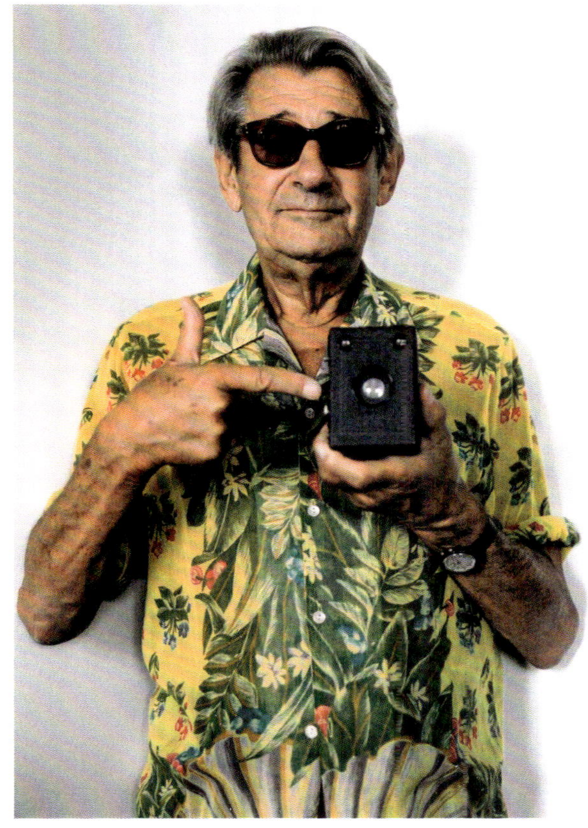

**With his Box Tengor,
Monte Carlo, 2000**
Photo: Alice Springs

Imprint

**EACH AND EVERY TASCHEN BOOK
PLANTS A SEED!**
TASCHEN is a carbon neutral publisher. Each
year, we offset our annual carbon emissions with
carbon credits at the Instituto Terra, a reforest-
ation program in Minas Gerais, Brazil, founded
by Lélia and Sebastião Salgado. To find out more
about this ecological partnership, please check:
www.taschen.com/zerocarbon
Inspiration: unlimited. Carbon footprint: zero.

To stay informed about TASCHEN and our
upcoming titles, please subscribe to our free
magazine at www.taschen.com/magazine,
follow us on Instagram and Facebook, or e-mail
your questions to contact@taschen.com.

© 2024 TASCHEN GmbH
Hohenzollernring 53, D–50672 Köln
www.taschen.com

© 2024 for the work of Helmut Newton and
Alice Springs: Helmut Newton Foundation, Berlin

© 2024 for the introduction and picture
commentaries: Sarah Mower

© 2024 for the chronology:
Philippe Garner

German translation:
Kirsten Riesselmann

French translation:
Sophie Lecoq

Printed in Italy
ISBN 978–3–8365–9400–4

Front cover
**Daryl Hannah, American *Vogue*,
Los Angeles, 1984**

Back cover
**June Newton's favourite portrait of
her husband, taken on the terrace of
their apartment, Monte Carlo, 1984**
Photo: Alice Springs

Page 2
Self Portrait in Yva's Studio, Berlin, 1936